Books should be returned on or before the
last date stamped below.

NORTH EAST of SCOTLAND LIBRARY SERVICE
14 Crown Terrace, Aberdeen

D1437197

DEFEAT AT THE FALKLANDS
GERMANY'S EAST ASIA SQUADRON 1914

Defeat at the Falklands

Germany's East Asia Squadron 1914

EDWIN P. HOYT

ROBERT HALE · LONDON

© *Edwin P. Hoyt 1981*
First published in Great Britain 1981

ISBN 0 7091 8863 3

Robert Hale Limited
Clerkenwell House
Clerkenwell Green
London EC1R 0HT

Photoset by
Specialised Offset Services Limited, Liverpool
and printed in Great Britain by
Clarke, Doble & Brendon Ltd., Plymouth
Bound by Redwood Burn Ltd., Surrey

Contents

List of Illustrations

Credits

Photographs from the Imperial War Museum: 2, 3, 4, 5, 6, 7, 9, 15, 16, 17, 18, 19, 20; the remainder supplied by the author.

Maps

1

The Kaiser's Navy

On 10 February 1906 the dockyards at Portsmouth were festooned with bunting and high officialdom from London came down in droves to participate in the launching of the *Dreadnought*, the most powerful warship in the world, representing a new concept of naval warfare. For years the officers of the Royal Navy had been asking for just such a ship: a floating gun platform that would be able to blow all enemies out of the water with such speed and dexterity that it would suffer no harm to itself. The range of *Dreadnought*'s guns was such that this seemed perfectly possible.

But this purely military calculation was as naïve politically as it was advanced strategically, and as even the most dunder-headed politicians in Parliament must have known, what one nation can do another can do also, if not perhaps quite as quickly. The *Dreadnought* boasted ten 12-inch guns that could throw projectiles of 850 pounds over a distance of more than ten miles. A line of dreadnoughts was said to be the equivalent of two lines of pre-dreadnought battleships. In single combat a dreadnought was evaluated as three times as strong as anything else afloat.

In Potsdam, Kaiser Wilhelm II looked upon the launch of the *Dreadnought* with chagrin and yearning. Wilhelm had always envied his English cousins; indeed, his favourite uniform was that of a British admiral, which he was entitled to wear as much through his relationship with the British Royal Family, as through diplomatic falderal. Had matters been slightly different, Wilhelm probably would have been quite content to live out his life as a member of the English royal house, and a working officer of the British Royal Navy.

However, as the reigning monarch of the German state Wilhelm's interest in British naval affairs assumed an attitude of competition. He wanted an important navy for Germany, as much for prestige as for any legitimate political purpose. Dreadnoughts were more or less out of the question, for the Kiel Canal had not been built to carry ships of 18,000 tons. He would have them, he decided, but they would have to come in smaller numbers.

By the end of 1906, Britain calculated that in three years she would have nine big ships, six dreadnoughts and three 'battle-cruisers', large vessels with relatively heavy armament but no deck armour, which relied on speed and their big guns for superiority.

This plan created divisions within the German naval staff. Some officers said the Kiel Canal must be sacrificed if need be, to retain and increase German naval power in relationship to Britain's. Other officers suggested that the traditional German policy of building

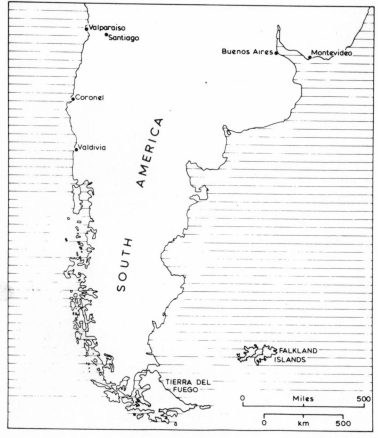

Coronel and the Falklands

cruisers and destroyers should be retained. Admiral Alfred von Tirpitz, the chief of the German Navy, believed in the big ships, and it was his intention to match the British Home Fleet with a powerful force of his own. He had begun building big battleships of the same basic strength as *Lord Nelson*, the 16,500-ton ship that was last of the British pre-dreadnought class. Germany, preoccupied with a national paranoia whose centre was a concern over encirclement by Britain, France, and Russia, began worrying about the relative naval strengths anew. But even the Kaiser realized that Germany could never match Britain's naval strength, nor was there any legitimate reason to do so save fear of Britain. The German concept of the cruiser force was completely sane, given her international position. Germany was a land power, whose fleet could sail into the wide world only by passing Britain. Outside Europe, Germany's fleet requirements were for naval vessels that could show the flag and if necessary move against shore installations or naval forces in Africa and the Pacific Ocean. Outside Europe, cruisers were totally adequate for Germany's needs.

The only possible threat to German interests in the Pacific could come from Japan, which had built a large fleet of its own to wage the Russo-Japanese war. Certainly the Japanese were to be watched, for they had shown a remarkable proficiency in adopting European colonial yearnings. But at the moment they were not stirring, and the cruiser concept seemed safe enough. During the next five years, Germany and Britain fretted with one another at the diplomatic tables, and Tirpitz built German naval strength as quickly as he could. The concept in Europe was to build warships as long as the British continued to do so, not to try to match Britain's total naval strength, which, after all, had to serve an empire on which the sun never set. The main aim was to make Germany strong enough always to hold a threat. The diplomats, particularly Prince Metternich, wanted to achieve peace at the conference table. Tirpitz, and particularly Kaiser Wilhelm, wanted to strengthen the fleet, and they did so in an atmosphere of secrecy that worried the British. Naval attachés found their activities limited and their questions unanswered. They did know of an enormous expansion of the Krupp armaments works and of the German naval shipyard at Kiel. By 1910 all these plans were in full preparation, a matter most confusing to Britain.

The diplomats argued endlessly about the relative strengths proper for the two navies; the Germans talked of maintaining a secondary position; they built furiously to try to match the British power in heavy capital ships. By 1911, in Berlin and London, diplomats were referring to the 'German Naval Party' which included the Kaiser and Tirpitz. The concern was lest the Naval Party assume complete dominance of German affairs. In the spring of 1911, a crisis developed in Morocco, where the French were furiously pursuing their colonial interests. An Arab uprising caused the French to send troops, and the Germans to send a gunboat and a cruiser to the port of Agadir, 'to protect German interests'. Since there were no German interests within a thousand miles of Agadir, this move seemed more than a little threatening to the French and the British. It was well known that the Germans coveted coaling stations in the area. So when the *Panther* arrived at Agadir on 1 July, so did international panic.

Lloyd George made a threatening speech in London, or so it was regarded in Berlin, where the Press aired its resentments. That whole summer the newspapers of London and Berlin did not help matters with a constant stream of veiled references to troop movements and warship sailings, as though the whole of Europe were about to explode at any moment. The Berlin stock market staggered under rumour, and the cost of British war risk insurance jumped. Lloyd's, which had been quoting a war risk insurance rate of 5s. per 100 on cargoes, jumped the rate to 15s. The crisis was very real. It also gave the 'Naval Party' a leg up. The Kaiser did not openly support that party – to have done so would have been to divide a nation that was even in 1911 only barely united from a conglomeration of petty states. But he did make his views clear enough in a speech at Hamburg in which he spoke vaguely of the enthusiasm of the people for an increase in the fleet. That was all Tirpitz and the naval party wanted. They managed to push through the Reichstag a new German naval law which would bring the ratio of German to British naval strength up to 2:3. The Navy was to have three new battleships, the Kaiser announced in the Speech from the Throne that opened the Reichstag on 7 February 1912.

By that time, the British were talking about building two ships for every one the Germans built, and Winston Churchill was talking about a reorganization of the British fleet. Britain would then have forty-nine battleships in home waters, compared to Germany's twenty-nine. The Germans responded with a forecast of their own: a fleet by 1920 that would consist of five squadrons of battleships, cruisers, and destroyers, with more in reserve. So the see-saw of naval armament see-ed and saw-ed, accompanied by large blasts of political bombast, on both sides of the North Sea. Lord Balfour wrote an article for the German Press which could be more or less summed up by the Japanese phrase *n desu ga*: which means 'everything that has been said before is just fine, but ...' Britain did not want a 'preventive war' (as some Germans claimed), *but* ... Britain was disturbed about certain features of German national policy, *so* ... The Balfour position was occasioned by a time-honoured concern in Britain: without a superior fleet Britain's existence was always threatened. The Germans could starve out or invade England with their enormous armies. The British could neither starve out nor invade Germany.

By 1913 British and German naval estimates agreed that the next year Britain would have twenty-nine dreadnoughts and Germany twenty-one. Britain was not happy about this, and *The Times* warned Britons of the fate of the Roman Empire. The warning was occasioned by an offer from Canada and the Malay States to put ships into service that would be considered a part of the British fleet in times of trouble. When citizens of Rome looked to the outreaches of empire for support the empire collapsed, warned *The Times*.

Everyone, of course, spoke of 'defence'. Tirpitz talked of attaining and maintaining a relationship of ten to sixteen against the British. 'It gives us such a measure of power that it is difficult to attack us ...' Churchill spoke of the need for a strong force. 'Margins of naval strength which are sufficient when the time comes to compel a victory, are insufficient to maintain a peace ...' They all saw peace as a particular national prerogative. By the spring of 1914 the politicians were talking about a ratio of eight British ships to five German ships in home waters. This gave the Germans a new idea: build ships for the German Empire; they could later be brought back and meanwhile they would not count in the ratio.

This naval jockeying increased in tempo as the century wore on. One result of the Agadir affair was more British naval construction. By 1912 the British boasted of having more dreadnoughts than all the rest of the world navies put together. Another result — or perhaps a symptom — was a growing nervousness about war. Sane statesmen pointed to the balance of power and said there could be no war. But everytime either nation slipped another new hull down the shipyard ways heads that were not so sane wondered; with both sides calling loudly for arms reduction while they continued the race.

In the winter of 1913-14 war fever began to develop. In the Balkans, the Austro-Hungarian Empire was threatened by rebellion of Slavic groups, who claimed kinship with Russia. If the Hapsburgs moved against Serbia strongly enough to bring Russia into action, then France would join Russia, and Germany would back up her

Austro-Hungarian ally, and Britain ... what would Britain do? That was the question. She had alliances with Russia and France, but claimed the most sincere desire for peace. But Kaiser Wilhelm was not lulled by such talk. 'The final struggle between the Slavs and the Teutons,' he wrote on the margin of one report from a diplomat, 'will see the Anglo-Saxons on the side of the Slavs and the Gauls.' So that winter Germany prepared, and in the naval sense she prepared well; sensing the impending crisis, her naval constructors turned to the building of U-Boats, cheap and quick to manufacture. Learning of this, the British concern deepened. In March, 1914, Winston Churchill, First Lord of the Admiralty, went to the House of Commons with estimates for the next year's naval expenditure. The full fleet would be in commission and four new dreadnoughts were to be built.

After years of diplomatic talk, the gloves were off. The arms race was wide open. Each side blamed the other, but neither now tried to heal the split. The Germans, whose industrial growth in the Ruhr had begun to frighten Britain, renewed their efforts to increase manufactures. Kaiser Wilhelm no longer made any pretences: it was his fondest hope that one day his fleet would equal, or surpass, that of Britain in strength. All he needed was a little more time.

2

Summer 1914

June was the glorious month for navies. In Europe it signalled the coming of Kiel week, Germany's naval regatta, which was the Kaiser's favourite celebration. He loved to go to Kiel, and live at sea for this week, and race his yacht against all comers of the class. The German Navy always made much of the event; it was a showcase for the *Kriegsmarine* and the ships were there in new paint and all their bunting. As the week opened, four British dreadnoughts and three cruisers came steaming into port, under the flag of Vice-Admiral Sir George Warrender, Commander of the Second Battle Squadron of the Home Fleet. Admiral Warrender flew his flag in HMS *King George V* as it came majestically into port. The ship was followed by the *Centurion, Ajax* and *Audacious*, and then the cruisers. Many eyes were turned to the British battleships as they moved through the bright sunshine, serenaded by the booming of the twenty-one gun salutes, and moored near a line of five of the Kaiser's latest battleships.

At first the reception was rather cool. The British officers boarded the German flagship, *Friedrich der Grosse*, but no one seemed to have much to say. The German naval attaché to the London Embassy went about warning his fellow officers that the British were ready for war, and this visit could only be explained as an attempt to spy on the German Navy. Particularly, he warned about any British interest in German U-Boats, which had been artfully concealed about the harbour so that the British could get no accurate estimates. Sir George invited the German officers to visit his warships and look over them from engine room to bridge. Tactfully, he did not say that the wireless rooms and fire control stations had been closed off. The Germans were blunter; there were parts of German ships that no one outside the navy was allowed to see. Yet in spite of the amenities' shortcomings, British officers did visit some German ships, and the Germans came aboard Royal Navy vessels for a look.

The leavening factor in the proceedings was Kaiser Wilhelm, who arrived in his yacht *Hohenzollern*, once the naval vessels were on display. She came through the canal, and down the line. Ships' bands struck up, and the battleships thundered their salute to the Emperor of the Germans. He was very pleased, as he always was at a naval celebration, and his enthusiasm broke the ice. Next day the Regatta began, with parties, dances, banquets and boat races, from the majestic yachts to the lifeboats manned by struggling Other Ranks and Matelots.

At the same time, Vice-Admiral David Beatty was visiting St Petersburg with the battle-cruiser squadron, to allay any feelings that Britain might be prepared to sacrifice her alliance with Russia. The St Petersburg visit was even more splendid than the German affair, with champagne and high kicks, swirling skirts, medals and shiny swords whirling about the decks of the warships that were suddenly transformed into floating palaces for a night or two.

Across the world, similar celebration was taking place at Tsingtao, capital and major port of the German colony of Kiaochow on the Shantung coast of China. The acquisition of Kiaochow had come in 1897, as Germany had joined the race for footholds on the China coast. Since that time Germany had pursued an aggressive colonial policy, building up one of the finest ports in the world in the half-moon bay of Tsingtao, and creating a German city of brick and stone on the plain and hills around the port. There was no finer town in Asia than the German settlement at Tsingtao, with a proper water works, and power stations, paved streets, neat public buildings, and a busy port that handled merchant shipping and housed Germany's naval might in the Pacific, the German East Asia Cruiser Squadron. The cruiser squadron consisted of two heavy cruisers, the *Scharnhorst* and the *Gneisenau*, and three light or unarmoured cruisers, the *Emden*, the *Leipzig*, and the *Nürnberg*. Their purpose, established years earlier, was to show the German flag and put down petty rebellions against German power in various colonies. The flag had been shown several times in China, to protect German commercial interests in that divided and confused country. Cruisers had occasionally been sent to the Pacific islands, to deal with some minor problem so ruthlessly that repetition was unlikely. One would not say that command of the German East Asia Cruiser Squadron was the next step to chief of the naval staff, but it was vital and pleasant duty for reasons that were apparent in that summer of 1914.

Tsingtao was 'the pearl of the east' and while British businessmen and officers from Asian posts flocked to Weihaiwei in the north for summer respite from the Oriental heat, the Germans and many others came to Tsingtao where the summer weather was delightful, warm sunshine from above and almost always a cool breeze from the sea. The young officers of the squadron were much in demand for soirées, balls, garden parties, and beach parties on the white sands of the half-moon bay. The horse races were held weekly, band concerts were a Sunday feature in the square, good German beer could be found in all the restaurants, and the girls of summer were extremely pretty, they said. So summer duty in Tsingtao was considered a treat. The tensions that gripped Europe that summer of 1914 were apparent in Tsingtao, but overlaid by the cushion of luxurious colonial life. Even the lowly seamen enjoyed special privilege and special status here. In Europe, when a naval vessel needed fuel, the sacks of coal were carried below decks by the seamen. In Tsingtao, the sacks were carried by Chinese coolies, and even an ordinary seaman was so rich by Chinese standards that he could have a servant ashore. The crews ate and drank like nobles, with fresh produce, eggs and chickens supplied by the Chinese farmers who clustered around the port.

The commander of this enviable naval establishment was Rear-Admiral Maximilian von Spee, a count, or *Graf*, who had chosen the naval service instead of the Army for his career. He was a dapper and even dashing officer of healthy middle age, with a clipped beard and the manners of Berlin. He had commanded the squadron since the late summer of 1912, and had already seen more than a little trouble. Indeed, when he arrived to take charge he found a ticklish situation in China which necessitated the dispatch of several vessels to the Yangtze. Various warlords were kicking up their heels against the new Republic of China's policies, and German traders in the ports along the river were threatened. So were those of Britain, France, and other countries, and the Europeans banded together to apply their combined strength to put down threats against European life and property. That local union was one of the anomalies of service in the Far East; no matter the situation at home, Europeans had hung together 'out here', and sometimes it was hard to remember that enmities were growing out of suspicions back at home.

This summer there would not be too much time to enjoy the amenities of Tsingtao. The squadron had a busy schedule, and already was scattered over half the world. The two big cruisers were in port at Tsingtao that spring, along with the *Leipzig* and the *Emden*, but only for a brief few weeks. Early in June the relief ship came in from Wilhelmshaven, carrying mail, naval supplies, and replacements for the ships and shore battalions. The government of Tsingtao was also a naval matter, with authority rested in Captain Alfred Meyer-Waldeck, a professional naval officer and intimate of the Berlin court. Governor Meyer-Waldeck was in charge of the colony, but Admiral von Spee was in charge of the squadron, whose responsibility extended to the shores of America. The two men were on the friendliest of terms; all that Meyer-Waldeck asked of the squadron was that it keep order; all that von Spee asked of the colony was that it provide a base. The relief ship *Patricia* brought the new men who were apportioned among ships and shore, and the squadron could then resume its many functions.

The light cruiser *Leipzig* had been waiting only for the new draft of men to fill her complement. Early in June she sailed, bound first for Yokohama and then for the west coast of Mexico. There she would replace the light cruiser *Nürnberg* on station. Political affairs in Mexico that summer were thoroughly confused, with a rebellion in progress, and with it all the concomitant fears and dangers to the German trading population. Fregattenkapitän Johannes Haun, the commander of the *Leipzig*, had his work cut out for him. Fully half his crew had been replaced that spring, with the new draft from the relief ship. That meant the ship must be worked up on the voyage across the Pacific, for Captain Haun had no idea what sort of trouble he might encounter in Mexico. Conceivably the ship would have to fight, and so must be ready.

On 10 June when *Leipzig* sailed into Yokohama Bay and passed the big Japanese naval base at Yokosuka, Captain Haun saw most of the Japanese fleet at anchor. This fleet was the most powerful in Asia, and one of the four most powerful in the world. Captain Haun had little but professional considerations on his mind as he looked the ships over, but when he got to shore that day the German naval attaché greeted him with a wild look in his eye and a tale of crisis. Reports in Japan of almost certain war in Europe had triggered discussions among the Japanese of extending their own empire. *If* war came, said the naval attaché that evening over after-dinner cigars and brandy, *if*, mind you, then they might expect that Japan would come in. On whose side, asked a naïve Captain Haun? On the side of Britain and France, of course, said the naval attaché. The Japanese coveted Tsingtao, *and* the Carolines, *and* the Marshalls, and any other bits of territory they could get their hands on. It was too bad that Haun was going the wrong way, for the naval attaché would very much have liked to send an informal message to Admiral von Spee. That officer was widely known as one of the most astute in the service, and he might be able to help. The naval attaché (Captain Knorr by name) had been warning the German ambassador and the diplomatic staff of danger for months. The ambassador had been too busy going to parties to listen, and the secretaries and counsellors were too much wrapped up in their own affairs to pay attention to what the attaché had learned from drunken Japanese naval officers at a series of carefully planned dinners. Japan would join the Triple Entente for the simple reason that she would then be free immediately to attack Tsingtao. Even as the naval attaché said these words, he knew the futility of trying to tell von Spee. What could the Admiral do about it? Given time, perhaps von Spee could persuade Berlin to strengthen the defences in the Pacific, but how much good could that do? For coal was the rub; coal existed for the Germans only at Tsingtao where it came down from the mines of Shantung province, and in Japan. There was no coal on the string of tiny islets in the Pacific, and very little else but coral and sand. If war came, and Tsingtao was besieged, then what would the East Asia Cruiser Squadron do?

Admiral von Spee had been contemplating that question for a long time, and he was no closer to the answer than he had been in the beginning. For everything depended on what happened, and how. If war came — and he meant war with Russia primarily — then Vladivostok would be his aiming point. If the French came in, then Indo-China would also be a target. All this depended on his freedom of movement, and that, in turn, depended largely on what the British did. For the British, with bases and colonies that ringed the Pacific, could strangle the East Asia Squadron simply by denying it coal.

The most frustrating aspect of it all was that there was absolutely no way that intellect or courage could change the situation, and all the messages in the world from Yokohama would make no difference. Survival was a matter of perseverance and luck. The Admiral could do nothing about the latter, but everything about the former. What it involved this summer was a heavy schedule of training for the squadron. With the tensions hanging over Berlin it seemed a bit odd that discharges from the service were still permitted, but the peacetime ways could not be discarded as long as there was peace. A cloud was descending over Europe, and its shadow fell across the Pacific, but perhaps it would blow away, and as long as there was no storm, then the old ways would continue.

Even before the *Patricia* came with her contingent of recruits, Admiral von Spee had planned a training programme for the squadron's summer. Captain Karl von Müller, the commander of the *Emden* was told that his ship would remain on station in Tsingtao for the summer until August, when it would make a call at Shanghai to look over the Shanghai river gunboats that were part of von Spee's responsibility. *Vaterland, Tsingtau* and *Otter* were stationed on the Yangtze near the big port. Three other gunboats, the *Iltis, Jaguar*, and *Luchs* also ranged Chinese waters, from the Pearl River off Canton to Taku Bar off Tientsin, moving where they were needed to assist Germany interests. All these would also be von Müller's responsibility during the summer months, as would administration of the activities of the torpedo boat *Taku* and the small steamer *Titania*, which were auxiliaries of the squadron. Von Müller would be in charge because Admiral von Spee intended to be gone almost all summer. It was the custom for the ships to visit all the South Sea colonies: New Guinea and Samoa in particular, to remind the Australians and the New Zealanders that this was German territory, no matter how much these *Englanders* might covet the land. In 1913 the heavy cruisers had not made the trip; the revolution against President Yuan Shi-kai's China government had made it necessary for von Spee to stay in Chinese waters, and *Emden* had been sent alone to remind the world of the German presence. It was all the more necessary then that the commander of the fleet put in an appearance this year.

Von Spee's plans were interrupted by a message from Vice-Admiral Sir Thomas Jerram, commander of the British China Squadron, that he was coming by and would drop in at Tsingtao for a visit. Jerram knew very well that the Germans changed their guard in the early summer, and that they did not relish visits for at least a month or so after the relief ship had left. No one liked to be caught in a situation that demanded protocol and competition with an untrained crew. So Admiral von Spee was a little annoyed by the British insistence on a visit at this particular time. He also suspected that the British had a reason for coming: to see for themselves if the Germans had added any strength to Tsingtao or the squadron in the last few months. But there was nothing to be done in politeness save break out the bunting and the champagne and give the British a party. When the *Minotaur*, the armoured cruiser that was Jerram's flagship, moved in past Chaliento lighthouse in the outreach of the bay, and was recognized and reported, Admiral von Spee was ready. The *Minotaur* came in slowly under the guidance of the German pilot, and passed Cape Yatau that stood sentinel above the entrance to the bay, then glided in at slow speed, her guns opening up in salute, and those of the port responding. The pilot brought the British cruiser squarely in to the berth designated by Admiral von Spee, next to the flagship *Scharnhorst*, and across from the *Gneisenau*.

It was 12 June, the height of the British visiting season, it appeared this year. By early afternoon, all was shipshape aboard the *Minotaur* and Admiral Jerram began his round of duty calls. He called on von Spee aboard the *Scharnhorst*, and then on Governor Meyer-Waldeck at the residence. Von Spee then called on Jerram and so did Meyer-Waldeck. The squadron Chief of Staff, Captain Otto Fielitz called on the Chief of Staff of the British squadron. The *Scharnhorst*'s captain, Felix Schultz, called on the *Minotaur*'s captain, and so did Captain Gustav Maerker, the commander of the *Gneisenau*, and Captain von Müller of the *Emden*. It was late afternoon before these formalities ended, and nearly time for the officers to change for the formal dinner and dress ball that Admiral von Spee was giving aboard the *Gneisenau*. The German cruiser was polished and dressed with canvas curtains that concealed the instruments of war, bunting, strings of electric lights on the afterdeck, and potted plants brought aboard for the night. A dance band played discreetly during the dinner, and then warmed up for the evening. Admiral von Spee had sent out a hurried call to all the belles of Tsingtao to help out, and most of them came to make the ball a grand success. It was late at night before the electric lights were turned out as the last guest went ashore.

Admiral von Spee gave a dinner aboard the *Scharnhorst* for the senior British officers. Governor Meyer-Waldeck gave a ball at the governor's great stone palace on the hill overlooking the harbour. The *Gneisenau* officers gave another reception. For four days the celebration continued on ship and shore. The officers of the *Minotaur* challenged the officers of the *Scharnhorst* to a polo game, and *Scharnhorst* won. The crew of the *Minotaur* challenged the crews of the two German cruisers to a whaleboat race, and the Germans won. The ships put up champions for boxing matches at every weight, and the Germans won most of the contests. But then came the football match. The Germans started out strong, and soon ran up a three goal lead. But the British then got their second wind, and came back to win the contest four goals to three, which gave them possession of a silver cup Admiral von Spee had donated for the event.

While the athletes were competing, many of the British suddenly became outdoor enthusiasts. So many officers and petty officers decided to go mountain climbing that the Germans were hard pressed to find guides, and painted directions on the rock walls. It was an interesting coincidence that the mountains they climbed also housed the major defences of the ring of hills around Tsingtao. Some of the British seemed to get lost for hours, and worried their hosts until they appeared again. Admiral Jerram decided he must have a drive in the country, and travelled around every road in the vicinity of Tsingtao all one day.

The last event of the visit was a grand ball given by the British visitors aboard the *Minotaur*. It was as impressive as the German entertainments had been, and the women and girls of Tsingtao society enjoyed themselves immensely. Next day, Admiral Jerram left the port for Weihaiwei, the British squadron's summer headquarters. The flags flew in the offshore breeze as the *Minotaur* was escorted out to sea by a small flotilla of harbour craft, and then she turned north and the boats came back into port. The visit ended with Admiral Jerram's final signal: 'Live well and good-bye until we meet again.' No one quite knew when that would be, but in spite of the tensions of Europe, here in the Far East there seemed not so much cause for concern. The interests and activities of all the Europeans were apparently similar, and sometimes it was hard to know what the people back home in Berlin and London were arguing about.

With the departure of the British visitors, Admiral von Spee lost no time in getting ready for sea. He wanted to take the two armoured cruisers down to the Pacific islands as quickly as he could get there. Berlin had also indicated recently a more than usual interest in the daily affairs of the squadron. In that sense, the tension was communicating itself to the eastern world. *Leipzig*, for example, left Yokohama with Captain Knorr's warnings about war ringing in Captain Haun's ears, and sailed for Honolulu, training the new crewmen in gunnery and seamanship as she went. She moved off the regular steamer lanes and into the quiet waters where gunnery would disturb none but the fish. There the men practised for a week before the captain was satisfied. Then he resumed course for Hawaii, arriving at a Kauai landfall on 26 June, and entering Honolulu harbour the next day. *Leipzig* had no sooner arrived than London had that word. Francis Swanzy, the managing director of the British trading firm of Theo H. Davies Ltd, was also British consul, and recently he had been advised to keep a sharp eye on the movement of any German vessels. He complied with a will, for Swanzy was a loyal Englishman. *Leipzig* was provisioned by Hackfeld and Company, a German firm, but Swanzy kept an eye on her all during the stay.

In Tsingtao, Admiral von Spee conferred with Governor Meyer-

Waldeck and Captain von Müller on administrative matters, since he would be away for three months. The coming of the British had resolved one problem: at least Meyer-Waldeck and von Müller would not have to worry about being dropped in on without notice. So there seemed no reason that von Müller's *Emden* should not go to Shanghai in July as planned.

Gneisenau was sent into the dry-dock for some minor repairs and coaling. A crane lifted baskets of coal up from the dock to the main deck and then down into the holds. The crew of the cruiser worked from flat-bottomed scows that carried the coal, and then carried bags up the gangways into the coal hold. Normally the ship would be coaled by the dock coolies, but Admiral von Spee was in a hurry and he felt the new hands could use a little hard training. So the crew did work quite unusual for them in East Asia surroundings.

Gneisenau sailed on 20 June for Nagasaki, and Captain Maerker was very glad to be going. The coaling had been a dirty job; hurried and unpleasant. The ship was filthy with coal dust, the black had permeated every cranny down to the lockers where the ship's crystal was stored. Glasses, linens, the corners of the galley, were all covered with a film of black and must be scoured clean. The sailing was a relief. From his bridge Captain Maerker could see the dust beginning to blow away as the ship rounded the horse-shoe reef and headed out of the harbour. Soon the lighthouse at Arkona Island passed and then faded from view, and finally even Laushan Mountain, the highest in the colony, was only a bit of purple grey in the distance, and all around them was the blue water of the East China Sea. As the ship reached deep water, the captain ordered her cleaned and the hoses were brought forth. The men were happy at this work, getting rid of the grime. They scoured the paint work and scrubbed the wooden decks until they whitened. They were happy to be at sea and even happier because they were headed for Nagasaki, one of the best leave ports in the Pacific. The men would have shore leave – it had been promised – and they might have to stay for several days. For the purpose of the visit was really to pick up the squadron's mail, which had been directed to this port. The mail ship that had left Germany two weeks before had collected all the letters and packages for the squadron. Perhaps the ship would be delayed by storms; at least the men could hope. But there was no such luck, on the very day that *Gneisenau* arrived at Nagasaki, so did the German mail steamer, and there was no further business to be done except top off with coal. It did not take long to load a mere 400 tons of coal, so the men knew

the ship would sail next day. She did sail, and on 26 June, the day
that Admiral von Spee and the *Scharnhorst* made ready to sail from
Tsingtao for the south Pacific, the *Gneisenau* crossed the Tropic of
Cancer; and the next day the ship arrived at the edge of the Marianas
Islands chain. For the new men of the crew of the *Gneisenau* it was all
a remarkable and novel experience. Before them lay the island of
Urakas. Some had expected the South Seas to be a tropic paradise,
with palm trees waving in the gentle breeze and grass-skirted girls
strumming ukeleles on white sandy beaches. Urakas, the landfall they
made at the Marianas, was a lifeless volcano, whose rocky shores had
not attracted enough rainfall to create vegetation. The crater rose
above, a peak with its top popped-out, a thousand feet above the sea,
and the only sign of life was the myriad of sea birds that swirled and
floated above the island.

Captain Maerker moved the ship down the long Marianas chain,
coming in close ashore by day to show the ship to the people of the
islands, but moving out to sea by night. The Marianas had never been
completely charted and the captain was concerned lest his cruiser pile
up on a tropic reef. But no mishap befell the *Gneisenau*, and on 28
June she arrived at Pagan, the German capital of the colony.

Pagan was always regarded by the squadron as a difficult port of
call. The place had no proper harbour for an ocean-going ship, and so
the captain anchored outside the reef. In a sense this was self-
defeating, for the ultimate effectiveness of the visit would have called
for the *Gneisenau* to pull up alongside a pier, all white and shining, to
impress the populace with German might as well as German
efficiency. From the standpoint of the squadron, there was little
enough to attract at Pagan, however, and the ship was as well off outside the reef. The place consisted of a few tin-roofed shacks, and a
large number of thatched huts and coconut palms that provided a
mainstay of native diet. The Marianas colony made a proud
impression on the maps, but in reality it was of very little value to
Germany; its main export being copra, in a world where copra was
hardly in short supply.

There was very little to do on the island that lay before the ship, and
the officers were well aware of the dangers of doing anything. The
year before, when the squadron sent representative ships south,
Gneisenau and *Scharnhorst* had come here first. A party of young
officers had gone ashore on the first day to have a look and had hiked
up the side of one of the two volcanoes on the island. One of the
youngest officers had strayed from the group, a fact unnoticed until

they returned to the ship in small groups aboard the liberty boats. When he was discovered missing a boat was sent ashore, and then, when the boat crew found no one, a search party was organized. Two hundred men went out with torches and lamps to retrace the party's steps. They had found him on the side of the mountain, in a patch of scrub vegetation, dead from fatigue and the hot sun.

The story of this misadventure was related to the crew before the leave parties went ashore. No one was to wander away to the mountains. The group was to stick together close to the landing. And so it was. The men came ashore, found the general store, drank a little beer, and wandered about in their uniforms, perspiring in the heat. They saw few women and fewer beauties. Then, after two or three hours, they went back to the ship. No one was lost or hurt, although one of the liberty boats capsized in the surf going across the reef, and the whole crew got a dunking. But since no one was lost or even injured, it was regarded as a fine joke by the rest of the crew. As darkness fell, officers and men came out on the decks of the warship to smoke and talk. The officers sat on the fantail looking out across the calm waters at the volcanoes, playing chess or smoking companionably. The men assembled on the foredeck and sang of love and loneliness, for there was much about these tropical waters that reminded them just how far they were from home. It was a peaceful night, and as far as the men of the lower deck were concerned, the first of three full months of relaxed duty here in the South Seas. It was 29 June on this side of the international dateline. In Berlin, and at a little town called Sarajevo in Serbia, it was 28 June.

3

The Saddest Month

On the morning of 28 June Archduke Franz Ferdinand of Austria-Hungary prepared for his participation in a parade down the main street of Sarajevo to the government buildings. He had come to Serbia as an ambassador, to remind the people of the power of the Empire of the Hapsburgs. The sending of the heir-apparent to the throne was calculated to quiet the unrest that had been disturbing Serbia for a long time. He did not know, although some of his official hosts did, that an organization called The Black Hand had decreed that he was to be killed this day on the line of march.

The parade assembled in late morning. The Archduke and his consort entered the ornate carriage kept for state occasions, and the guards, on their splendid horses, lances at the ready, moved into position and the parade began, along the dusty boulevard. Suddenly out from the crowd stepped a young man named Gavrilo Princip, who came purposefully toward the carriage. There was an explosion, the carriage sagged, and the Archduke of Austria-Hungary was dead.

The woeful news of the assassination reached Kiel late in the afternoon. Kaiser Wilhelm at that moment was racing his yacht, *Meteor*, and could not be reached. But one officer knew how important was the telegram handed to him, and he braved the possible wrath of the Emperor of the Germans to take the message out to *Meteor*. The Kaiser reacted as he had expected; the race was stopped, a state of national mourning declared, and the festivities brought to an abrupt end. Admiral Warrender had planned a splendid series of celebrations to show British hospitality. They were reduced to a single subdued luncheon for Admiral Tirpitz and other leading naval figures. When Warrender sailed, flying his signal flags in a message even he could only hope might be true: 'Friends today, friends in future, friends forever ...'

The big battleships took the outside route home to England, but the 'friends' aboard the three British cruisers which had come to Kiel moved into the Kiel Canal, which gave them a shorter route. The events of the day before had made their observations of changes in the locks and passing points of new importance. The changes were carefully observed and noted. No one in the Royal Navy knew just what would come next, but all knew it might be disaster.

In Tsingtao, the news was greeted next morning with the detachment that events in Europe were given by the great distances involved. The British Vice-Consul, R.H. Eckford, called on Governor Meyer-Waldeck, and they agreed that the situation was depressing, but they could hope for the best. Captain von Müller of the *Emden* did not have to make any judgements about what had happened; it was his task to inform Admiral von Spee and all the ships of the squadron of the events, and he had begun that process on the night of 29 June when the news had come in from Europe. Admiral von Spee was in mid-Pacific, going to join the *Gneisenau* in the Marianas. The *Gneisenau* was still at Pagan. The light cruiser *Leipzig* had just left Honolulu under the suspicious eyes of Acting Consul Swanzy, and Captain Haun got the news by wireless from the American station in Hawaii. Captain Karl von Schönberg of the *Nürnberg* also had the message while at sea off the coast of Mexico. For the moment Admiral von Spee did not contemplate any change in plan. Politically speaking, nothing had actually happened. But it was apparent that Vienna would not let the assassination go unpunished. And in the tinderbox of the Balkans, with the Serbs agitating for independence and Russia backing their claims, anything might happen. The Russians were bound to the French, and the British to both of them. Germany was allied with Austria-Hungary, and so, supposedly was Italy. Admiral von Spee did not wear his heart on his sleeve, nor did he confide to many of his officers. But he was seriously concerned. The war plans came out: one for war against Russia, one for war against England, one, even, for war against Japan. Any of these and all of them were distinct possibilities, but no more than that and under the circumstances there was nothing specific to be done, except one thing: get the squadron ready for war.

For the next week, the Tsingtao Press was filled with speculative stories: Kaiser Wilhelm had not changed; the yacht *Hohenzollern* would leave Kiel and cruise into the Baltic beginning 7 July; Admiral Tirpitz, the chief of the Navy, was 'taking the cure' before going to Switzerland on holiday, and he did not move. That was the news for the public. But the Tsingtao wireless station also had confidential telegrams for Admiral von Spee, and they were less optimistic. Consequently on 7 July the Admiral made up his mind: it was no time for von Müller to be going off to Shanghai, and leaving Tsingtao unprotected. Von Müller was to stay on instead of sailing the next day. Further, he was to give Admiral von Spee in the next few days a careful review of all German naval units in Asia. The Admiral particularly wanted the bare facts of their preparedness for war.

Captain von Müller began assembling the information. *Emden*, of course, was in harbour at Tsingtao, and, except for the training of the new men, respectably ready for action. The gunboat *Jaguar* was on the Yangtze River, quite where he did not know, but somewhere upriver. The gunboat *Luchs* was in Shanghai, and he had intended to meet her in a few days. The gunboat *Tiger* was in Tsingtao harbour, undergoing a few repairs. The *Iltis*, another gunboat, was in the dry-dock at Tsingtao, where major work was being done on her engines and hull. The river gunboat *Tsingtau* (smaller than ordinary gunboats) was on the West River, and her sister ships (*Vaterland* and *Otter* were on the upper Yangtze above the gorge. The torpedo boat *S-90* was in Chefoo. Also in Tsingtao for repairs was the old unarmoured cruiser *Cormoran*. And that was the strength of the squadron, impressive enough if one contemplated the maintenance of order against bandits, but not very strong if one contemplated a major war against multiple enemies.

On 7 July as Admiral von Spee ordered Captain von Müller to assemble all this information about the ships, Kaiser Wilhelm sailed for the Baltic, giving every indication of a man preoccupied with a holiday. Actually, the wireless room of the yacht *Hohenzollern* twittered day and night with messages. German ambassadors around the world were briefed daily about the political situation. So were military and naval commanders throughout the Empire. Secretly, the German fleet was mobilized; extra supplies of coal and ammunition were hurried to Danzig, Heligoland and Kiel. Wilhelmshaven was on a war footing. Work had been progressing normally on three new battleships and a cruiser; now it was done around the clock, as orders went out to the fleet detaching crews for the new ships. The battle-cruiser *Goeben* had been stationed in the Mediterranean for some time, and her captain had complained that her boilers were in serious need of repair. No one had paid much attention to the plaint; captains were forever bedevilling the Admiralty with requests that meant spending money. But now *Goeben* was hurriedly ordered to the Austrian port of Pola on the Adriatic coast, and not trusting the abilities of their Austrian allies, the *Admiralstab* sent specialists from German naval yards to do the work. The High Seas Fleet, Germany's answer to the Home Fleet, was off the Skagerrak on its usual summer cruise. The plans were not changed, ostensibly, but the fleet was warned to be ready for anything at any moment. In Berlin supply officers argued for bringing the fleet back to Germany immediately for refurbishment, but the foreign office argued that such a move would only add to the political excitement and Admiral Tirpitz agreed. He was sure the 'thunderstorm' would pass without any lightning striking, and that is what he wanted; he told the Kaiser that the German Navy would not be ready for war against England for at least six years. Let the politicians remember that and keep on talking.

Admiral von Spee was ordered to keep in 'certain and constant communication' with Berlin. The orders came on 7 July, and were taken seriously. Admiral von Spee considered the possibilities of war. The first thing he must do was guarantee the security of the squadron, and he was in a poor position at the moment to do so. The Marianas had very little of what he wanted or needed in case of war, although Truk harbour in the Carolines was excellent for defensive purposes. Until this point, Admiral von Spee had not disturbed his captains with his worries. Von Müller, in Tsingtao, had to know because he was functioning as the Admiral's right arm. But Captain Maerker had been allowed to take *Gneisenau* from Saipan over to Rota so his officers could have some sport in a goat hunt; hardly the course one took when preparing for battle. But by 7 July the two big cruisers were anchored in Truk's Eten harbour, between Toleas and Eten Islands, with twenty fathoms of water under their keels.

That day two more vessels arrived in the harbour. They were *Titania*, the squadron's despatch ship, and *Fukoku Maru*, a Japanese collier that had been chartered for the summer to supply coal for the squadron during the long South Pacific voyage. The presence of the Japanese ship now gave the Admiral a distinctly uncomfortable feeling; it reminded him that one of his enemies might well be Japan, with a fleet that could easily overwhelm the squadron. It also emphasized his desperate situation in case of war. The southern colonies had small supplies of coal on hand, but every ton of it had been brought down from Shantung province, Manchuria, or Japan. There was not a single known vein of coal north of Australia; these islands, which had seemed so desirable to the builders of empire, had no resources on which von Spee could draw.

The situation was dramatized for the Admiral by Captain

Maerker's observation that it was time for him to coal. Since topping off on 22 June at Nagasaki, Maerker had steamed at 10 knots (her best cruising speed) across the Pacific, and yet two weeks later he was short of coal. Captain Schultz of the *Scharnhorst* announced that his ship's condition was even more demanding. The Admiral had ordered the ship to speed across the Pacific to catch up with *Gneisenau*, and the flagship had burned twice as much coal in less time. Von Spee had planned for all this. The German collier *Elsbeth* was scheduled to meet them later, and meanwhile they had on hand the *Fukoku Maru* and the *Titania*, whose holds were also filled with coal for the squadron. And yet in case of trouble this tiny supply meant nothing. Admiral von Spee told Captain von Müller in Tsingtao that his next order of business must be to locate and charter every conceivable collier along the China coast. They must be filled up and made available to the squadron. The Admiral did not know what he would do in case of war; everything would depend on circumstance. But the need for a fuel supply was inexorable.

So the ships coaled. The senior officers, except for the first officers of both cruisers, fled ashore with the Admiral, to get completely away from the dust. Anyone who could find an excuse at least went over to the *Titania*, to sit on the deck and drink beer while watching the black clouds rise above the ships. But Commander Alfred Bender of the *Scharnhorst* and Commander Hans Pochhammer of the *Gneisenau* were stuck with supervision of the dirtiest job in the German Navy. They put on their oldest uniforms and told the men to strip down to shorts and undervests. Then they coaled. This time the job was done with more enthusiasm than usual, because a third of the crew had never coaled before from a steamer. The process involved the movement of the *Scharnhorst*'s boats to both sides of the *Fukoku Maru*. The men clambered aboard the steamer, the boats moved out, and the two ships were brought together, with rubbing gear protecting their plates. The steam hoists of the cargo vessel were fired up and the loading began. In the hold of the *Fukoku Maru* men sweated and strained to bag coal, which was stacked aboard the cargo nets below, and then brought up and hoisted over into the coal holds of the cruiser. In the morning it went well, but by about ten o'clock the sun was high and the heat began. By noon it had reached the 90°s F on deck, and in the holds it was well over a 100° F. The coaling was stopped at midday for three hours, and then resumed again. When the process was completed at nightfall, the *Scharnhorst* was filled with coal and covered with coal dust from end to end. The collier moved over to the *Gneisenau*, where spotlights and searchlights were rigged to give nearly the light of day. *Gneisenau* coaled then, while *Scharnhorst* scrubbed, and only when both ships were fuelled and the paint and bright work had been cleaned, did the crew get a rest. For the next few days the men had liberty almost for the asking. The officers commandeered boats to go fishing and sailing. The Admiral commuted between ship and shore in his launch, a vessel 30 feet long, with a tall stack that kept the soot away from the open stern where von Spee sat in a deck chair.

Part of the reason for the trip had been to show the flag. The native chiefs came in a drove to see the great white ships one day, and clambered up the sides of the two cruisers on ropes and assembled on coconut fibre mats on the decks. About the flagship they gave a performance of native dances. The German officers, even those who had seen it all before, were fascinated by the dark warriors in their feathers and anklets, clutching spears and warclubs and dancing with a ferocious enthusiasm. The girls, in grass skirts, shell necklaces and flowers, sang and clapped their hands to beat time, and the drummers sent forth strange cadences into the afternoon air. The Admiral smiled and pulled on his vandyke beard, and made it a point to hold an interpreted conversation with every chief aboard. It was well after dark before the ship's searchlights were turned on to light the way back to shore for the war canoes.

During the second week of July 1914, war fever simmered in Berlin and Vienna. Admiral von Spee was in touch almost hourly with Tsingtao's powerful wireless transmission station, but the news was anything but definitive. In Berlin the cabinet argued among themselves as to policy. In London it was much the same. But as the politicians talked, the forces of violence assembled, and with each day of delay it was apparent that no concessions were going to be made by anyone, and that without concessions war would surely come in a matter of weeks. On 15 July Admiral von Spee could stomach the tension no longer without release, and he sailed the ships out of harbour for military manoeuvres at sea. They went out of Truk at night, for the specific purpose of practising night navigation, and night battle techniques. Next day Admiral von Spee arranged for *Scharnhorst* and *Gneisenau* to go to sea and practise their gunnery. He took the 30-foot launch and went off, accompanied by his staff, to contemplate courses of action as he visited the uninhabited island atoll of Oroluk. For a long time he had wanted to see the place and write a record of his findings for the German nature magazine. This was considered to be extremely good form; all over Asia ardent foreigners made such observations and collected them for posterity. The Germans had nothing quite so imposing as the Royal Asiatic Society, but they had hopes, and a proper European gentleman always took note of his surroundings. There was an even deeper reason for the Admiral's sudden turn to love of nature. It might be expected that Captains Schultz and Maerker would witness some very poor performances by gun crews just out from the Fatherland, and it was best if the Admiral avoid any direct confrontation with such inefficiency. By the time the ships returned, it was to be most ardently hoped, the crews would have been whipped into shape and any further gunnery would be up to par. No captain liked to be embarrassed before his Admiral, Schultz and Maerker were not responsible for the circumstances that forced them to train the crews in front of their commander, and von Spee had a delicate sense of protocol; it was one of the aspects of his character that endeared the Admiral to his officers and men.

When Admiral von Spee approached the islands, he was startled to see a Japanese schooner just offshore. As the Germans came up the Japanese broke out fishing gear and began fishing furiously. But it was apparent that until they saw the Germans they had not been fishing at all. What were they doing? Undoubtedly they were making observations for charts. Further, they were certainly in this area because of the announced coming of the German cruisers. Von Spee was indignant but he had to accept the fact that this incident was of a parcel with the unexpected intrusion of the British into his lair at Tsingtao the month before.

The Admiral did not let his discovery of the Japanese keep him from his self-appointed task. He went ashore, trailed by his staff and prowled around the islands looking for wild life and plants. For two days he enjoyed the beauties of nature while his men trained. First *Gneisenau* towed a target for *Scharnhorst* while the experienced members of the gun crews taught the youngsters how to shoot. Then the process was reversed, until on 17 July, when Admiral von Spee went aboard the flagship and the cruisers put on a gunnery demonstration for him, he was able to give his approval without reservation.

Usually on such cruises as these, Tsingtao made frequent announcements to the world that the squadron was moving about the Pacific. But not this year. Tsingtao was making no announcements at all, and the ships moved in as much secrecy as possible. On the 17th they moved to Ponape, the most important island atoll in the Caroline group. The harbour was not much; *Scharnhorst* anchored off Langar Island and *Gneisenau* under the Djokadj rock, but Captain Schultz and Captain Maerker were uneasy. The weather was foul with high seas and squalls outside the reef. The typhoon season was not far off. Finally Captain Schultz grew unhappy enough to move his ship into deeper water in the middle of the lagoon, where she was safer, but developed a nasty pitch.

Hourly, the messages came in to the wireless telegraphy office of the flagship. Much of what was transmitted was rumour, and there was plenty of it: all pointing to a declaration of war by Austria against Russia. That course seemed by far the most likely, but as of the middle of the month nothing had been settled. Among the messages were various advisories of a political nature, some of them concerning the future of Tsingtao and the other German colonies. There was only one or perhaps two ways in which Tsingtao could be protected in case of war. Suddenly it became absolutely clear that there was no way the German East Asia Cruiser Squadron could do much to help. Indeed, the squadron was becoming a political liability as the chance of war increased. If Germany declared Tsingtao absolutely neutral, and dispersed the cruiser squadron with orders not to operate in Asiatic waters, then Berlin could claim that her China colony was harmless, and perhaps thus avoid the opening of a theatre of war in the Far East. The other chance, slim at best, was that Germany could invoke a clause of the Treaty of 1898 with China, which provided that Germany could at any time transfer her leased territory back to China, receive indemnification for her out-of-pocket expenses for improvements, and accept a 'more suitable' leasehold, at some future time. Thus Tsingtao could be given back, the war waited out, and a new colony taken over.

But these plans did not take into account Japanese expansionism and the strong chance that if the allies of Russia became involved in the war, Japan would join them for the purpose of seizing the German possessions. Still, they were the only diplomatic routes open to Berlin, and here in mid-July Admiral von Spee was made cognizant of his own difficult situation. But the diplomatic decisions were no surprise to the Admiral; he had long known that in case of war with Britain, Tsingtao was indefensible and the squadron must either be bottled up there and sacrificed, or moved out of the restricted waters. In the whole Pacific, there was absolutely no base for her, given hostilities against Britain, France, Russia, and Japan. The United States might offer haven, but the United States was certain to observe a strict neutrality, according to her history. What role the cruiser squadron could play in the war would have to be determined. The most sensible course, given the yearnings of the politicians, was for the squadron to head immediately for Germany, and join the High Seas Fleet, waiting for a major action against the British.

The trouble with all this discussion which raged in the wardrooms of the cruisers, was that it depended entirely on postulations of unknown positions. Just conceivably the crisis could pass, as Admiral Tirpitz so devoutly hoped. Then all the arguments would disappear in a round of entertainments. But at the moment there was nothing to do but wait as patiently as possible. Since there was no military reason for their presence in Ponape, and no reason either to move until the political situation had been clarified, the crews of the two ships enjoyed more than the usual shore leave. The officers of *Scharnhorst* organized an expedition into the interior of Ponape Island, to examine archaeological ruins. Admiral von Spee led a group of senior officers in paying homage to fallen comrades. In 1910 the natives had rebelled against German rule, and the cruiser squadron had sent vessels to put down the uprising. Men had been killed, one warrant officer in an assault against Djokadj rock, where the rebels had made a final stand. The Admiral climbed the steep rock, his staff puffing along behind him, and then visited the cemetery in Ponape town to dedicate a memorial to the fallen. He had brought with him from Tsingtao a stone memorial, and a ceremony had been announced. This was the real business of the cruiser squadron's visits, to cement the stones of empire. Accompanied by the village priest, and an honour guard from the police department, the governor, the police chief, and the doctor and other notables, he went to the churchyard and dedicated the memorial, as the *Scharnhorst*'s band played sentimental music. In such ways did the Admiral and his men spend the anxious days of waiting.

All this while Admiral von Spee was in daily touch with all the ships of his squadron, although the messages were stale and sometimes went astray. There was no such thing in 1914 as a wireless transmitter that could reach around the world. Messages for the ships on the American station had to be sent by cable over a tortuous path, so if Admiral von Spee wanted to be in close touch with Captain Haun of the *Leipzig*, he would have to bring him back to the squadron. But no orders from Berlin had indicated the advisability of any such course, so the *Leipzig* was left alone.

The *Nürnberg* was already on her way to rejoin the squadron, and might be expected to go into dry-dock at Tsingtao almost immediately for major overhaul. Captain von Schönberg had greeted Captain Haun on 7 July when the *Leipzig* arrived at Mazatlan on Mexico's west coast, *Nürnberg* having just come back up the coast from Panama. Neither captain knew a great deal about the war threats in Europe since the wireless message service was so spotty. Most of their information came from Mexican and American newspapers and was not considered reliable. Besides, as Captain von Schönberg explained to Captain Haun, the troubles in Mexico were real and not rumoured. The German colony faced economic and even physical harm from the series of assassinations and coups that had been occurring since 1911 when Francisco Madero ousted the government of Porfirio Diaz, and then was overthrown and murdered to boot, by Victoriano Huerta. Just the year before the Huerta regime had been challenged by another Mexican general, Venustiano Carranza, and now the country was deep in civil war. All the big powers were taking strong action to protect their 'rights'; the Americans had occupied Verz Cruz on the eastern shore of Mexico; Britain and Germany maintained warships in Mexican waters.

Under such tremulous conditions, it behooved Captain Haun to find a guaranteed supply of coal, that did not depend on the resources of any Mexican town. Captain von Schönberg had already seen that need, and made arrangements through the German consulate in San Francisco to charter a British collier named the *Citriana*. She had just arrived a few days earlier and lay in Mazatlan harbour. The men of the *Leipzig* looked across at her, a rustbucket so forlorn that one officer suggested her British owners had sent her to Mexico in hope that she would be lost through an act of war and they could claim the insurance. But she was there, available, and if her coal was crumbly and burned with a fierce yellow after flame and sent off clouds of noxious gas, still it was coal. The German government had arranged for stores of coal to be laid in at Guaymas, Mazatlan, San Blas and Manzanillo, but no one knew, in the atmosphere that prevailed in Mexico, when and how it would be available. The country was overrun with revolutionaries or, one might say, revolutionary bandits, for no one quite knew who was going to triumph. Carranza claimed to have the true faith, but so did Huerta, and Carranza's first lieutenant, Pancho Villa, was about to set up in the revolution business for himself. The town of Mazatlan was cut off from most of the rest of Mexico by Carranza's forces. There was no food supply for the

Leipzig (she did not need it) and even the water for the local brewery came from springs that were in the rebel hands. If it had not been for the foresight of the German colony in laying in an immense stock of beer, the officers and men of the *Leipzig* might have been reduced to drinking tequila.

On the night of 7 July Captain Haun had boarded the *Nürnberg* for a conference with his departing predecessor. They discussed the politics of two hemispheres, and concluded that *Leipzig* must be prepared for almost anything. Haun went back to his ship and detached his commissary officer to ride up to San Francisco with von Schönberg and send a telegram to Berlin for another collier. She should also have extra tinned foods, for although *Leipzig* had brought half a dozen pigs on her deck from Japan, and now turned the fore-deck into a hen-house to supply eggs and chickens, more would be needed. The future of the region did not look very stable, so Haun must shift for himself. If this instability needed emphasis it came the next day: Haun ordered the collier *Citriana* alongside so he could replenish the coal supply of *Leipzig* after the voyage from Honolulu; the cruiser's steam pinnace was towing a boat to speed the process of moving men to the collier, and the coxswain swung about in a wide circle that took him close to shore on the far side of the harbour. Captain von Schönberg had warned that this shore was held by the rebels, but the reality of danger had not percolated down to the crew of *Leipzig*. The German boats came within a hundred yards of the shore, and suddenly bullets began flying about the pinnace, and the crew ducked. Captain Minister, the master of the *Citriana* was aboard the pinnace, directing operations along with one of the junior officers of the *Leipzig*. They ducked too. As they lay, face down in the cockpit of the pinnace, Captain Minister apologized to his new acquaintance. The bullets were not an insult to the Germans, he said; they were meant for himself. He had been around the Mexico shore for a long time, and his ship had been chartered by the Americans to carry troops to Vera Cruz during the recent occupation. Pancho Villa and his friends seemed to carry a grudge for that.

No one was hurt in the shooting, and the coxswain of the pinnace soon had the boats far from shore. *Leipzig* coaled, and then so did *Nürnberg*, which sailed that day for San Francisco. So did Captain Minister; the coaling of the two cruisers had exhausted his supply, so he was heading back to the American bay city for more coal. But by the time they left, *Leipzig* was already out of port on urgent business of the Kaiser, which showed quite clearly what she was doing in these waters.

For several weeks, Pancho Villa's men had been moving in on Guaymas, which they had besieged for months. General Tellez, the Huerta government commander, had been able to resist, largely because his troops were surrounded and could not desert without getting shot at by both sides. But Tellez was faced with a wholesale uprising of his men because they had not been paid for weeks. Also, he was almost out of guns and ammunition. These latter could be brought in by ship, but they had to be paid for and Tellez had no money, nor did Huerta seem anxious to provide him with any. Repeated pleas for help from his commander had brought nothing more than platitudes. So Tellez had turned to the foreign community for aid, and now threatened that unless the foreigners made him an enormous 'loan' they would be shot. The German community had acted with unusual speed when that word was given out, and managed to send a small vessel along the coast to Mazatlan to pass the message to the cruiser on station. So Captain Haun was to go to Guaymas, and 'reason' with General Tellez, even if it meant training and even firing the cruiser's guns on the General's headquarters. He steamed out immediately and three days later arrived in Guaymas to the immense relief of the nervous foreign colony. On the arrival of the German warship General Tellez's demands on the foreigners ceased immediately.

Still, there was work for the German warship. The rebels were very near to the gates of the city and General Tellez was ready to leave it to them. Five steamers and two sailing ships had been brought to Guaymas to evacuate the government adherents, and on 12 July hundreds of soldiers, followed by their wives and children, streamed into the city square. They organized there and marched raggedly to the ships, led by a drum and bugle corps. On 14 July the ships were all loaded and the government gunboat, *General Gueraro*, led the flotilla out of the port and toward safety in the south. The exodus was complete by 15 July, and the city was quiet. Sailors from *Leipzig* roamed the streets and were welcomed by restaurants and bars that suddenly had no business except from the people of the town. But on 16 July the rebels arrived, shouting *Viva Carranza*. If they were bent on looting the property of the businessmen of Guaymas they were disappointed; the sailors from *Leipzig* were in the streets, armed, and so were sailors and marines from the American warships *Raleigh* and

Annapolis which were guarding American lives and property. These two cruisers were much larger and more imposing than *Leipzig*; together the three of them made sure that there was no violence in Guaymas in the transition.

For a week the sailors patrolled the town. The rebel General came out to the *Leipzig*, accompanied by a German soldier of fortune named Major Maler, who had once been a Hussar in Torgau. The General protested that there was no need for foreigners to carry arms on Mexican soil; the rebels would protect everyone; and Captain Haun smiled and said, in effect, 'we'll see'. The officers and men of the tiny international squadron exchanged visits. The Germans were pleased because the American ships had motion picture projectors and many reels of film. The Americans were pleased because the German ships had wine, beer, and spirits, which American warships did not. (The Woodrow Wilson administration's Secretary of the Navy, Josephus Daniels, was the man responsible for drying up the Americans – a state of affairs that has persisted, at least officially, for all the years since.) On 23 July however, the little idyll was brought to an end by an abrupt order to the German warship to return to Mazatlan, to join an international squadron there. The revolution had spread across all of northern Mexico and some decisions about protection of property must be made. *Leipzig* hauled anchor, too, and went to Mazatlan. There Captain Haun, who had been out of touch with events in Europe except for the meagre gleanings from the wireless, discovered that the tension in Berlin, Paris, Vienna, St Petersburg, and London had grown much, much worse. Haun found himself in harbour with the USS *California*, a modern battleship; the heavy cruiser USS *Albany*; the Japanese heavy cruiser *Idzumo*, and the British warship *Algerine*. Captain Haun needed coal again, and *Citriana* was supposedly bringing it down from San Francisco. But would she arrive? Or would the British, in view of the temper of the times, put a stop to her sailing? Captain Haun was not very happy to have his fuel supply in the hands of a potential enemy, but there was nothing to be done on such short notice. It would be weeks before the German collier requested earlier could reach the west coast of America. Meanwhile there was nothing for Captain Haun to do but wait.

Meanwhile, *Leipzig*'s sister ship, the *Nürnberg*, had reached Honolulu after a leisurely voyage, and the men were looking forward to some recreation on the white beaches under the palm trees. The troubles of Mexico and even those of Europe seemed far away. But at the offices of Hackfeld and Company, Captain Haun found coded messages awaiting him from Admiral von Spee. He was to coal immediately, and sail immediately thereafter for Ponape. Admiral von Spee did not like the look of events as reports were transmitted to him from Tsingtao. He was assembling his fleet around him.

In Tsingtao, Captain von Müller assembled all the information about German and foreign warships that he could collate, and transmitted it to von Spee. He sent cautious messages to the captains of the gunboats on the China rivers, warning them to move down near the mouths of the rivers so they would not be trapped upstream in case of sudden trouble. The public was unaware of the intensive activity in the harbour these days, for von Müller took care to keep up appearances of peaceful ennui. Tsingtao could be presumed to be alive with spies, particularly British and Japanese, and no information would be given the enemy about German plans if von Müller could help it. The public read the newspapers and saw the reports of political difficulties in Europe, but there had been many crises before, and in the drawing rooms of the big houses, most of the matrons and their guests presumed that like all the others, this one would soon pass. They were surprised, then, when the Austro-Hungarian cruiser *Kaiserin Elisabeth* appeared without notice off the harbour entrance. The word was about town before the ship came into the inner harbour and moored beside the *Emden*. There Captain Richard Makoviz came ashore and made a hurried call on Governor Meyer-Waldeck. He had been ordered to Tsingtao from Chefoo; 'unobtrusively and with economic speed', said the message from Vienna. What did it mean? Governor Meyer-Waldeck could not shed any light on the orders, nor could Captain von Müller, but privately they drew their own conclusions. As far as help was concerned, the *Kaiserin Elisabeth* could offer little. Makoviz reported that he had shaken out the engines for the first time in years, and the ship had trembled from stem to rudder. No, the old unarmoured cruiser would be of little help to the squadron. Her reason for coming to Tsingtao was obvious; she was seeking shelter in a friendly haven in case of war. So much was also obvious to the good businessmen of Tsingtao, and for the first time they began to worry seriously about the state of the current crisis.

Kaiser Wilhelm, aboard the *Hohenzollern*, was in constant communication with his fleet, still in Norwegian waters, and with Berlin. When the Austrian ultimatum to Serbia was handed over, he had the news within hours. And from the decks of the *Hohenzollern* it looked very much like war. In London, most attention was focused on the Irish problem, which had been giving the British government serious worry for several years, and seemed to be approaching a crisis. Lloyd George was talking about the future of the continent in the most glowing terms. He was particularly pleased with progress of British relations with Germany, and on the day that the Austrian note was delivered, he forecast a long period of co-operation between London and Berlin. The Germans had been aroused by a test mobilization of the Home Fleet, but Admiral Sir George Callaghan was on that very day dispersing the fleet, and sending the ships of the Reserve to their home ports where they would pay off the crews. A Flag Officer's conference was scheduled for Portland, where the Admirals would talk over the results of the recent exercises; but no one in authority was seriously considering war.

All this occurred without knowledge of the contents of the Austrian ultimatum, which spelled out terms so hostile that it would mean the end of Serbian independence entirely. Further, the Serbian government was given only forty-eight hours in which to reply, another indication of the fury with which Vienna was addressing the problem.

So, while on the day of the ultimatum, the future looked rosy in northern Europe at least, on the morning after, the newspapers were full of the threat of war, and ambassadors scurried about chanceries, trying to do what they could to keep governments from growing excited. The British cabinet was meeting that day, and the Foreign Secretary, Sir Edward Grey, was suddenly interrupted by a messenger from the Foreign Office, with the bad news of the ultimatum spelled out in details that left little to the imagination. Sir Edward read it out to the ministers, and the whole tenor of the cabinet meeting changed. Winston Churchill went back to the Admiralty shortly afterward and addressed himself to the impending crisis. The 1st and 2nd Fleets were still at Portland, and would remain for two days. He would see what must be done. That evening Churchill dined with a German representative, Albert Ballin, who was sounding out the water for Chancellor Bethman; what would Britain do if Germany were 'forced' into war with France and Russia? Ballin had dined with the Prime Minister, and with Foreign Secretary Grey, and had spent several days with his ear to the ground. He had heard no rumblings; he had the definite impression that if Germany went to war, unless she 'swallowed up' France, Britain would stay out. But Winston Churchill was of quite a different opinion, and he warned Ballin that Britain was not committed to any policy and would not guarantee neutrality.

Ballin went home with that warning, but nothing stronger; an unequivocal statement from the cabinet that Britain would intervene in behalf of France was not forthcoming.

Probably even such a strong move would have done no good. Kaiser Wilhelm was already rattling his sabre. He ordered the High Seas Fleet home to Germany, and his yacht headed for Kiel, in spite of his Chancellor's pleas that he remain aloof and add no militaristic gestures to an aggravated situation. He ordered all approaches to the harbour secured against Russian torpedo boat attack, which set off a mighty rumour, and then he ordered up his train for Potsdam.

Within the forty-eight hours, the Serbs did reply, in an ingratiating way that pleased most chanceries, but infuriated the Austrian war party; somehow war must be declared to resolve the Slav problem once and for all. This was the situation that existed on 27 July, when a messenger from von Müller's communications centre sweated his way up the hill to the governor's mansion, to deliver a sealed envelope. The governor was at luncheon, entertaining a number of distinguished guests, when the sailor burst into the room, with a flustered butler behind him. Before Governor Meyer-Waldeck could say a word of reproval, the sailor thrust out the envelope, and when the governor saw the seals, he knew it was indeed important. He excused himself, and opened the letter. Inside was a brief note: the message was for his eyes only, it was still encoded, and he would have to decode it for himself. So he left the room, and set about the laborious job of deciphering a code he did not know very well. It took him a good deal of time and luncheon was half over by the time he returned to the table. Berlin warned that the crisis was real, and that war might come at any moment. He must prepare. But the governor said nothing to his guests, and only when the last of them had been taken to the door did he call his staff together and tell them that the colony must prepare. Leaves were to be cancelled. The harbour was to be patrolled constantly. The railroad stations were to be watched and so were the roads. Any odd activity of any sort was to be reported immediately to the governor's mansion.

For the next two days Berlin seemed to indicate that the difficulties might be resolved, but on 30 July Governor Meyer-Waldeck learned that war had broken out between Serbia and Austria-Hungary. Anything might happen from this point on; as if to underscore that fact, Governor Meyer-Waldeck regretfully suggested to a high ranking group of Japanese diplomats who were visiting Tsingtao that it would be best if they went home to Japan, pending resolution of the war problem. Baron Yasumasa Fukushima had been asked to investigate the German bureaucracy in Kiaochow, with an eye to making it more efficient. But he packed his bags, and that evening the colony's officials gave a farewell dinner, marked by dozens of toasts and fervently expressed wishes for peace; both sides knowing that the chances they would be at one another's throats in a matter of days were far better than even.

On the last day of July, the governor learned that Kaiser Wilhelm had ordered full mobilization of the German military forces for 2 August. The war clouds were lowering, and Meyer-Waldeck had little time to order Germans from all over Asia to hurry to Tsingtao. On 2 August came the news of war between Germany and Russia.

For three days Captain von Müller had been as busy as the governor, carrying out the duties assigned him by Admiral von Spee. He ordered all the gunboats home to Tsingtao as quickly as they could get there. But the results were anything but uniform.

The gunboat *Tsingtau* was tied up on the Pearl River in south China, next to the British gunboat *Teal*. On the day that the orders came, the German and British gunboat captains had just made an appointment to go hunting together. They conferred and went hunting anyhow, had a drink when they returned, and that evening Captain von Moller of the *Tsingtau* slipped his buoy in the darkness and steamed for Canton. But he got no further. As war between Germany and Britain was declared on 4 August, von Moller realized his gunboat could not run a British gauntlet, and he ordered the crew to abandon ship and make their ways in small groups to Tsingtao. With five men, von Moller set out for Germany, crossed the Indian Ocean in a small boat, landed on the Arabian coast, and headed for Constantinople. They nearly made it, but not quite: they were assaulted by a band of roving Bedouin and every last man was killed.

The gunboat *Jaguar* was in Shanghai harbour when the recall came from Captain von Müller; Lieutenant Commander Luring went ashore that night and made a great show of appearing at all the night-clubs, while his executive officer took *Jaguar* quietly to sea. The gunboat slipped past the Russian cruiser *Askold* in the darkness but the Russians saw them and followed, and it seemed likely that the *Jaguar* would be taken the moment war came. On the day before (1 August) Lieutenant Erich Mathias escaped with a desperate gambit. He fired two recognition shells from the gunboat at the *Askold*, and not having orders to retaliate, the Russian cruiser moved away and *Jaguar* escaped to make port at Tsingtao.

By this time, Captain von Müller and the *Emden* were gone from the harbour. Von Müller had left an officer in charge of the garrison and the naval mission, which was to assure a stream of supplies heading southward to Admiral von Spee and the squadron. Von Müller would go to sea to be ready, and when war with Russia was announced he *was* ready. On the day that the German government sent its ultimatum to Russia, the panelling of the civilian-oriented Navy was removed from the wardroom and the officers took all the bric-à-brac from their cabins and stored it ashore. The *Emden*'s gunnery officer, Lieutenant Ernst Gaede, loaded ammunition and torpedoes all day. That evening the ship coaled, beginning at six o'clock and the men and the Chinese coolies worked through the night until the job was finished. On 31 July von Müller sailed, worried lest he be caught in port by war. Captain von Müller was a student of naval history, and he recalled from his reading how during the Russo-Japanese war of 1905, the Russian warships *Warjag* and *Korejetz* had been surprised, and blockaded by the Japanese at the Korean port of Inchon. In the gloaming, with the collier *Elsbeth* tagging behind her, the *Emden* steamed out of Tsingtao harbour and headed south-east into the Pacific, it seemed. But the course was partially a ruse to confuse spies, and partially a protective device to set the *Elsbeth* safely on her way; the collier was really going to the squadron. As for von Müller, an hour before midnight he turned away and headed for Chejus Island, on a course that kept him just off the steamer lanes. Slowly the *Emden* headed north, waiting. Captain von Müller could do nothing else, for war seemed imminent, but had not yet come. The tension grew. So nerve-racking was the waiting that the ship's First Officer, Lieutenant Commander Helmuth von Mücke spent much of the day in the wireless room, looking over the shoulders of the operators and examining almost every message for a sign. At three o'clock in the afternoon, von Mücke was there again. 'Any strange traffic?' he asked, and without waiting for answer, picked up the receiver and held it to his ear. From the instrument came a crackling sound so loud that von Mücke jerked the receiver away. The wireless operator was tuned into the British naval frequency, and the loudness meant the British ships were very close. He went to the bridge to inform Captain von Müller. Just how close, the captain learned within the hour; they passed the lingering wake of the British, and could ascertain that one large vessel and a number of smaller ones had gone by. Indeed they had, the wake came from several ships of the British East Asia Squadron, which had been lying at anchor in Weihaiwei,

north of Tsingtao. They had been ordered to proceed to Hong Kong by
Winston Churchill, First Lord of the Admiralty. Admiral Jerram had
then taken the *Minotaur* south, obeying orders, although with some
reluctance. He had announced to his staff that if war came, what he
wanted to do was steam into Tsingtao harbour immediately, take the
guardship (*Emden*) and then lie at the entrance to the port, taking
German ships as they came to and fro. But Churchill had other plans
for the squadron, so *Minotaur* went south.

The tension aboard the *Emden* continued, until 3 August, which
was a Sunday and usually a day of light work aboard a warship. But
not this Sunday. Even church services had been conducted for the
men in their dirty fatigue clothes rather than dress whites. They were
making the ship ready for war so there was no time for nicety. At two
o'clock in the afternoon, Captain von Müller mustered officers and
crew, and appeared on the poop deck, to announce that Germany was
at war with Russia. Now they could do something; he set a course for
Vladivostok.

By so moving, Captain von Müller ran the danger of encountering
Askold, the heavy cruiser that had given *Jaguar* such a fright a few
days earlier. But although von Müller knew the danger he ran he also
remembered the German naval officers' code, and the tradition of the
service, which reminded him that the task of the cruiser squadron was
commerce raiding in time of war. He might avoid *Askold* and meet
Yemtschuk, the light cruiser of the Russian Far East fleet, which was
just about a match for *Emden*. More particularly, he might avoid both
and reap a harvest of merchant ships heading for the Russian Pacific
port.

On the next day, von Müller had more opportunity to consider and
more enemies to worry about. France and Germany went to war, and
so he must also look out for the heavy French cruisers *Montcalm* and
Dupleix which might be anywhere between Vladivostok and Saigon.
But there would also be more steamers, French as well as Russian, if
he could find them. To do this, von Müller brought into his confidence
Lieutenant Julius Lauterbach, a rotund, merry merchant captain in
peacetime who had just happened to be aboard *Emden* for his yearly
reserve officer's stint when she sailed for the danger zone. Lauterbach
suggested that the captain move into the Tsushima Strait, which lies
between Japan and Korea. This was the route from Shanghai to
Vladivostok; Lauterbach knew, for he had brought his own ship along
this way dozens of times. The danger of this move, of course, was that
the Japanese might suddenly enter the war, and instead of finding an

easy prey at Tsushima, the *Emden* could be surrounded by a score of Japanese warships, and be doomed. But the benefit was that by moving north von Müller did not have to worry about the British just then. Britain was not yet in the war, but most officers of the *Emden* would have taken bets on her entrance any hour. Under those conditions, von Müller would just as soon not be encountering any of his British friends.

Having listened to Lauterbach's advice, von Müller acted on it and soon *Emden* was moving through the night at 15 knots, heading into the strait, and then north. The sky was dark, there was no moon to betray the German warship. Below, the engineers were careful not to make unnecessary smoke, and the only visible sign of *Emden*'s passage was the phosphorescent wake.

Captain von Müller stayed on his bridge until midnight. He had slept only an hour or two in the past two days, and the quiet of the night lulled him until he gave up the bridge gladly. The day before he had put the ship on 'war watch' which meant that von Müller and First Officer von Mücke shared watch responsibility. The captain's starboard watch was off duty until 4 a.m., so he went into his sea cabin for some sleep, with the order that he be called at the first sign of the unusual. Von Mücke took the bridge for the next four hours.

At four o'clock a seaman awakened the captain. There was nothing to report, said von Mücke. All had been completely quiet for the past four hours. The false dawn had begun to break a little later when suddenly something loomed ahead and the look-outs shouted the alarm. The call to action stations rang throughout the ship, bringing every man up to his post. But it was nothing but a dark cloud, and soon the ship was quiet again. An hour later the wireless room sent word to the bridge that unusual traffic nearby had been detected. But once again, nothing came of it; there might have been an enemy warship somewhere off in the gloom, but no one knew.

Before the day watch began, the weather began to roughen up. When the weather grew worse, Captain von Müller turned south, and toward the western channel of the strait, off the coast of Korea. This should be good hunting ground, said Lieutenant Lauterbach. But the hours went by and nothing was seen, and the foul weather chased them and caught them that night again. During a squall, at about 2 o'clock in the morning, the look-outs sighted the stern light of a vessel ahead. Then the cloud and rain closed in on the *Emden* and nothing more could be seen. But it seemed obvious that the vessel was moving south and west, as they were, and that by maintaining speed they would come up with her in time, unless she had seen them and turned away, a most unlikely manoeuvre in bad weather in these waters. The captain waited confidently. Four hours later his confidence was rewarded when the look-outs reported the masts of a ship ahead. Just then the weather cleared, and the other ship spotted the German warship. It was apparent in a moment that she was trying to escape, turning and sending up a smoke cloud, which meant a sudden increase in speed demanded of the engines. Captain von Müller ordered the same, and told the quartermaster to call the men to their battle stations. He also hailed Lieutenant Lauterbach to the bridge for consultation. The weather was good enough now that Lauterbach could take the glass and have a clear look at the ship ahead as she headed in toward Tsushima Island, in Japanese territorial waters. If she could reach the three-mile limit, under international law she would be safe. And as far as *Emden* was concerned that was all that could save her, for Lauterbach immediately identified the two golden funnels of this steamer as the Russian mail ship *Rjasan* which ran regularly between Vladivostok and Shanghai. Lauterbach was an old friend of the captain of that ship, and had spent many hours on her bridge talking.

She was fast, a ship of 3,500 tons, and she had wireless. That last bit of news meant that *Emden* did not have much time to waste. Already, he knew, the ship must be sending distress signals that would warn every French and Russian warship in the Pacific of the plight of the *Rjasan*. Further, she must be making at least 17 knots, for at her flank speed of 19 knots *Emden* was overhauling the steamer more slowly than von Müller liked. It seemed that she might indeed make Tsushima Island.

Von Müller wanted this first prize badly. He ordered a shot fired across her bows, and one of the 10.5 centimetre-guns sent a shell ahead of the other ship. Her captain ignored the ominous message. Captain von Müller ordered the signalman to run up the 'stop at once' flag, and it was done. Then von Müller told gunnery officer Gaede to start firing regularly across the *Rjasan*'s bows, bringing each shot closer to her, until, if necessary, he was to begin shelling the ship. Eleven shots were fired then, each some 50 yards closer, until the last plunked into the water so close by that the Captain of the *Rjasan* saw that there was no further hope. He turned back toward his enemy and stopped.

When Captain von Müller had learned that Lieutenant Lauterbach knew Captain Austin, the Englishman who commanded the Russian ship, he decided to send Lauterbach to head the boarding party. The tubby lieutenant clambered briskly into a boat, and the oarsmen sped away. Just then First Officer von Mücke came to the bridge to tell the captain that the Russian was trying to send a wireless message.

'Do not wireless', was the signal run up on the *Emden*'s foremast, but the dit-dot-dit continued, until Lieutenant Lauterbach reached the Russian ship, and clambered up the boarding ladder, his armed men behind him.

From the deck of the cruiser, Captain von Müller saw Lauterbach swaying on the ladder, and the cutter dipping and banging against the side of the Russian ship. He was so dismayed that he ordered another boat out to assist Lauterbach's party, but even as the men rowed the boat away from the *Emden* he saw that it was not necessary. Lauterbach had gained the deck, obviously there was no resistance, and all was going as it should. He knew that when the wireless operator came to the bridge to announce that the tapping of the man on the *Rjasan* had suddenly been cut off in mid-word. Obviously Lauterbach had given the captain a piece of his mind.

Actually, the encounter had not been nearly so harsh. Lauterbach had taken possession of the wireless room of the Russian steamer and stationed Wireless Operator Wille and several armed German seamen at the doors. Then he had gone to the bridge, where Captain Austin had bowed stiffly. Lauterbach bowed also.

'I am awfully sorry, Captain,' he said in German, 'but it is my duty to make your ship a prize of war.'

'I do not know what you are saying,' Captain Austin replied in English. 'I don't speak German.'

Lauterbach began to laugh and shrugged his big shoulders. 'You have certainly forgotten a lot. You knew German well enough a fortnight ago when we were drinking beer together in the club at Tsingtao.'

Austin grinned sheepishly then, and had to laugh. It was true. In those days, even on the brink of war, the camaraderie of the European in Asia had held. Only now had it all changed.

Lauterbach took the ship's papers in hand and went to the wireless station. Operator Wille took the key and reported back to the *Emden*. *Rjasan* was carrying about eighty passengers and the Russian official mails, but not much cargo. What was to be done with her?

Captain von Müller considered that problem for a little while. The ship could be sunk, the passengers put into lifeboats and set free. But 'free' was not a very meaningful word in this weather, with the seas still running very high; there was a very good chance that the passengers would never make the shore. As for the ship she was new, and she would make a good raider. Back in Tsingtao the Austrian *Kaiserin Elisabeth* was lying, of little use to anyone with her slack plates and wheezing machinery. But she did have guns, and the Russian ship had speed, she was almost as fast as *Emden*. So why not augment the German naval force in Asia with a new auxiliary cruiser? That was what Captain von Müller decided he would do, and he sent the message to Lauterbach: he was to keep a dozen of his twenty-two men and maintain control of the *Rjasan*. The cutter would return to the *Emden*, and they would all head back for Tsingtao as quickly as possible.

The wisdom of von Müller's decision was shown within an hour or so, at least as far as the neutral passengers were concerned. The storm was a typhoon, and the eye kept moving toward them. An hour after the cutter was picked up by the *Emden*, the seas were so high that no small boat could have been launched. Lieutenant Lauterbach looked at those tall grey waves, and ordered the lifeboats of the *Rjasan* loosened, just in case. Then he informed Captain Austin that they were going to Tsingtao, and that if anyone interfered he was ordered to scuttle the ship. Austin protested, as he must. He was in Japanese territorial waters when captured, he said. The whole affair was a disgraceful breach of international law. He would report to the Hague, to London, to anyone who would listen. Lieutenant Lauterbach sent this word to Captain von Müller, and in reply had a strong message for the English captain of the Russian ship. Let there be no nonsense, said Captain von Müller. The *Rjasan* was captured in international waters: and he gave the co-ordinates: 35°5′N 19°39′E. This wireless message was intended for all listeners, Japanese, English and others. Von Müller wanted no misunderstandings about the German respect for international law.

Still, Captain Austin continued his protests to his old friend Lauterbach. The word came from von Müller to steer a course southward; that was not the way to Tsingtao, said Captain Austin, and as a prisoner of war he had the right to demand internment. He did? Captain von Müller disagreed, and in his next message he told Lauterbach that if Austin continued to make trouble he was to put him in irons for the rest of the voyage. Captain Austin subsided then, but Lauterbach was kept busy by the eighty passengers, most of whom came up to protest their treatment. It was outrageous, they said, that their voyage should be interrupted this way. The old merchant skipper was as genial as he could be, and he refrained from

1 Tsingtao just before the First World War began. Note the huge half-moon harbour and the characteristic German architecture

2 His Imperial Majesty's *Kreuzer* SMS *Scharnhorst*. The four stacks and the underslung dreadnought bow were typical

3 Admiral Sir Christopher Cradock, commander of the British cruiser squadron. He went down with his ship at Coronel

telling them that it was just their good luck that a number of them were not already dead. The last shot of *Emden* had passed just five yards ahead of the *Rjasan*'s bow, and that had been the clincher for Captain Austin. Had he waited another few minutes to surrender, Lieutenant Gaede would have begun firing on the steamer's bridge to stop her.

Lauterbach had lots of time, and not much to do except be sure that the Russian ship kept pace with *Emden*, just about 1,200 yards ahead of the shepherding cruiser, and that Captain Austin kept quiet and the members of the crew did not try any tricks. Examining the ship's log, Lauterbach noted that she had been in communication with the French cruisers *Dupleix* and *Montcalm* during the chase. He hastened to inform Captain von Müller and von Müller changed course to stay out of the way, if possible. There was no point in risking suicide, which would have been the fate of *Emden* under the circumstances. Obviously the two French cruisers were travelling in consort, and they might also have destroyers and torpedo boats with them. That surmise was proved correct later in the day when the look-outs aboard *Emden* sighted five wispy smoke plumes off to the west, in the waters through which *Emden* should be passing had von Müller chosen the most direct route to Tsingtao. Von Müller did not hesitate, but turned due east immediately, and ran. Only after dark did he set a course for Tsingtao.

Darkness brought new problems. The *Rjasan*'s blackout precautions were not very effective. Neither the crew nor the passengers gave a fig for blackout; quite to the contrary, they were hoping someone would see the ships and rescue them from the clutches of the Germans. Lauterbach and his men were kept busy all night long dousing lights, as ordered by the officer on the bridge of the *Emden*. No sooner was one light properly extinguished or shielded and the ship secure, than there came another message from *Emden*: 'light showing port amidships ...' and the search and the scolding had to begin all over again. Finally, Lauterbach resolved the problem by stopping all generators aboard the *Rjasan* save those actually needed to run the engines.

As morning came, so did a ship on the horizon. The look-outs watched the smoke, and when the masts showed, they were obviously those of a merchant ship. Of course it could be an armed auxiliary cruiser flying either the French or Russian flag, but von Müller had nothing to fear from such a vessel, so he let her come on. When she came within hailing distance her colours were clear, Japanese, and she was very polite, dipping her ensign to the German warship as she passed. Nor was there any sound of wireless – at least until she was over the horizon. Then the chattering began. There was nothing to be done about that; von Müller's little flotilla passed another Japanese steamer *en route* from Shanghai to Yokohama a bit later, and the performance was repeated. Japan was still neutral, he did not know how long that would continue, but for the moment he had nothing to fear from even the powerful Japanese Navy.

On the evening of 5 August von Müller had the sobering news that England had declared war against Germany. He was expecting it, but the fact was a shock, none the less. For as von Müller had learned throughout his career, the natural enemy of the German Navy was England. Now, of course, all Asia save Japan would be turned against the German East Asia Cruiser Squadron. Only from Japan could they obtain coal, and if Japan maintained strict neutrality the coaling situation would not be easy.

But if the news of England's entry into the war was sobering it also was heartening in a way: there would be plenty of hunting in these waters for a German warship; every vessel she encountered was likely to be fair game. Chinese shipping was largely confined to junks, and so the Japanese were the only neutrals bringing many ships into China waters, and particularly north of the Whangpoo.

Von Müller's major worry at this point was the whereabouts of the English squadron. He did not know that Churchill had called it back to Hong Kong; all he knew was that the flagship had passed close by, heading south on its voyage to Tsushima. What if she was lurking off Tsingtao, just waiting for him? (His mind worked very much like that of Admiral Jerram.) Von Müller wirelessed Tsingtao, asking that one of the gunboats be sent out to the harbour entrance to check. The answer came back: it had been done, and no sign of any warships had been seen by the searchers or by the lighthouse or the shore stations. Satisfied, von Müller ordered Lauterbach to make fullest speed. *Emden* was supposed to be in the South Seas within the week, to join Admiral von Spee. So they hurried straight toward Tsingtao, the *Rjasan* leading, until they came within an hour of the land. Then von Müller ordered the men of the *Emden* to battle stations, and told Lauterbach to drop back and let the cruiser lead. The wisdom of his precautions seemed emphasized when suddenly the wireless station of the cruiser reported the crackling of enemy messages – they were known to be that because of the code and the hand of the operator. Von Müller set course for the Chaliento lighthouse, and hoped for the best, as night began to fall. At three o'clock on the morning of 6 August a bright light was sighted and the look-outs brought the ship to battle stations. But it was a false alarm; they ran in through a fleet of Chinese fishing junks and at dawn reached the entrance to the mine field that had been sowed in the past few days according to von Müller's orders. They stopped there and waited for the pilot boat *C.S. Leiss* which came out and brought them in safely through the mines. Inside the harbour entrance the ship was greeted by the gunboat *Jaguar* and by six o'clock that morning, the ship was inside, with the view of Tsingtao's red and white buildings sprawled out ahead. The men looked at the city, and some were surprised because it seemed totally unchanged. But it was they, the men of the *Emden*, who were changed. For unlike the others of the colony, they had already been to war.

4

The Plan for War

On the afternoon of 5 August 1914, Admiral von Spee was waiting as patiently as possible for the light cruiser *Nürnberg* to appear at Ponape. A week had passed since he began earnest preparations for war, which included the storing of his personal silver service along with all the other non-regulation furnishings that a peacetime navy acquired. Everything had gone ashore to be stored with the Jaluit Company at Langar until the coming of a better day. On 3 August the Admiral had announced the coming of war with Russia and France, on the quarterdeck of the flagship *Scharnhorst*. So what was he waiting for? *Nürnberg*, the little cruiser which had been off the Baja California coast, had already been re-routed from a previously arranged rendezvous at Samoa. He must wait for her; and then of course there was *Emden*, on her way in the next few days from Tsingtao.

The Admiral had announced the war with France and Russia, but he had also made it clear to the men of the squadron that he firmly expected war with Britain within a matter of hours. That was his way; he was a man of strong convictions and he did not fail to speak them. 'We must also regard English ships as enemies,' he told the crews of *Scharnhorst* and *Gneisenau*, and while technically he was wrong, he knew that actually he was right. It was just a matter of hours.

In those two days between the declaration of France and that of Britain, the Admiral reassessed his war position. He dismissed the Russian Navy as a threat of little consequence. The Tsar had only two cruisers in Far Eastern waters. To be sure, the staff had amassed detail on dozens of gunboats and torpedo boats and submarines, but these were not capital ships of the sort that made a difference to Admiral von Spee. The French posed a more serious threat with the two armoured cruisers, *Montcalm* and *Dupleix*. But the real problem was going to be the British squadron. It consisted of the battleship HMS *Triumph*, the heavy cruisers *Minotaur* and *Hampshire*, the light cruisers *Newcastle* and *Yarmouth*, plus eight destroyers and all the other torpedo boats and floating bric-à-brac that was eminently effective in solving colonial problems, but quite meaningless in terms of real naval warfare. Considering the fact that *Leipzig* was off on the American west coast, the British outnumbered him and outgunned him by a wide margin, in Jerram's squadron alone. That did not include the Australian forces, the battleships *Australia*, the *Swiftsure*, and ten armoured cruisers and one light cruiser. So, even if Japan stayed out of the war, and this seemed unlikely to Admiral von Spee, given his knowledge of Japan's ambitions toward the Shantung Peninsula, the German East Asia Cruiser Squadron was facing overwhelming enemy power. The fact did not make Admiral von Spee tremble, but it did pose some difficult questions. How could he best employ his force to do maximum damage to the enemy, and for the longest period of time? Just now he had at his disposal the two heavy cruisers. In a day or so, *Nürnberg* would arrive, and then *Emden*. And then what?

On 3 August von Spee had some new intelligence from German offices in Australia. If hostilities broke out between England and Germany, the Australians would immediately move the 17,000-ton battleship *Australia* and six of the heavy cruisers to the China station to augment Jerram's force. That being the case, it was foolhardy to consider return to Tsingtao, and the Admiral discarded the idea as a possible course of action.

On 4 August, Admiral von Spee had several interesting bits of intelligence. He learned of *Emden*'s capture of the *Rjasan* from the international broadcasts. He learned of the progress of the Mexican revolution, and the *Leipzig*'s adventures as part of the international squadron that was protecting Europeans. From the German wireless station at Yap he learned that *Nürnberg* should be arriving in the next forty-eight hours. He could not wait for *Emden*, he would have to meet her elsewhere. Meanwhile, he ordered the two heavy cruisers *Scharnhorst* and *Gneisenau* out to sea for serious gunnery practice — with no more worry lest ammunition be wasted. And as the ships sailed, Admiral von Spee left word that the Japanese collier *Fukoku Maru* was to be ready to coal them on their return. They came back into port at the end of the day, and stripped the last of the coal from the Japanese ship, then sent her on her way to Samoa to pick up more coal. Actually, von Spee was sending the collier on a fool's errand, for he had no intention of remaining in Ponape harbour, to await the *Fukoku Maru*'s return. He did not trust the Japanese captain or crew, certain as he was that England would enter the war, and then Japan would follow. Von Spee was a prescient and careful man. He assigned a 'civilian' from the Ponape colony to accompany *Fukoku Maru* to Samoa 'on business'. The real reason for the man's presence was to make sure that the collier did indeed go straight to Samoa. *Fukoku Maru* carried no wireless, but it was conceivable that she could have arrangements with some other vessel for a rendezvous, and this should be prevented. *Fukoku Maru* sailed, her captain was told to come back as soon as possible, and that was the information he was able to give the allied forces later. Admiral von Spee was taking no chances on *Australia* or half a dozen cruisers showing up to blockade him in this South Seas port.

So by the afternoon of 5 August, Admiral von Spee had done all within his power and he had nothing more to do but wait for *Nürnberg*. He was waiting when the word came: England had just declared war on Germany. When the Admiral learned the news it became even harder to wait, but if there was ever an officer capable of total calm it was Admiral Maximilian Johannes Maria Hubert Graf von Spee. He was a totally disciplined man, and that was why his star was rising steadily in the Imperial German Navy.

Just now he was Vice-Admiral, but it seemed apparent that with the retirement of the Tirpitz age-group von Spee would become one of the two or three major figures in the German Navy. He was 53 years old, in vigorous middle age and he had every attribute, including friends at court. As for himself, he spent little time in that sort of atmosphere. Since the spring of 1878 he had been an active seaman, first a cadet in the Kaiserliche Marine, and then, four years later, an Unterleutnant zur See. His years thereafter were spent in the slow, steady climb up the ladder of promotion. Leaves were spent at his father's castle at Heitorf on the Rhine, not far from Düsseldorf. He had begun his officer's career as a deck officer aboard the gunboat *Moewe* in South-west Africa. His next assignment was as port commander at Cameroon. Then he was appointed an instructor of cadets, and served aboard the training ship *Moltke*. In 1889 he was a junior lieutenant, and married that year, eventually to raise five sons. He was made lieutenant (Kapitänleutnant) in 1892 and adjutant of the cruiser *Bayern*. In 1899 he became lieutenant commander and in 1904, commander. He was only 44 years old when he made the huge peace-time leap to captain (Kapitän zur See).

All this while, von Spee's name was mentioned occasionally at court, but he was not really known there except as son of his father.

But in 1897 he was made aide to Rear-Admiral Prince Heinrich of Prussia. When that Admiral took over command of the 2nd Division of the Cruiser Squadron, the Kaiser paid especial attention to the unit, and in the course of time von Spee was brought favourably to the Kaiser's attention. From that point on his future was assured. Those in power had seen that he had every sort of experience: minelaying, minesweeping, first officer of a battleship and commander of a cruiser (*Hela*, which represented Germany off Taku Bar during the Boxer Rebellion). He had served on the staff in Berlin and had been promoted there to rear-admiral and chief of staff of the North Sea naval district. In 1912 he was appointed to command the East Asia Squadron, which gave him another step up to vice-admiral. He could look forward to even dizzier heights – but he had to get back to Germany to do so. And that fact was paramount in von Spee's mind as he considered his position on this first day of the war against England.

His urgent problem was coal. In the past week, at Tsingtao, Lieutenant Commander Fritz Sachse, the officer left in charge by Captain von Müller, had despatched a number of freighters loaded with drinking water, provisions, ammunition, and coal – 19,000 tons of coal – for the squadron. These were now sailing to various points of the Pacific, so that no matter what Admiral von Spee finally decided to do, he would have supply – if the ships were able to avoid the British. The ships were the *Gouverneur Jaeschke* (Lieutenant Lauterbach's old command), the *Longmoon, Markomannia, O.I.D. Ahlers, Staatsekretar Krätke, Senegambia, Frisia*, and *S. Frederick Laeisz*. But 19,000 tons of coal for four cruisers was little enough, and whatever action von Spee took, it must be swift, and he must somehow secure more coal in future. Berlin had just despatched another 10,000 tons of coal for Tsingtao. If it arrived it still would do von Spee no good, for he had had no intention of returning before, and now he learned that the Japanese were already beginning to march. If possible, Berlin ought to stop or divert the coal, but the trouble was that most of the colliers carried either no wireless or one so inadequate as to offer no hope of long distance transmission.

It was apparent on this day of war, that von Spee would have to rely upon himself and his officers for their salvation. In this, he was not unlucky, for even as he had been chosen for the highly independent command of the squadron, he had made sure that the officers who served under him were of more than usual independence. His Chief of Staff, Captain Otto Fielitz, had already enjoyed the same brilliant rise that had marked von Spee's career; Fielitz had become a captain at 42 and once they reached Germany, unless they fell completely apart, he could look forward to having his own command and an Admiral's flag.

The commanders of the five cruisers were not perhaps of such calibre, but they were good stout men. Captain Felix Schultz, the commander of the *Scharnhorst* was 45, was a Prussian, a task-master, and proud of the reputation of running a 'taut ship'. Of course he had to do just that, with the Admiral aboard, and the Admiral's staff. His job, indeed, was the least enviable of that of any of the captains. Captain Gustav Maerker, the commander of the *Gneisenau*, was an entirely different sort. Like all the rest of the senior officers of the squadron (save von Müller) he wore a moustache and vandyke beard, but the ferocious look of the whiskers was belied by the gentle and humorous eye of this Westphalian, who regarded Prussians as just a little amusing in their fervour. Maerker ran a stout ship, but he was satisfied with results and paid less attention to form. His officers did not click their heels so loudly, or bark at the men so peremptorily as did the officers of *Scharnhorst*.

Captain von Schönberg, of the *Nürnberg* was 42 years old, and he had just been promoted from commander as he was racing across the Pacific to join von Spee and the squadron. The other two, von Müller of the *Emden*, and Haun of the *Leipzig*, were both commanders, but both had already shown brilliance in their work that indicated rapid promotion, particularly now that war had begun.

Of the men of the squadron two-thirds were experienced and one-third raw recruits. But the training programme had been in effect since the moment the *Patricia* arrived with the recruits in June, and Admiral von Spee was well enough pleased with the results that Schultz and Maerker had achieved, and could assume that his other captains had done as well.

On 6 August when *Nürnberg* arrived at Ponape, Admiral von Spee had completed his plan of action: he would take the squadron across the Pacific, around Cape Horn, and dash north-east across the Atlantic to Germany to join the High Seas Fleet. *Leipzig*, however, would not join them. It was to stay on the American station as a raider. Von Spee had learned that Captain Haun was able to buy coal from the Americans, and as long as America stayed neutral that meant the *Leipzig* would have a source of fuel supply. The ships of the squadron that would make the dash halfway across the world were *Scharnhorst, Gneisenau, Nürnberg* and *Emden*.

That decision was communicated to Captain von Schönberg almost immediately after his arrival at Ponape harbour that morning of 6 August, and he was told further that he must strip his ship for action and coal her, *and be prepared to sail at dusk*. Impossible? Not at all, if the officers and men of the two armoured cruisers turned to, and that is what they did. Boats raced back and forth from ship to shore, carrying food supplies and ammunition from the Ponape dump. The butchers aboard the ships slaughtered the livestock they carried in peacetime, and salted down the meat. The seamen of *Nürnberg* and details from the other two ships surrounded *Titania* in their boats and began moving the coal by sacks. By four o'clock in the afternoon the dirty job of coaling was completed and the men were cleaning up. Another detail was sent to fill water casks at the fresh water creek ashore, and when that was done, Admiral von Spee ordered all the surplus boats, including his barge, left behind. The squadron had to be lean and taut for action. Everything pertaining to peace must give way to everything pertaining to war.

One of Admiral von Spee's perquisites as commander of the East Asia Squadron had been his freedom to choose his own officers. Among the officers were two of his five sons, Otto, a lieutenant aboard the *Nürnberg*, and Heinrich, a lieutenant on the *Gneisenau*. As everyone knew, the Admiral was completely matter of fact about the boys, and they did not receive any special treatment in terms of their duties. But this day was a little special. Admiral von Spee picked up the two boys at the landing stages of their ships, and took them ashore in Ponape that afternoon. They headed straight for the Roman Catholic church, three tall handsome officers; they made their confessions, then returned to duty.

As the day wore away, the harbour was alive with small boats. Friends from shore came aboard the ships to say good-bye to the squadron, and have one last drink, to wish Godspeed and bad fortune to Germany's enemies. Then, as the gloom of night began to descend, the boats pulled away, and *Scharnhorst*'s departure flag was run up the mast. In an hour all three vessels had moved out of the lagoon through the reef's channel, and into the sea, with *Titania* trailing along behind. The squadron set a course for Pagan, a thousand miles away. In a few days they would meet the *Emden* there, and several colliers and provision ships. Admiral von Spee would send these supply vessels out to pre-arranged rendezvous points, and from Pagan would begin his war against the British. Expecting the Japanese to join the war at any moment, von Spee's movement to the Marianas was audacious but completely in keeping with his character. Audacity would have to see him through the next few months if the squadron was to fight effectively against England.

'Larboard watch mask lights', was the order from the Admiral as the ships began moving into the dusk. For the first time in years, the squadron was blacked-out. The war came home to every man just then. While the larboard watch (port) ran the ship during those first four hours at sea, the officers and men of the starboard watch slept, then at midnight the watches changed, and then again at four o'clock in the morning. When the watches changed at eight o'clock, the whole ships' companies were mustered, and the orders of the day read out, and a brief summary of the wireless news garnered by the operators was given to the crews.

During the daylight hours, the off-watch cleaned ship and checked stores. At two o'clock in the afternoon all hands were mustered again for battle drill. For two hours the guns were run out and firing simulated. Damage control parties worked on specific problems presented them. A few rounds of live ammunition were fired at towed targets. At four o'clock the guns were cleared and the ships prepared for night. They sped on towards Pagan, the same routine followed the next day and the next.

In Tsingtao, Captain von Müller was making the *Emden* ready for her voyage to Pagan. On arrival he had reported to Governor Meyer-Waldeck, and announced that Admiral von Spee had called him to join the squadron. Meyer-Waldeck had expected it, just as he expected the news he had that day from Tokyo: Commander Knorr had sent an urgent coded message reporting that the Japanese were loading ships with troops to attack Tsingtao. It was not news to the governor; already the 'bamboo telegraph' had told him, and proof lay in the arrival of several ships and a whole flotilla of Chinese junks which took much of the Chinese population away from the city. When asked why they were leaving, one Chinese had replied in Pidgin: 'Master ... Japan ... Tsingtao soon much boom-boom ...'

On 7 August the *Emden* took on additional crew members, most of them reservists who had made their way to Tsingtao from many points in China. She had three new officers and twenty new enlisted men to crowd in with the others. Captain von Müller conferred with Governor Meyer-Waldeck most of the day, while First Officer von Mücke directed the filling of the ship's holds with coal. Von Müller also directed the removal of the guns from the gunboat *Kormoran* and their installation on the *Rjasan*, which was rechristened *Kormoran*.

She would become an auxiliary cruiser and a raider. For that purpose a number of naval guns had been brought to Tsingtao. Now the 9,000-ton passenger vessel *Prinz Eitel Friedrich* was converted to an auxiliary cruiser too. Such ships, making 19 or 20 knots, could be invaluable in raiding the commerce of the enemy. They did not appear to be warships and thus could maintain the element of surprise until ready to attack. Of course even a destroyer could sink any auxiliary, but there were not enough destroyers to go around in any navy in the world, so the raider concept was sound enough.

Captain von Müller also conferred with the merchant ship captains, one by one. They were given their orders: to load with coal and head to the points indicated in the master plan. The collier *Markomannia* would join the squadron at Pagan, and she was made ready to sail. She was loaded with coal, and the crew changed her appearance as much as possible. She was given the markings of an English Blue Funnel liner. *Prinz Eitel Friedrich* was changed to resemble a British P & O liner. The other ships also altered their appearances. By nightfall of 7 August, Captain von Müller was ready to leave. His instructions were all delivered; everyone now knew that Governor Meyer-Waldeck would soon be fighting a siege battle against the Japanese, but there was nothing von Müller could do about it. He would leave the old *Jaguar* and the torpedo boat *S-90* in Tsingtao; they were too slow to keep up with the squadron. The Austrian *Kaiserin Elisabeth* was also too wheezy for any normal wartime purpose, and she would stay to offer whatever assistance she might in the defence of the colony.

By nightfall on 7 August the *Emden* was ready. She had been called Swan of the East since her christening six years earlier and her proud white lines had impressed all who saw her. But the white paint was all gone, she wore wartime grey, and her decks − even the main deck − were heaped with bags of coal that changed her lines and made her seem dumpy and bulky. Von Müller gave the order, the engines were started, and with the ship's band playing on the poop deck, she began to head out to sea, accompanied as far as the outer harbour by a fleet of small boats. She was taken through the mine field by *S-90*, and the *Markomannia* and the *Prinz Eitel Friedrich* followed. *S-90* went on ahead to Cape Yurnisan, to make sure that no British warship was lying just beyond the harbour to attack. There was nothing to be seen. *S-90* accompanied the little convoy as far as Cape Yatau, but there turned back, and the others went on in to the night.

The darkness was complete. The throbbing of the ship's engines lulled the men off watch to sleep. Then, suddenly, the alarm bell rang throughout the *Emden* and every man turned to his battle station. It was Lieutenant Gaede, the gunnery officer, just making sure that his men would be able to go into action in a matter of seconds if need be.

For the next few days *Emden* steamed along at her best cruising speed, about 12 knots, which moved her steadily toward her destination, without sacrificing fuel. She moved along through the China Sea. Several times wisps of smoke appeared on the horizon, and Captain von Müller turned toward them. But every ship proved either to be a German or a neutral. Several Japanese ships were approached, but Japan had not yet declared her intentions, and the ships had to be treated as neutrals.

On 8 August the perfidy of the Japanese was made perfectly clear. The wireless operators picked up a message in the clear sent to all English ships at sea in Asian waters. The *Emden* was out there, said the report, and she was accompanied by two captured British ships. Captain von Müller laughed at that report: the Japanese had been fooled by the new markings on *Prinz Eitel Friedrich* and *Markomannia*. He could also hope that the British would be fooled when they parted company, which would be soon enough. They did part, and each steamed off alone on a slightly different course, so as not to attract attention from busybodies.

Life aboard the warship was not so much different from peacetime. They steamed along through the sunny weather. After four days they had burned enough coal that the deck loads could be shifted to the bunkers and the ship cleaned, properly. Captain von Müller stuck mostly to the loneliness of his bridge and the cabin. On Sunday he came to the wardroom after church services as was his custom, for a drink with his officers before the Sunday dinner. But the task of managing the ship was left to First Officer von Mücke. He ran orientation courses for the men about the progress of the war. In Europe that progress seemed wonderful, as the German army moved into Belgium. As far as the Navy was concerned the most remarkable feat was that of the cruisers *Breslau* and *Goeben*, which had been manoeuvring in the Adriatic on the outbreak of war, and had made a dash through the Mediterranean and the entire British Mediterranean Fleet to reach the haven of Constantinople.

The *Emden* had not been properly prepared for war in one sense. Von Müller's dash out to strike the first blow at Tsushima had kept him from tearing away all the peacetime appurtenances of the wardroom. But now he decided the wooden panelling and the carpets and the overstuffed furniture all had to go and it did, over the side or into the furnaces.

On 10 August the *Emden* made rendezvous with the *Prinz Eitel Friedrich* and gave her crew lessons in gunnery. The cruiser towed a sleeve target for the auxiliary cruiser, until von Müller and gunnery officer Gaede were satisfied that the auxiliary's shooting was adequate. They waited at this point for a whole day for the *Markomannia*, but she did not show up. Late on the next day came a mysterious message, in the clear.

'Am at rendezvous. Give your position,' said the wireless. And it was signed with *Markomannia*'s call letters.

When Captain von Müller had the message he smelled a rat. *Markomannia* had no business sending in the clear. All their communications were coded as ordered. Further, the request for position sounded very much like that of an English warship just waiting to pounce on the *Emden*. He did not respond to the message, but instead, sent a wireless message in code to the squadron, asking for information about the *Markomannia*.

'Do not use your wireless,' was the reply from the *Scharnhorst*. So Captain von Müller had to continue on, in the dark as to what had happened to *Markomannia*.

On 12 August the *Emden* came in sight of land. Captain von Müller had not told the crew where they were going, but when a distinctive volcano appeared on the horizon, many of the members of the crew knew they had reached Pagan. Around noon they were skirting the island's coast, looking for the entrance to the harbour, when suddenly a ship came out and steamed directly toward them. It was the *Titania*, sent by Admiral von Spee to welcome the *Emden* and speed her along to the rendezvous. The cruiser followed the supply ship inside the harbour, and there before them were the other three ships of the squadron, *Scharnhorst, Gneisenau* and *Nürnberg*. The *Emden* came in close, and found an anchorage between the shore and the *Scharnhorst*. Almost immediately the *Emden*'s steam pinnace was put over the side and Captain von Müller went to the flagship to pay his respects and report in detail on the events of the capture of the *Rjasan* and the situation at Tsingtao as he had left it. The men of the ship looked around them and counted the merchant ships in the harbour, at least half a dozen. They could see that *Nürnberg* and *Gneisenau* were coaling, which meant that something was going to happen soon. Then Captain von Müller came back from the flagship after his interview with Admiral von Spee. It had all gone satisfactorily, and he was smiling. He confided to First Officer von Mücke that the next day there would be a meeting of all the ships' captains aboard the *Scharnhorst*, and that Admiral von Spee would then announce their war plan. Meanwhile *Emden* was to fill up once again with coal from one of the colliers.

That afternoon, a boat came over from the *Scharnhorst* inquiring if the *Emden* carried the squadron's mail. No, said Lieutenant von Mücke, they had despatched the mail with the *Elsbeth* some two weeks ago. She had been laden with coal and provisions and all the mail. Had she not arrived? Was she not out there in the lagoon with the other merchantmen of the squadron line? No, she was not, said the first lieutenant of the *Scharnhorst*. She had not been heard from, and now it seemed certain she would never be. So the men of the *Scharnhorst*, *Gneisenau* and *Nürnberg* were not to hear from home. There was another reason to strike a blow at the damned Englishmen!

5

Southward Ho!

As the other ships of the squadron lay at anchor in Pagan harbour, waiting for their Admiral's orders, *Leipzig* was carrying out her war orders, too. Admiral von Spee had instructed Captain Haun to go immediately to San Francisco and through the German consulate there to secure a steady supply of coal. He was to use the *étappe* system developed by the cruiser squadron on the premise that they would never have adequate coaling stations. Instead, the Germans planned to employ a whole system of colliers, to be stationed at various points. Thus, *Leipzig* might have half a dozen colliers under contract, all carrying coal for her so that she might harry British shipping up and down the west coast of the Americas. Obviously British ships could not be so employed, but those of every state in the Americas except Canada certainly could be. So the *Leipzig* on 7 August was heading for San Francisco with a full load of coal, including a deck load of 50 tons. Captain Haun listened carefully to the radio broadcasts and his wireless operators followed the morse reports with equal care. Between the sources, they managed to put together a picture of the shipping situation. The Canadian cruiser *Rainbow* was in Vancouver. The British sloop of war *Algerine* was somewhere off the Mexican coast and the sloop *Shearwater* was supposed to be somewhere south of the Mexican border. Also rumour had it that two submarines recently purchased by Britain from Chile were working the west coast, looking for German shipping. Haun also learned that the German steamer *Alexandria* was in San Diego. He considered commandeering that ship, which as a naval captain he had a perfect right to do, but then backed away from the idea. He had no knowledge of the local conditions. *Alexandria* might well be shadowed by the British, who were just hoping he would call her up, and they might follow her and put an end to *Leipzig*'s career even before she got started on her commerce raiding. No, he would leave *Alexandria* completely alone and rely on American sources for supply.

On 7 August then, he was doing just as Captain von Müller was, stripping his ship while at sea, dismantling the awnings, carpets, panelling and all the niceties of civil life that could be introduced into a warship in peacetime. Nearly all the furnishings went into the furnace. Indeed, for four hours that evening, the stokers did not burn any coal at all, but furniture and panelling were thrown into the maws of the furnaces.

For two days *Leipzig* steamed northward in steadily worsening weather. Their landfall was to be the Farallone Islands off San Francisco but they did not see them when they thought they should. The ship's wag suggested they had overshot, and that the next land they would see would be one of the Aleutian Islands – it seemed that cold. Also, on the second night, the weather grew absolutely foul in a summer storm, and many of the men were seasick. They could hardly wait to reach San Francisco. They steamed northward very slowly, against the storm, and did not reach the Farallone Islands until 14 August. They were blacked-out at night, of course, and staying well off the sea-lanes, for the wireless had brought traffic that indicated the Canadian cruiser *Rainbow* was now out searching for them.

The weather was dreadful, foggy and cold. The helmsman could not see the ship's bows. The look-outs could not see anything ahead or behind for that matter. Just before nine o'clock on the night of 14 August, by dead reckoning they brought up at the Golden Gate light-ship, and the fog cleared for a moment so that they could see the ship – and the stern of a large grey vessel that looked very much like a warship.

Captain Haun was extremely nervous. He was on the look-out for two major warships, the *Rainbow*, which would shoot on sight, and the *Idzumo*, a heavy Japanese cruiser. Captain Haun did not know the status of the Japanese at the moment – he had heard nothing of a declaration of war, but he could remember the Russo-Japanese war from his study of history. That war had begun with a surprise attack by the Japanese fleet. There was no reason to expect that the Japanese were not willing to undertake such a stroke again.

Actually no one knew what the Japanese intended, except that the Chinese were certain they would strike Tsingtao. Back in that city, Governor Meyer-Waldeck was trying desperately to find out what the Japanese intentions were. He had sent pleas for information to the German consulates at Yokohama, Kobe, Shimonoseki, and Nagasaki without result. He had asked the embassy in Tokyo to amplify the naval attaché's early report, without getting any satisfaction. Tokyo

4 The armoured cruiser *Königsberg*

5 The visit of the Admiral von Spee to Valparaiso in November 1914
after Coronel

6 One of the 5.9 inch guns of the small cruisers. Against a battleship
they were nothing, but against merchantmen they looked like
Big Bertha

7 The *Nürnberg* at sea, on her way to Palau on what began as a
good-will trip and ended up as a major war

was alive with rumour, the embassy was certain that the Japanese would move, but no one knew quite when. Meyer-Waldeck sent an emissary to Peking, and there he learned that it was certain the Japanese would make *a casus belli* of the German occupation of Kiaochow. But what really convinced Meyer-Waldeck that the Japanese were about to attack was the sudden closure of *all* Japanese business firms in Tsingtao, and the disappearance of the Japanese overnight. The bank closed suddenly and the staff disappeared with the funds in one day. The Japanese Press throughout Asia suddenly began angry attacks on the Germans they had favoured so long. And then, from the consulates and the Tokyo embassy came a string of reports of ship and troop movements that could leave little doubt. But on 14 August, the Japanese had not yet made an overt movement.

What was Captain Haun to do if the ship was indeed Japanese? He had no doubts; he was ready for a fight. The alarm rang and the men rushed to their battle stations as the *Leipzig* felt her way through the fog. Then suddenly the fog swirled away and they saw the ship – two ships, not one – and Captain Haun recognized them as an American battleship and an American heavy cruiser. They were the *South Dakota* and the *Pittsburgh*, just leaving the Golden Gate, heading for San Diego naval base. With immense relief Captain Haun ordered an exchange of greetings, and the ships passed one another. Soon the *Leipzig* was hailed by the lightship, whose captain reported that somewhere out there the German consul was floating around in a small cabin cruiser searching for the cruiser. A pilot was taken aboard, and he passed the gossip of the day. It included the report that just the day before the *Rainbow* had actually been in San Francisco harbour, but that she had sailed, and the last report the pilot heard put her a hundred and twenty miles north of the Golden Gate. Captain Haun was so relieved that he did not find it in his heart to be annoyed with the consul for taking such foolhardy and wasteful action. He anchored near the lightship, and waited, and in about two hours the small boat showed up and the bedraggled consul came aboard the *Leipzig*. He introduced himself as Vice-Consul von Schack. He also introduced Dr Reimer of Mazatlan, who needed no introduction. The doctor had been a good friend to Haun for several weeks; he had arranged for coal for the cruiser in Mexico, and he had made this current trip north to San Francisco to help solve the cruiser's supply problems. Also in the little boat were three San Francisco newspaper reporters, whose presence Captain Haun lamented, but must accept. The consul said the publicity would be good for Germany, so the Captain gave the reporters the run of the ship and they buttonholed every officer who could speak English and stored up an enormous amount of information, much of it erroneous. They over-estimated the size of the cruiser, and her guns – making of her an armoured cruiser instead of a light cruiser. That was good for British consumption, Captain Haun knew. They also came to the conclusion that the *Leipzig*, single-handed, intended to blockade the west coast against British shipping. This was not such good publicity, for it would alert the British and cause them to divert several ships to this area to hunt down the *Leipzig*.

Any remaining irritation of Haun's however, was erased when Consul von Schack revealed the reason for his apparently foolhardy adventure in the foggy sea. He had to stop Haun from entering San Francisco port until they had conferred. Everything was going wrong. Dr Reimer had ordered 2,000 tons of American coal, as Haun had asked him to do. But when the coal arrived in San Francisco, it was promptly confiscated. The American government announced that this was war material and the government was not permitting the sale of war material to either side in this war.

Captain Haun was indignant. Coal a war material? Coal was fuel. No ship could move without coal.

That was true, said Vice-Consul von Schack, but there was no point in arguing truth with the Americans. The fact was that the Yankees had already begun to show a marked leaning toward the British, no matter what their government said in Washington. He had to deal with the world as it existed, and the facts he had just related were reality.

Captain Haun was speechless.

Worse, said Vice-Consul von Schack, the *Leipzig* would have to be out of San Francisco in four days. The Japanese cruiser *Idzumo* had asked for mooring facilities and supplies on 18 August. It would be wiser for *Leipzig* to be far away, particularly since no one knew precisely what the Japanese were planning, although all reports from the Pacific indicated an attack on Tsingtao. (The Japanese had already prepared, but not yet delivered, an ultimatum to Governor Meyer-Waldeck to evacuate Tsingtao and Kiaochow colony by 23 August.)

Captain Haun then made arrangements with the consul for dockage, and a supply of coal and food to be delivered on 16 August. The Americans would allow anyone to load up bunkers with coal, it was the idea of maintaining a supply base that they refused to entertain. Those arrangements made, the vice-consul and Dr Reimer boarded their little motorboat and went back to San Francisco. They carried with them several suitcases filled with the civil belongings of officers of the *Leipzig*.

Captain Haun took *Leipzig* out to sea then, his mind awash with a dozen thoughts. In a few minutes his entire war plan had been scotched by the news that the Americans would *not* entertain the *étappe* concept. There was only one alternative: to achieve surreptitiously what he was denied openly. Consul von Schack was going to have to begin moving mountains, and find ships that could be chartered to carry coal for the cruiser. This would be an enormously difficult assignment, because the captains must be friendly to Germany and there could be no doubt about it. Finding such men in America might be hard. But until a stream of colliers could be brought from Germany there was no alternative. Having settled that problem in his mind, Captain Haun turned *Leipzig* toward the shipping lane, and headed north, hoping to come across some British ship bound for Vancouver. The wireless operators listened for transmissions from the *Rainbow*, and when they came they were sufficiently faint to indicate that she was far away.

Early on the morning of 15 August, the *Leipzig* sighted Cape Mendocino, and two hours later turned around and began running back toward San Francisco. Under the Hague convention the ship was allowed only twenty-four hours in a neutral port, and the consul had advised that they run into the Golden Gate at midnight, and go out again under cover of darkness the next night. That would give them the entire day for resupply. As they came down the coast, close inshore, Lieutenant Schiwig, who had pretensions as a world traveller, called the junior deck officers to the port rail to observe 'the Rocky Mountains'. What he saw, of course, was the High Sierra fifty miles inland, not the Rockies, which were a thousand miles east, but the snowy peaks were impressive enough to the young men who had never set foot in America.

Late that night, they passed the lightship again, and picked up a pilot to take them in through the Golden Gate. They entered the harbour, saw the stern grey outline of the Federal prison on Alcatraz Island before them, and came to dock at the Embarcadero, below the city that sprawled up the hills on the southern shore of the bay.

Almost immediately the ship was boarded by Dr Reimer and Lieutenant Jensen, a naval reserve officer who was also second officer of the German steamer *Serapis*, which was in the harbour – the twenty-four hour rule applying only to warships. Reimer and the consul had asked the *Serapis* for help; and it had been the *Serapis'* motor launch, in fact, that the consul had used to search for the cruiser. They had made a dreadful mistake in allowing the reporters to come along, for they had splashed their stories of the 'mighty *Leipzig*' all over the front pages of the local Press, and these had been picked up by the wire services. What the stories missed in speculative comment, they made up in misrepresentation, said Dr Reimer. For example, he and the consul had brought those suitcases of belongings from the officers back aboard the launch and then to the consulate for safekeeping. The San Francisco newspapers indicated the suitcases were full of mysterious secret documents, and Consul von Schack had been called on by the American authorities to explain, and when he had explained it was apparent that the Americans did not believe him. Today the newspapers were filled with charges that the Germans had committed a purposeful violation of the neutrality laws.

Having delivered this disturbing information, Dr Reimer and the merchant officer left the *Leipzig*. Almost immediately thereafter came a representative of the port authority, to tell Captain Haun that he must move his ship. They had come to the wrong pier. Suspecting that it was part of a plot to deprive him of reprovisioning, Haun protested, until told that his coal was lying in barges at the foot of Market Street, and he could take it or not as he wished. He moved the ship then, and the coal barges came alongside at the Market Street pier near the Oakland ferry slip at eight o'clock in the morning. The junior officers and the men of the *Leipzig* had their day's work cut out for them.

Captain Haun went off to do the honours of the port. He visited the American cruisers *Raleigh* and *St Louis*, made small talk, and came away. He travelled in the *Leipzig*'s steam pinnace, trailed by five motorboats full of noisy reporters and photographers. Each time he ascended or descended a gangway the cameras flashed and the reporters began crying out for interviews. Considering what the Press had already done, Captain Haun was hard put to hold his temper, and he did not give the reporters any news. At 10.30 he had completed his courtesy calls and returned to the ship. The reporters stayed aboard their boats, milling around the *Leipzig*, shouting up at crew and officers, and apparently making up their stories out of whole cloth.

Just before eleven o'clock the coaling suddenly stopped, with the bunkers not half full. What had happened, asked Captain Haun? The bargemen had not been communicative, they had simply disappeared and not come back. A Customs official did come aboard, and he began berating Captain Haun for that violation of neutrality in sending suitcases ashore without inspection. Haun was placating him when Consul von Schack appeared, red-faced from exertion, and much agitated. He had been rushing around all morning, he said, on the behalf of the *Leipzig*. The coaling had begun, but suddenly someone in the coal company had decided they must have cash for the coal. The German government's credit, which had never before been questioned, was no longer good. The consulate had an emergency account in a San Francisco bank, but it was in the name of the consul general, who just then was at home in Germany on leave, and vice-consul von Schack could do nothing to persuade the bankers to release the money. So he had rushed about, borrowing from German nationals in San Francisco, taken the cash to the coal company, and any moment now, the barges should be coming back. But that did not solve the problem, it seemed, for now the American authorities had intervened to question how much coal the Germans should have.

Across the bay, at anchorage, Captain Haun could see the German steamer *Alexandria*, laden with the 2,000 tons of good coal that he had ordered when he was in Mexico. Now, aroused by all the furore concerning his coming, the ship was interned because she was carrying war material. If in fact he had not come to San Francisco at all, the *Alexandria* probably could have sailed unnoticed for Mexico, and none would have been the wiser. But now the fat was in the fire, and Haun and von Schack had to do the best they could to retrieve the situation. They boarded the pinnace then, the reporters tagging along, and visited the Admiral of the American naval station at his headquarters on Goat Island, in the middle of the bay. The Admiral looked up his books on international law, to see how much coal the German should get. They wanted 500 tons, which seemed too much. But when he looked in the book, the Admiral saw that under the law the Germans must be given enough fuel to get them to the nearest German port. That was Apia, in Samoa, about six thousand miles away. The 500 tons would not get them there. How about taking along the *Alexandria*? No, that would give them too much. The Admiral finally said they could have the 500 tons at San Francisco and another 500 tons would be waiting for them at Honolulu. Of course, it was understood that they were going to a German port immediately? Of course, said Captain Haun. So it was settled, at least in the minds of the American authorities. The *Leipzig* would leave San Francisco heading for Honolulu and be soon out of American waters and no further source of worry.

Captain Haun, of course, had no intention of going to Honolulu.

His orders were to conduct cruiser warfare against enemy shipping on the western coast of the Americas, and although this was not going to be as easy as he had hoped when he set forth from Mexico, he saw no reason to give up. He returned to the ship, and there found Lieutenant Jensen of the *Serapis*, who had decided to join the colours, and six seamen from the ship who wanted to come along as well. He also encountered a rebellion from the four Chinese laundrymen of the *Leipzig*. They were Shantung men, who had shipped aboard the cruiser in Tsingtao, with the understanding – at least in their minds – that their service would be in China waters. Now here they had been brought across the world, to a hot and sticky climate of Mexico, and now were half freezing in San Francisco, with the prospect of meeting a watery grave as well. They wanted to quit. Captain Haun reasoned with them. They were obdurate. They wanted to go back to China, and they were joined by several cooks and stewards. Captain Haun reasoned again, this time with wallet in hand. The second cook, his pay raised from $25 to $75 a month in one gesture, decided to stay on. But all the others opted to return to China. When Haun told the immigration men at San Francisco they were furious and first said the Chinese could not get off ship here. But when Vice-Consul von Schack guaranteed the passage of the Chinese home on the first available ship, the immigration men relented and let them go ashore.

Then came another difficulty, again with the immigration men. The cruisers of the city class (*Nürnberg, Dresden, Emden, Leipzig*) had all been adopted at launching by the cities for which they were named, and the businessmen of those cities undertook the fitting out of the ships with such niceties as furniture for the wardroom, silver service, and cups for various athletic events. In honour of the cities, each light cruiser so named undertook to spread the fame of the nameplace, and the loyalty was quite impressive. *Leipzig* carried with her a pet bear, the bear being the symbol of the city of Leipzig, and the bear had travelled far and wide with the cruiser. But with the war pressing, bear care was not on the agenda, and Captain Haun decided regretfully to confine his bear to the mercies of the Fleishacker Zoo in San Francisco, at least for the duration.

A bear? Leave it at San Francisco? A German bear? Absolutely not, said the immigrations men and the Customs men concurred. They were not animal trainers, they advised Captain Haun. Let him ship his bear back to Germany, or better yet, take it back himself. They began searching their manuals covering the abandonment of bears in American ports. Captain Haun and his officers spoke rudely and not quietly about the state of freedom in this country that was completely in the hands of a very unpleasant sort of bureaucrat. Consul von Schack intervened, and took charge of the bear, to argue the matter out later with higher diplomatic authority, and the immigration and Customs officials departed the ship, muttering.

All this activity consumed the daylight hours. At 8 o'clock on the night of 16 August the coal was all safely aboard, the bear was safely ashore with Vice-Consul von Schack, and the captain was ready to sail. The men of the *Leipzig* were ordered to battle stations as the ship left port. No one knew what they might find immediately outside the Golden Gate. All an enemy had to do was trail them out, past the three-mile limit, and then attack.

The ship was in the hands of an American pilot, but the moment they passed the lightship he would be put off, and *Leipzig* would be on her own. They moved slowly through the night, even though in this neutral port the lights of the city shone brightly and those of the ships were distinguishable around the bay. Suddenly, the ship was jolted on the starboard side.

'Torpedo', someone shouted. But it was not a torpedo, it could hardly be, in the haven of a foreign port, even though Lieutenant Schiwig suspected it was a torpedo and so said.

No, the ship had collided with something, and it did not take Captain Haun long to figure out what, and why. The American pilot who had come aboard the *Leipzig* late in the afternoon had made for the wardroom, and had sampled heavily of the cruiser's hospitality. He was, in a word, dead drunk. In the darkness he was taking the ship toward the narrows of the harbour, past a small English sailing ship, which was anchored near the old San Francisco World's Fair Grounds at the edge of town. Her anchor lights were bright, but the drunken pilot had mistaken them for the lights of a buoy, and had run the cruiser up on the anchor chain of the sailing ship. The crack and shudder had been caused by the breaking of the sailing ship's jib boom, which had become entangled in rigging of the *Leipzig* and created a dreadful mess.

The pilot was sent under guard to a cabin to sleep off his drunkenness and Captain Haun took over. The first officer reported that the sailer's jib boom had torn loose the armour plate of No.5 gun, and torn the gun partly loose from its mounting.

The impact had ripped the sailing ship's rigging to pieces. By rights, they should have stopped, gone back into port, and waited for a court of inquiry. But when they learned that the ship involved was an

Englishman, they had no such intention. They hoped that the damage would sink her before she could be repaired. The waggish Lieutenant Schiwig suggested that the drunken pilot must have German sympathies underneath it all, to have acted so bravely in their behalf. Captain Haun did not think that a very funny remark. The pilot was hustled over the side at the lightship, and told to report the incident and himself to the authorities. But of course, even as Captain Haun said those words he realized how silly they were, for of course the pilot would go back to San Francisco and tell how the Germans had intentionally run into the English ship on their way out, and there would be no one to set the story straight. At this point, Captain Haun could not give a fig for American public opinion. He had found the Yankees thoroughly disagreeable, English-oriented, and totally unaccommodating. When with the American Admiral he had asked what would happen if he came into San Francisco bringing prizes. Could he capture a collier on the high seas, for example, and then claim her as a prize of war? The treaty of 1828 between Prussia and the United States so stipulated and it had never been abrogated. The American was not as familiar with his naval history as the German captain, but he knew what he intended to do none the less, and it had no bearing on the Treaty of 1828. If Captain Haun brought prizes into San Francisco Bay, they must be taken out again within twenty-four hours or they would be interned. Nor would Captain Haun be allowed to unload the booty (coal) and trans-ship it in American waters. So Captain Haun's last hope about America vanished. He had wanted to send prizes back into port, and then call them out for coal when he needed it. But the Americans would not permit it, so the Americans had to be written off as unfriendly. He would head south and see if people down there were not more reasonable.

Of course he pretended now – his last discussion with the Admiral having ended in his profession of intent to go to Apia – to head off in the direction of Hawaii. Leaving the vicinity of the lightship, he steered a course due west, for seventeen miles. Then, having passed over the lightship's horizon, Haun turned due south. The Americans would be fooled. When *Idzumo* pulled into San Francisco Bay, she would be told that the *Leipzig* had left, heading for Honolulu and Samoa.

Captain Haun had one stroke of luck in San Francisco, and he was relying on this to help him through for a time. Consul von Schack had told him of the existence of a firm named Jebsen and Company in San Francisco. The owner was a good German, and he had already agreed to help the *Leipzig* as much as he could. One of his ships was the

Mazatlan, which travelled up and down the coast under the Mexican flag, since labour and labour laws there were superior to those of the United States for shipowners. Dr Reimer and Consul von Schack had made arrangements for the *Mazatlan* to pick up 500 tons of coal for the *Leipzig* in San Francisco, and take it, ostensibly, to Guaymas. At least that is how the bill of lading read. But the coal was for the *Leipzig* and it was to be off-loaded in a rendezvous off Baja California. For five days *Leipzig* cruised back and forth along the steamer lanes from San Francisco south, and found nothing. Even travelling at 10 knots the ship burned a good deal of coal, and could only go twenty days thus without refuelling. But Captain Haun firmly expected to refuel from the *Mazatlan*. On 23 August, north of Magdalena Bight and Bellena Bight, the *Leipzig* anchored and waited.

He waited three days with growing impatience. On 26 August the *Mazatlan* appeared, and he made ready to receive coal. But when the liner's boat came over to the cruiser, an agitated Dr Reimer appeared to announce that the plan had been foiled by the unfriendly Americans. They had grown suspicious of Jebsen and Company and had allowed the *Mazatlan* to sail only when a Mexican government official was placed aboard to be sure that the coal was loaded off at Guaymas, not anywhere in between. Captain Haun was thoroughly disturbed, but the captain of the *Mazatlan* took him aside and confided something in his ear that made Captain Haun smile once again. He yielded gracefully to the *force majeure* of the Mexican government presence, and soon raised anchor and steamed away south, leaving the impression that he was heading for South American waters.

6

The First Move

Admiral von Spee was worried, and he had good reason to be. The wireless brought him messages from Tsingtao that left no doubt about Japanese intentions, although the Japanese were certainly taking their time about it. If he had planned to return, it was obvious that the way would soon be cut off. But more immediate was the danger to the squadron where it lay. From intercepted messages the Admiral learned that the British had begun to scour the South Seas for his squadron. They had last been reported in the Carolines, and the radio station at Yap implied it had intercepted messages indicating that the British were using a process of elimination to find the squadron. It was too dangerous to remain in Pagan for long, and now that *Emden* had arrived, and most of the German merchant ships that had been ordered to meet the squadron, the Admiral was just about ready to move out. Admiral von Spee was well aware of the danger that he posed to Britain. As long as his squadron was loose, the British would have qualms about shipping men and materials anywhere in the Pacific. What was needed was a few sinkings, a bit of what the Germans called *Kreuzerkrieg* and the French called *Guerre de course*, the destruction of merchant shipping. If he could take a half dozen British ships moving from Australia toward Europe, he could paralyse Australian shipping. If he could take several ships in different places at about the same time, he could paralyse an entire ocean. And of course, that was one reason the Admiral was so pleased to have the *Leipzig* on the Pacific coast of the Americas. It gave him another dimension.

Once more in these last hours, Admiral von Spee reviewed his possible courses of action. Firstly, return to Tsingtao, a possibility if Japan did not enter the war, but was to be written off with the certain knowledge that hostilities with Japan were just days away. But he could travel to the east coast of Africa and harry everything that moved in the Indian Ocean. British East Africa was a natural prey,

Zanzibar, Madagascar, and of course, India, and all the shipping that went through the Indian Ocean. The disadvantage to this plan was that it brought him too close to the British Mediterranean fleet. Besides, the cruiser *Königsberg* was in those waters, and it had its own orders. Further, it was hard to see how von Spee could ever battle his way, on this route, through to Germany, unless he went around the Cape of Good Hope. That, of course, was a definite possibility. He could attack South Africa, and perhaps raise the ire of the Boers once again against England. But that was more a political move than a naval action, and the Admiral did not relish it.

Further, it was necessary to remember his purpose – the *raison d'être* of the German East Asia Cruiser Squadron. Its task was to deal out the utmost destruction to the British, and his task was to determine just how that might be done. Several of his captains had suggested that they operate in the Indian Ocean, around India and Burma, but there were two arguments against this: one was Jerram's China squadron and the other was the British East Asia Squadron – not to mention the augmenting force offered by the Australians. True, the Dutch were neutral and he could use their facilities, but the British would never allow the Dutch to let him stay on for more than the twenty-four hours allowed by international law. So the disadvantages of British might and lack of havens made the Indian Ocean a difficult choice for the squadron. The British could bring up two battleships, eleven heavy cruisers, sixteen light cruisers, fifty destroyers, thirteen submarines, and countless auxiliaries to oppose him, and once the Japanese got into the fight, they could add and certainly would, another thirty or forty ships. The odds were just too great.

There was another alternative, nearly as intriguing as the Indian Ocean, and that was the coast of Latin America. Britain relied heavily on Argentina for meats, and several other Latin countries for tin and copper and other supplies. If he could work off Latin America he might disrupt Britain's shipping in the south, and this would be a serious blow. Latin America was welcoming for another reason; the governments there were not too difficult about such matters as supply and neutrality, particularly if one slipped a little gold to the proper people at the proper times. He could count on the diplomatic corps and the consulates throughout Latin America to help him in this, and if Germany had no colonies there, once past Central America, neither did the British. For a number of reasons the Germans had built a strong position in Brazil and Paraguay and Argentina, and the British had at least their fair share of enemies in these areas. Further, much of the coast of South America was only vaguely charted, which presented him with countless hiding places where he was unlikely to be found by his enemies.

On 13 August Admiral von Spee was ready to meet his captains. One by one they were piped aboard the *Scharnhorst* and were escorted to the Admiral's quarters. Von Spee was seated in the middle of one side of a long conference table. Chief of Staff Fielitz on one side of him, and his lesser staff members taking up the rest of that side of the table. The captains sat down opposite, as they always did for conferences, because the Admiral wanted to see their expressions as they talked.

The Admiral outlined all the possible courses of action, without indicating which he proposed to follow. It was his method of drawing out the captains, to see if they might offer some arguments he had forgotten. But of them all, the absent Captain Haun excepted, none had any specific ideas apart from Captain von Müller of the *Emden*. He was heard most respectfully, for he was the only one so far who had struck a blow against the enemy. He wanted to go into the Indian Ocean and conduct cruiser warfare to disrupt the British trade with India, Burma and the China trade too.

Admiral von Spee nodded, apparently approving. But, he said when von Müller had finished, where would they coal? In the whole Indian Ocean there was not a friend of Germany. And what would they do when the British sent ships from the Mediterranean, ships from Australia, and ships from Hong Kong to box them in? Von Müller had to agree that these were weighty considerations. From the point of view of the big armoured cruisers, the plan seemed hardly possible. *Scharnhorst* and *Gneisenau* needed great quantities of coal to survive. They carried about 2,000 tons of coal each. Steaming at 10 knots, their most economical speed, they used not quite half a ton of coal for every mile travelled. That meant they could steam for twenty-one days without coaling, and no more. But if they got into action, those figures were meaningless, for at 20 knots, the *Scharnhorst* consumed more than twice as much coal per hour as she did at 10 knots. Generally speaking all the cruisers, large and small, must coal about every five days when they travelled at high speed. To secure and maintain enough colliers in the Indian Ocean to keep them going would be a herculean task even if there were no enemies searching for warships and colliers, and everyone knew that the moment they began operations the search would be intensive, and might utilize fifty or sixty English warships. If von Spee had fifty colliers on hand it might work. Instead he had about a dozen available to him, and it was apparent that the squadron could never successfully manage such a mission.

Captain von Müller accepted that argument without demur. But he said, what about a single ship that would enter the Indian Ocean, with perhaps one or two colliers at its disposal? It could work the length and breadth of the ocean, moving swiftly and erratically, capturing enemy vessels and living from their coal. To be sure, the ship might not survive for too long, but while it did survive, it would tie up the whole Indian Ocean, from Trincomalee to Mombasa. The British would be afraid to use the Indian Ocean to move goods from Australia, or if they were not, then the single cruiser would have good pickings.

Admiral von Spee was well aware of Berlin's view of the East Asia Cruiser Squadron. It had been made quite clear in recent days in the absence of any orders from the Admiralty. The squadron was expendable, and was already written off the books for all practical purposes. So while it was apparent that the mission of a single ship in the Indian Ocean was really suicidal, there was no good reason to stop it from the point of view of maintaining the force, and von Müller's arguments were sound enough. The damage wreaked by one fast-moving ship could be enough in a few weeks to justify that ship's loss, and there was no question about it. He gave his assent – for of course it was apparent to all that Captain von Müller had been talking about himself and the *Emden* as he spoke of the opportunity, and with his capture of the *Rjasan* he had certainly earned the right to be first chosen. It was established then, that the *Emden* would be detached and sent into the Indian Ocean.

The news from America was very uncertain. Consul von Schack had cabled the Admiral his information about the seizure of *Leipzig*'s coal, and his impression that the Americans were determined to observe the letter of neutrality. That was not so good, but Admiral von Spee believed the opportunities for the *Leipzig* on the eastern Pacific shore were so great that the small cruiser should run the risk of fuel shortage and remain on station. Meanwhile, von Spee would lead the rest of the squadron across the Pacific to the shore of South America and conduct raiding operations there. He felt certain that with friends in the area, and the many havens, and colliers he should be able to secure from Germany, he would be able to operate for a considerable length of time. After he had arrived there, he would see what was to be done later.

The meeting broke up then, and Captain von Müller went immediately to the *Emden* to get ready to depart. The ship coaled, and he made several transfers of personnel. Kapitänleutnant Hermann Mezenthin, an experienced merchant captain, was sent to the *Gneisenau* to become prize officer, although he had first been destined for that job on *Emden*. But when Lauterbach had been dispatched to the *Rjasan* because he knew the captain, the rotund merchant officer had proved so successful that von Müller wanted to keep him as prize officer, and *Gneisenau* was badly in need of just such a person. In trade, Captain Maerker gave von Müller two of his young professional lieutenants for deck officers.

Captain von Müller was worried about one thing: he had hoped to take the collier *Markomannia* with him on his adventures, but the *Markomannia* had never showed up after leaving Tsingtao. He asked von Spee for another collier, and one was about to be assigned that day, when suddenly the *Titania*, which prowled back and forth at the entrance to the bay like a watchdog, came rushing inside to announce that the *Markomannia* was coming in with the 5,000 tons of coal she had brought from Tsingtao. Her captain came aboard the flagship, and von Müller came over too. Von Spee and von Müller discovered that the captain of the merchant ship had mistaken the co-ordinates in Tsingtao when jotting them down, and so had waited for three days at the wrong rendezvous point before coming along to Pagan. Von Müller then asked about the strange message he had received when at the rendezvous. No, said the captain of the *Markomannia*, he had not sent it. His wireless had been out of order or he would have asked the squadron for information. The Admiral grunted, and von Müller went away still mystified. He never did learn who had sent that message asking for his position, but he was sure by now that it must have been one of his British enemies.

As Captain von Müller got the *Emden* ready for departure, making sure that he had all the charts he would need, Commander von Mücke supervised the coaling. Lieutenant Lauterbach, the old skipper of the *Staatsekretar Kraetke*, took a boat over to that ship and personally conned his old command back to the side of the cruiser and brought her to as smoothly as if she had been a launch. She came up on the port and the *Gouverneur Jaeschke* moved up on the starboard side, and the men coaled from both ships, to speed the process. Prince Franz Joseph von Hohenzollern, a nephew of the Kaiser, supervised the coaling from the *Staatsekretar Krätke*, a job which befitted the new rank given him that very day by order from Berlin. He was advanced from sub-lieutenant to lieutenant along with several other young men of the squadron who had completed their three years of service.

Coaling from these two mail and passenger ships was hard work. They were not built to carry cargo of that sort, and their holds were deep and the coal inaccessible. The men had to tramp up long steep gangways with the sacks on their backs. But the work was made lighter by the band of the *Emden*, which turned out morning and evening (it was too hot to coal at midday) and there were extra rations of food and beer for all concerned. Had there been none of that, the men of the *Emden* would still have turned to eagerly. For the talk around the scuttle-butt had it that they and their captain were going off on high adventure. For once the rumour was right: they were going into the Indian Ocean as the gossips said. Morale could not have been higher, and the dirty job was completed that evening.

Aboard the *Staatsekretar Krätke*, Lieutenant Lauterbach spent a pleasant afternoon helping to demolish the supply of wines he had laid in in those peacetime days that seemed so long ago now. He also decided, after several bottles, that First Officer von Mücke had gone too far in totally denuding the wardroom of the *Emden* of panelling, furniture and even all but one picture of the Kaiser. He conferred with other officers from the *Emden* and they decided to take some of the niceties from the liner, which certainly was not going to need them on its new business. So they employed seamen from the liner to fill the ship's boats with cases of wine, beer, whisky, and easy chairs, some pictures, and Lauterbach's extensive private library. The enthusiasm on the *Emden* was complete, and when von Mücke saw them coming and heard the praises of Lauterbach ringing from the skies, he made it a point to go and examine the yard-arm so he would not have to take official notice. Indeed, he had been heard to note regret that he had gone quite so far in interpreting Captain von Müller's order in the first place.

Lauterbach, while assembling all these luxuries, encountered three familiar figures hiding in the kitchen galley of his old ship. They were the laundrymen from the *Emden* who had decided they did not want to go to war, and that the *Staatsekretar Krätke*, which they knew well from the old days, would be returning soon to Tsingtao. They wanted to go home to China. Now this matter was of the gravest concern, for the officers of the *Emden* must have clean linen, and not one of them had ever washed anything himself in his life. The departure of the laundrymen would create havoc in the wardroom.

Lauterbach, at his most expansive argued with the laundrymen in pidgin, but they were unmovable. They would not stay, they said, and if they were forced to stay, they would not wash.

Besides, they said everyone was going ashore. The officers of the liner told them that all the Chinese were being evacuated from the ships here by order of the Admiral. They were non-combatants and it was not fair to take them into the war, the Admiral had said. Lauterbach knew this was true. It was the most discussed topic in the wardroom of the *Emden*; what were the officers going to do about their spotless white uniforms? And their coaling costumes which ended up black with soot at the end of a watch? The most serious loss, as everyone knew, was to the *Titania*, which had been entirely crewed by Chinese. But reserve officers and men would take over the *Titania*. So it had been ordered that all the Chinese would be put ashore, with two bags of rice for each man, and they would be trans-shipped by island steamer to a neutral port and thus sent home.

All this had been decided and the Chinese knew all about it – until Lauterbach began. He had conferred with Captain von Müller and they had decided that the Admiral would not be hurt by events that he would know nothing about on his departing cruiser *Emden*, so that if Lauterbach could manage discreetly, they would entice the three laundrymen back aboard the *Emden* and take them along.

Lauterbach shrugged his shoulders helplessly, overtaken by superior moral force. What could he do? It was unfortunate, he said, that no ships were returning to China again until the war was over. But they could be taken to Samoa, perhaps, or to Fiji, and put ashore there, if the ships stopped anywhere at all which seemed unlikely. The laundrymen had not contemplated a life during which no one stopped anywhere, but it seemed most likely that the foreign devils would fight a war that way, and certainly they did not wish to stay in the bleakness of Pagan. Still, there was the terrible question of going home, and also the laundrymen had been insulted deeply by von Mücke and a whole succession of junior officers who had been shouting at them for three days. Lauterbach calmed them down. He tripled their salaries, which made them smile. He gave them a bottle of whisky, which made them laugh. And in an hour they agreed to return to the *Emden* and their wetwash laundry just off the galley.

Von Mücke made the rounds of the other ships, discovering what surpluses existed, so the *Emden* might be properly provisioned on her lonely voyage. Everyone wanted to help: von Mücke got extra yeast from the *Scharnhorst* and medicine from the steamer *Yorck*. The *Prinz*

Eitel Friedrich's ample cold storage lockers yielded up fresh fruit and many cases of beer. The steamer *Holsatia* gave them tins of cigarettes and soda pills so the officers could enjoy sparkling water with their whisky. A shore party replenished the *Emden*'s water casks and brought back a whole boat-load of coconuts which were given to the thirsty *matrosen* when they completed the coaling in late afternoon.

Just at that time a boat came over to *Emden* from the flagship, with the Admiral's final orders. The mission was reconfirmed, and *Emden* could sail that evening for her war in the Indian Ocean. Captain von Müller told von Mücke that the ship was to be ready to sail by 5.30, for at that time the entire squadron would leave Pagan harbour. At the appointed hour the ships weighed anchor and formed into two lines, the warships to port and the merchant ships on the starboard. The flagship *Scharnhorst* led the way, and *Emden* tailed. They headed south-east. During the night the weather worsened and the starboard column of merchant ships broke up. At dawn the warships had to break formation and go back and round up the stragglers. This task was completed by eight o'clock in the morning, and the squadron steered almost due east. From the flagship, came the signal: '*Emden* detached. Good luck.' The *Emden* turned south to make the passage into the Indian Ocean, and soon was out of sight with a smoke cloud trailing on the horizon, the mark of the collier *Markomannia* which would tag after her on the long voyage. The *Emden*'s course was south-south-west and the speed 12 knots. She was on her own, but at least she had her three laundrymen.

Having left the *Emden*, the squadron moved east, through an especially filthy Pacific day toward the Marshall Islands. The procession was ragged and the going very slowly. Little *Longmoon*, smallest of the freighters, was always falling back, and twice before noon very nearly broached in heavy seas. Patiently the Admiral waited, and at 1.30 in the afternoon had the temerity to order a battle drill among this unwieldy squadron. It began at 1.45 and lasted all afternoon, the cruisers running out their guns and loading and reloading, and the warships taking turns as 'the enemy', whom the Admiral expected to encounter soon.

The real enemies of the squadron were just then forming up. In London, First Lord of the Admiralty Winston Churchill had decided the Far Eastern and Pacific forces would be grouped under two flags, those of Sir Thomas Jerram, with the nucleus of the China Squadron, and the whole augmented by French, Russian and Japanese ships; the second, under Rear-Admiral Sir George Patey, which was built around the battleship *Australia* and consisted mostly of Australian and New Zealand vessels. They were already out looking for von Spee.

But from the English standpoint, von Spee had proved as elusive as a cat in a jungle. They had all sorts of reports: the whole squadron was together around New Guinea; the whole squadron was at Pagan (that was the best report as of 12 August); the *Scharnhorst* and *Gneisenau* had split up and *Scharnhorst* was in Samoa. But the Pagan report, while accurate to within one ship, was pure conjecture and nobody believed it and the other reports were completely inaccurate. Admiral Patey was absolutely certain that the squadron was off New Guinea, and he tried to persuade Jerram to come south and help him surround the enemy and destroy them. Jerram had his orders from London, and they did not include a wild-goose chase to the South Seas, so he did not go. Patey headed for Friedrich Wilhelm harbour in German New Guinea, and found nothing. He then went to Simpson harbour on Neu Pommern, and found nothing. Admiral Jerram went to Yap − or he started to go to Yap. He was told to be ready for action. That meant getting the old *Triumph* ready for sea, and this took an almost superhuman effort, involving the transfer of the crews of several outmoded gunboats at Hong Kong, and the enlistment of a hundred soldiers from the Duke of Cornwall's Light Infantry Regiment as sailors. In the second week of August he managed all this, and went out with *Triumph*, the cruiser *Yarmouth*, the French cruiser *Dupleix*, and the cruisers *Minotaur, Hampshire* and *Newcastle*. In the South China Sea, they split up and *Triumph*, *Yarmouth*, and the French cruiser went up to see if von Spee was foolish enough to be trapped in Tsingtao, while the Admiral and the rest of the force went to Yap. *En route*, they had encountered the *Elsbeth*, with some of von Spee's coal and all the squadron's mail, and had captured her. The mail, hopefully, would provide some interesting intelligence. But it did not, for almost all of it referred to matters of a peacetime navy, and there was not a hint in the whole batch as to what had become of Admiral von Spee and his ships.

Reaching Yap, and not finding Admiral von Spee there, Admiral Jerram destroyed the German radio station by gunfire from offshore, which was the first unfriendly act of England against Germany in the Pacific. In fact, it was probably a mistake, for at that moment (11 August) Admiral von Spee was just seven hundred miles away from Jerram's superior force, and a lucky guess might have sent Jerram quickly to Pagan, which would have meant the end of the squadron then and there. The Germans tuned in to Yap constantly for the radio news broadcasts, and when they suddenly ceased in mid-passage on 12 August, as the 200-foot wireless mast fell under the *Minotaur*'s gunnery, von Spee sensed that a disaster had befallen the station. That, and the disappearance of the *Elsbeth* which must have been around Yap, confirmed his decision to move on 13 August, and thus he probably saved the squadron.

For nearly a week the squadron steamed steadily toward the Marshall Islands. The Admiral took this opportunity, facing eleven hundred miles of open sea, to train the men of the ships to as fine a fighting edge as possible. That meant drills for several hours every day, a process that was hardest on the stokers, because they worked down at their fiery furnaces (four hours on, eight hours off, in three watches) and then had to use their off-watch time in the daytime hours to pass ammunition and work in damage control exercises. But that was the fortune of war. The days were hot and filled with war work. The nights were more relaxed although the look-outs were posted carefully and the officers of the watch allowed no laxness. Until dark the officers had the run of the deck for exercise, but after dark the poop was cut off by a stern chain which kept men from wandering into the possible field of fire of the after turret, in case of a night engagement. The officers gossiped and drank and smoked cigars and talked about the war. Aboard the flagship *Scharnhorst* the formality was severe because of the presence of the Admiral, but aboard the *Gneisenau*, life was considerably easier. The wardroom was blacked-out and hot in this climate, but the junior officers played skat and chess, and the seniors smoked and listened to the guitars and piano that had been saved in spite of all aboard the *Gneisenau*. Captain Maerker came down from his bridge once or twice during the evening to hear a song or two, and pass a few words.

The ship was divided into regular officers and reservists, who were usually much older in grade. Lieutenant Mezenthin, a merchant marine officer of many years service who had been a captain for twenty years, was known as Uncle Hermann, and he had the respect of all for his accomplishments at sea. Uncle Hermann was a man of strong opinions, which were buttressed, it seemed, by the events reported by wireless from Belgium. They heard of the German drive through Liège, and the pushing back of the British armies. The war would be over in eight weeks, not longer, said Uncle Hermann with the air of a man knowing precisely whereof he spoke. The junior officers tended to believe him, but the seniors were not so sure. They recalled the naval might of England. Indeed, the traffic on their own wireless consisted largely of allied shipping traffic, and much of it emanated from English warships. They could understand very little, since most messages were now in code, but they knew the call signs of many of the ships in the squadron wireless rooms, and they could report that the enemy was on all sides of them.

Somehow the information that the enemy was around – all around – permeated the lower decks of the *Gneisenau* in particular, and Chaplain Rost, whose business it was to know such things, came up in mid-week to tell Captain Maerker that morale below decks was very low. He had a possible answer: would the captain allow him to give a series of talks on the lives of great German heroes, such as Field Marshal Gneisenau, the bearer of their ship's name, to instil new fervour and strengthen the patriotism of the men? Indeed Captain Maerker would do so, and the chaplain was assigned the task, although several of the officers suggested that arrival at a port out of the heat would probably do twice as much for morale.

Eniwetok was the landfall, and the squadron made it on 19 August, coming in through the south channel of the atoll to another in the deep inner harbour. It was a great relief, particularly for the stokers, and within two hours Chaplain Rost reported an upsurge in morale. This was partially dissipated by the Admiral's first order of business after the ships had all anchored: coal.

Coaling in wartime was not the same as coaling in peacetime, where civilians did much of the work. The ships of the squadron were virtually defenceless when coaling, and that is why every time a captain or commander found himself in a safe haven his first thought was to get the ship ready to fight, and coal. The gun muzzles had to be covered to protect them from the caustic dust, and they had to be pointed upward to get them out of the way. Tarpaulins were strung everywhere possible to cut down the spread of dust. Sacking and canvas walkways covered the decks. The doorways of the compartments were all covered to prevent seepage of dust. The small boats were moved away from the ship to protect them from damage. Then the crew was divided into four coaling divisions. In peacetime, coaling could be accomplished day or night, but in wartime, and here, Admiral von Spee did not want to attract any attention, so the coaling was laid off until dawn. At the first light, the stokers went into their bunkers and 'trimmed up', which meant levelling the mountains that had appeared as coal slid toward the opening, to make a flat and compact surface for the new coal. This was a filthy job, in which the unlucky stokers chosen covered their heads with towels, their eyes with goggles, and their faces with wet sponges, and still the acrid taste of the dust was always in their mouths and the sting in their eyes. The coal from the merchant ships was brought to the warships in sacks by the seamen, who then dumped their sacks down the bunker slides. The stokers stayed down, levelling the hills as they came and the dust rose, and rose, and rose.

On the stokers' end it was actually dangerous work in more ways than just running the risk of black lung disease. A stoker was stationed in each bunker with no other duty than to guard his fellows, and see that none of them collapsed and were buried under the coal. It had happened before. After two hours a stoker was relieved from this noxious duty and given a chance to wash himself in the sea water and drink all the cold tea or coffee he could hold. When the sun rose high, everyone took a two-hour break, and fresh water was allowed for washing, for, as everyone knew, salt water simply did not take off coal dust. After a hot meal, and a rest in the middle of the day, the coaling began again and continued until dark. If necessary, it could have been repeated next day, but on this occasion the bunkers were filled by day's end, and the dreadful task was over for a little while.

The next day, the squadron turned to other tasks, slaughtering more of the animals (which could not be done in high seas with any degree of safety), cleaning boilers, and renewing mechanical parts of the ship's engines.

Gneisenau had been last to coal, she had stood guard until *Scharnhorst* had finished the unpleasant job, and this fact caused her more than a little anguish that second day. She was just cleaning up when Eniwetok was struck by a sudden freak storm that came with no warning at all. One moment the sky was bright, and the next, a gust of wind swept across the anchorage, rippling the water, and then came an enormous downpour of rain, accompanied by swirling gusts of wind.

Scharnhorst and *Nürnberg* were battened down for the night already and suffered no damage. The *Titania* and the merchant ships bobbed like corks in the storm, but suffered no particular damage save some broken crockery. But *Gneisenau* was caught unprepared. First, *Longmoon*, the smallest ship, chose to slip her bow anchor, and the wind caught her and slapped her into a hundred and eighty degree arc, and came to rest with her bow facing the stern of *Gneisenau* on the starboard side, and only her stern anchor holding her from crashing into the warship. The steam pinnaces of *Gneisenau* and *Scharnhorst* were alongside the *Gneisenau*, where they had assisted in the coaling. The stokers had just gone into the pinnaces and were preparing to light up their fires and get them ready for more work around the ships the next day when the gust caught them and snapped the mooring lines of both vessels. Aboard the *Gneisenau* pinnace, one stoker had just come up from the engine room, and he grabbed the iron ladder of the warship and hauled himself up as the boat went out from under him. On the other pinnace, the fire lighter was not that lucky. He leaped into a rowboat as he felt the pinnace begin to move, but just then *Gneisenau* pitched in the storm, and the mooring lines of the row-boats broke, and the stoker's little cockleshell went into the tideway between the ships, sucked out toward the mouth of the harbour.

Lieutenant Commander Pochhammer, the first officer of the *Gneisenau*, was asleep in his bunk after a hard day of coaling, when he felt the ship tremble. Half-dressed, he swung up on to the bridge, to be caught on the quarterdeck by a downpour that soaked him through in a second. But he made the bridge, and found that the officer of the deck was doing all that he should be: he had already ordered the manning of the cutter, to go out and find those fugitive boats before they were lost. But just then, they were not found, and Pochhammer stood on the bridge, wondering how one explained to the captain, and to the Admiral, how boats got lost in the middle of a harbour.

Just then came a new crisis.

'Man overboard', was the shout. First Officer Pochhammer started and then ran to the port side of the bridge. The officer of the watch had seen it; a young seaman had fallen over the side between the cruiser and the steamer *Prinz Waldemar*. A life-ring was tossed into the water, but the boy could not reach it. The officer of the deck picked up another ring, dropped it overboard and leapt in. In two minutes he had the young seaman on deck, dripping and gasping, but alive. Pochhammer had just digested this excitement when the *Gneisenau*'s cutter arrived, with the steam pinnace in tow – the No. 2 steam pinnace. But the No. 1 steam pinnace had disappeared in the gloom. First Officer Pochhammer hoped fervently that Captain Maerker would be in a jolly mood in the morning, when he had to deliver the bad news that the No. 1 steam pinnace had blown away and was lost. But when morning dawned, and Pochhammer came on the bridge early to have one last desperate look around, he lifted his glasses and looked around at the quiet blue water of the Pacific, searching the beaches of the little islands, hoping for a sight of the pinnace on the sand. He saw it, not wrecked as he expected, but bobbing in the water on the other side of the reef. The pinnace had been carried out through the channel on the tide, and now stood offshore. The No. 2 steam pinnace was sent post-haste to pick up No. 1, and First Officer Pochhammer, with all boats and all men accounted for, began to hope that there was really nothing to bother Captain Maerker about at all.

But at nine o'clock came an officer from the *Scharnhorst* to see Captain Maerker and ask in tones that mirrored the acerbity of the Admiral, just what sort of games the *Gneisenau* had been playing last night, with all the racket, flashlights, and requests for boats from other ships. Maerker sputtered a little because he knew nothing about it, and then called on his first officer for an explanation as to why someone had gone to the *Scharnhorst* and tried to borrow one of their steam pinnaces. A fishing expedition, perhaps?

So then First Officer Pochhammer did have to explain, and received a thorough dressing down from his captain for carelessness in mooring the small craft. He passed it along to the officer of the deck, who passed it along to the chief boatswain, who passed it on to the stokers in charge of the pinnaces at the time of the accident, and to the man who had fallen overboard, indicating that he was nothing better than shark-bait. And so the incident ended. The Admiral had more important matters on his mind. He was planning the first strike of the squadron.

After the *Emden* left the other ships, she steamed along the east side of the Marianas and then headed for Yap, where the Germans had their wireless station. As they approached, the wireless operators called up Yap for hours, and, of course, had no reply. Captain von Müller sensed that something was wrong and gave the island a wide berth. He went then to Angaur Island in the Palaus, which had been leased by a German phosphate company. Von Müller hoped there to find another steamer that he could commandeer for his supply train. He had known from the beginning that *Markomannia* could not supply him for long, and if he sent her away to try to find more coal, perhaps to the Dutch Indies, he must have another collier to replace her. On the voyage von Mücke supervised the training and certain changes in the ship. Metal screens and screens of hemp were put up around the gun positions to protect the men from flying fragments.

The chief engineer ordered changes in the boiler tubes to replace the worn ones. All the torpedoes were taken apart, cleaned and put back together. The deck-hands spent most of their time cleaning up after coaling, a thankless task at the moment, for the ship's decks were piled with sacks of coal and the dust exuded from them. So all day long it was bucket and mop, and rags to clean the bulkheads. Then a hundred sacks of coal would be shifted down into the bunkers, and it all had to be done over again.

On 19 August, the *Emden* reached Palau. Captain von Müller had made arrangements at Tsingtao to meet a German collier here and had confirmed them once his freedom was guaranteed. She was the *Choising*, carrying about 3,000 tons of coal that he could use. But *Choising* was not at the meeting place. He must wait. He waited two days and then gave up, and moved to Angaur a few miles away. Carefully he worked the *Emden* completely around the island, which had no wireless sending station, because there were two anchorages, one on the north and one on the west and he did not want to anchor then find that his enemies were upon him. Finally he was satisfied that no one had come to Angaur, and he led the *Markomannia* into the north anchorage, where she tied up at a deep water buoy laid by the Germans much earlier. Again it was coaling time. He began to coal. At about that time a small boat appeared from shore, carrying officials of the phosphate company, who wanted news of the war. They had some news for Captain von Müller — disappointing news. Just three days before a steamer had left the harbour after filling up with phosphate. She was English. Captain von Müller could have cursed if he had been a swearing man. His hunch had been correct; just a few hours earlier and he would have had another prize for the Kaiser and another collier for himself. But the stop at Angaur was not wasted. Von Müller had made arrangements for the 10,000-ton German liner *Princess Alice* to meet *Emden* here, and she arrived later in the day. Like *Emden*, *Princess Alice* had already struck one blow for Germany in this new war. She had been travelling between England and Hong Kong, carrying four million dollars in gold destined for the Indian government from London, when her captain learned that the war had broken out. Instead of putting in at Hong Kong she had turned and gone to the Philippines, where the captain delivered the gold to the German consul. That was a brilliant stroke, taking the gold to the one place in Asia where it would most certainly be safe from British attempts to recover it, an American territory. At Manila, the *Princess Alice* had been told to load with supplies as if returning to Germany, and then to join the East Asia Cruiser Squadron as a supply ship. So the *Emden* was in great good luck. Lieutenant von Guerard, the ship's adjutant led a party of officers to the passenger liner. He went to enlist some of the crew, since the *Emden* needed all the trained men she could get. Captain von Müller expected to take many prizes, and each of them would demand a prize crew to move the ship into a neutral port where the prize would be safe. She had aboard thirty-four officers and three hundred and sixty men, and although this crowded her facilities, she needed more. In the next few hours, von Guerard enlisted another dozen reservists. Prince Franz Joseph, the mess officer and the purser also went with him, to requisition supplies, feeling lucky that they had been the first ship of the squadron to get a chance at *Princess Alice*'s luxury items. They wanted soap, beer, cigarettes and cigars, and the liner had plenty of all.

Captain von Müller learned from the captain of the liner that the Japanese had given an ultimatum to Governor Meyer-Waldeck, which von Müller had not known because the *Emden*'s wireless had some-how not picked up those broadcasts. This was sad but expected news, and it put the captain on the alert; Japanese vessels must be avoided at all costs or captured from this point on. There was no margin at sea for waiting.

As if to prove that point, by mid-afternoon von Müller was urging his officers to haste. They must be getting on, because these waters were too close to Japanese territory for comfort, and their assigned area of operations was still far away. As the sun was sinking, the *Emden* finished coaling and without stopping for the usual clean-up, von Müller ordered her to move out, with *Markomannia* behind him, and *Princess Alice* third in line. Captain von Müller had decided that *Princess Alice* should accompany him, even though when the captain learned of the *Emden*'s mission he was unenthusiastic. But since von Müller was senior naval officer present, his word had the force of law, and the *Princess Alice* came along − for a while. That night, von Müller had announced, he would make some changes in course. They would be signalled by lantern from the mast-head of the *Emden* to the *Markomannia*, and that ship would pass the signals along to the *Princess Alice*. In that way, von Müller would not break wireless silence, and would thus avoid informing his enemies − especially the Japanese − of the presence of unknown ships in the area. But the *Princess Alice*, through apparent design, 'missed' the signal and disappeared from the train. Von Müller had given the captain a rendezvous point in case of difficulty, but when he reached it, the liner was nowhere around. He did use his wireless then, and called the liner to him, but her captain argued that he was short of coal. Since Prince

Franz Joseph had been all over the ship and the engineering officer had told him that she had just filled with coal at Manila, von Müller knew the captain was lying, and as much as said so. Yes, said the captain, lamely, *Princess Alice* had coal, but it was the wrong kind and her boilers were sticky and it was much too dangerous to come. Von Müller was thoroughly exasperated but helpless for the moment. He could not sit out in the middle of the Pacific and argue all summer, while his enemies closed in on him. He could, and did give the captain of the liner a dressing down, and warned him that higher authority would deal with him later – and then he ordered the ship back to Manila, knowing very well that the captain could intern himself there and escape the Admiralty's wrath.

The *Emden* now headed toward the Moluccas. She would steam through the Dutch East Indies, and then turn into the Indian Ocean to begin operating. As she ran, the wireless room tried to get in touch with Tsingtao to learn the fate of the colony. They never raised the station there, but their transmission was picked up by the old light cruiser *Geier* which had been circulating among the Pacific colonies, running errands, more or less, since her ancient hull and engines made her an immediate candidate for oblivion in case of naval action. *Geier* had been at Yap when the British squadron attacked that place, but her captain, Korvettenkapitän Grasshof, had wisely hidden the old ship in a cove, and saved her. Now, Grasshof wanted to know what to do. Von Müller set a rendezvous point, and they met on 21 August to confer. After going over all the statistics, von Müller concluded reluctantly there was no possible use he could make of the *Geier*, so he sent her on to Honolulu, to intern herself rather than fall into the hands of the British.

That day, the purser began cursing the captain of the *Princess Alice*. While Prince Franz Joseph had brought back the luxuries for the wardroom of the *Emden* in his boat that day at Angaur, the captain's desire to leave had forced the purser to make arrangements for delivery of all his requests at the earliest opportunity at sea, and then the *Princess Alice* had defected, leaving the *Emden* without the supplies. Thus she very quickly ran out of food stuffs and was reduced by the time they reached the equator on 22 August to a basic ration of rice and corned beef. The cooks made curries and chili dishes. They fried rice and boiled rice and baked rice, but it was still rice, and corned beef was still corned beef. There was nothing to be done until the cruiser could reach a port, or capture an enemy, or find a haven where it might trans-ship some of the livestock and supplies that were aboard the *Markomannia*.

That day of the crossing of the line, Captain von Müller met a Japanese liner, which daintily dipped her flag to him, while her wireless buzzed furiously. What was he to do? He knew Japan was going to war, but there had been no declaration as far as the *Princess Alice*'s captain knew, and von Müller had since been unable to raise Tsingtao and learn what was actually happening. Should he capture the Japanese ship? He knew very well that she was an enemy, but he did not know the actual state of affairs. He considered taking her. The Japanese were already marching against Germany, but had pulled their old trick of holding up on a war declaration until ready to attack. But von Müller did not know this, and he still played the war game in the old-fashioned, gentlemanly way. He let the enemy ship go by unmolested.

The enemy was not all they saw; on Dutch East Indian waters they encountered a string of junks and sampans and all sorts of other small craft as they steered between Celebes and Halmahera Islands. They steamed slowly, partly to conserve fuel and partly to avoid attention, for they must assume that their presence in the Dutch Indies would be noted by British spies and reported quickly enough. The course was now set through the Moluccan Straits and to Timor, where Captain von Müller had arranged to meet the German steamer *Tannenfels*. Such matters were accomplished by a constant patrol of the airwaves; the wireless operators worked around the clock listening for German ships, and when they heard them, they lapsed into the German merchant code to question the officers about cargoes and destinations and see if they could make use of the civilian vessels. The *Tannenfels* had coal and other supplies aboard and she promised to meet the *Emden* at Timor. The *Emden* steamed ahead to the Nusa-berei Straits, which lie between the north-eastern shore of Timor and the island of Lerti. That was the point of rendezvous far off the steamer tracks. They could meet the steamship there and replenish without much chance of observation.

The *Emden* arrived a full day ahead of schedule, which gave the men a welcome respite from the tensions of the past weeks. They would have to coal again, for the bunkers were half empty and all the deck load had been burned. But they would not have to coal immediately, and that was the bright spot. They lay off the rendezvous point a few miles, so as not to run danger in case the *Tannenfels* had been trapped by the English and forced to keep the rendezvous at gun-point. Then, on the foggy morning of 25 August the *Emden* and the

Markomannia steamed into the deserted little bay where they were to meet the *Tannenfels*. No *Tannenfels*. They waited four hours, but the *Tannenfels* did not appear. Von Müller could wait no longer. He brought up the *Markomannia* and took 470 tons of coal from her, thus cutting deep into his reserves. The men had been waiting eagerly for the ship that would bring them a change of diet, but it did not seem they would ever see it. Morale sagged, and the coaling dragged in the heat of the day. Prince Franz Joseph shed his tunic and stripped down to his underclothes and picked up a sack of coal, put it on his brown back and carried it down to the hold. Only a prince could manage such a breach of naval etiquette, but once it was done, the other officers followed, and von Müller masked a smile. The Prince's effort changed the whole atmosphere. He shouted that he would beat the port watch with his starboard watch and he promised his men cigars if they carried more coal than the 'enemy'. The men were roused from their lethargy. Forgotten were the disappointments, the heat, and the tensions of the war in the little contest. Prince Franz Joseph's watch did win, and his men got their cigars, and the forward deck was redolent of tobacco that afternoon.

Some of the lucky ones were chosen to go on a foraging expedition ashore. The *Markomannia* still held six oxen, two pigs and several sheep, and they were badly in need of fresh fodder. They were threatened with the beastly equivalent of scurvy. So two of the *Emden*'s cutters went haying that day, and a dozen lucky men were given machetes instead of coal sacks, and sent on their way under an armed guard that included a machine-gun crew in case they encountered savages. The chart indicated that this was head-hunter country.

Making much of the danger, the adventurers set out, Commander von Mücke leading. One of the seamen, straggling, had to leap for his boat, and missed, fell into the sea and had to be fished out, but eventually they got to shore. They did not have to go far, just at the edge of the beach they found a meadow. The steam pinnace came around to stand offshore and guard them, while they went into the land, and there they cut two boat-loads of hay in very short time. Then von Mücke told them they could have a swim, so they stripped off their clothes and bathed under the envious eyes of their dirty friends afloat. The hay delivered, the boats back aboard, and the coaling ended, the two ships left the harbour, still having seen no sign of the *Tannenfels*, and they never expected to hear another word of her fate.

The next move was to get out of the Indies and into their chosen battle zone. They headed for the Strait of Lombok. On the morning of 27 August they arrived off the southern coast of Celebes, and there met a warship. The call to action sounded and the men rushed to their battle stations. From the bridge Captain von Müller looked the other ship over; she was an armoured cruiser, but of a design several years older than their own ship, and obviously slower. Finally he made out her flag: Dutch, as he had expected. The battle flags were run down from the mast-head and the crew told to go to the readiness position. He rang down half speed – the ships had been closing rapidly, and the ship seemed to relax. The other, they noted, was making an enormous amount of smoke, which indicated bad engine room management or poor coal. Von Müller guessed it was the latter; where they got their coal from the Lord could only know.

The Dutch ship came forward as von Mücke thumbed through the naval manual to identify her. He finally saw that she was the *Tromp*, rated as a battleship although obviously not that powerful in the days of the dreadnoughts. Von Müller noted that her guns remained pointed dead ahead, which indicated peaceful intentions, but then he still did not quite know. What position had Holland taken in this war? As far as he knew she was neutral, but he was so far out of touch with Berlin that anything might have happened and he would not know. From this point on, it would grow worse, von Müller knew; his wireless would never pick up a European station, and already Yap was out of the war, and he could not reach Tsingtao. So what was happening just now was an indication of the future. Every move would have to be played by ear.

Von Müller decided to meet this situation with fullest military courtesy. The bugler was summoned to the bridge and blew attention, which brought the whole crew to the rails, standing stiffly as they passed the other ship. The *Tromp* then led the way and invited the *Emden* to come into the little harbour before them. Both ships moved inside, and the *Markomannia*, which had dropped back, in case of trouble, came up too. Boats were let down, and formal visits were exchanged. The Dutch captain was courteous, if not overly friendly, but he disappointed von Müller sorely in two ways. First, he told the captain of the *Emden* that the *Tannenfels* had appeared as scheduled (although von Müller did not indicate that he had planned to meet her) but that the *Tromp* had driven her away, suspecting she was planning to meet a German warship and transfer supplies. Since these were neutral waters, that would be a violation of the Hague convention and of course, the Netherlands could not permit anything of the sort. Of course, said Captain von Müller a little grimly. Of course.

Captain von Müller would understand, said the Dutch captain, that he had to enforce the strictest rules of neutrality. So the *Emden* could only appear in East Indian waters once each three months and then could remain for only twenty-four hours.

This information sent a cold chill down von Müller's back, for he had hoped to be able to use the Indies regularly, darting into the Indian Ocean, making trouble, and then sending his captives out here, and following them. He had really expected the Dutch, as close cousins, to sympathize more with Germany than with her enemies, and now he found nothing of the sort could be managed. Concealing his disappointment, he masked his emotions in a show of haste, dropping the hint that this was a matter of no interest to him, for he had orders to move across the Pacific. The indication was that he was going to sail around Cape Horn and make a run for Germany.

When Captain von Müller returned to the *Emden*, he told von Mücke the bad news, and then said that they must move quickly to fool the Dutchman. Within the hour the *Emden* steamed out of the harbour, *Markomannia* in her wake, and headed north-east, indicating that their course was set for the Pacific Ocean and the Philippines, where von Müller had indicated he would coal before moving on. The *Tromp* accompanied them back to the three-mile limit of the island waters, then dipped her ensign in salute and turned back. The *Emden* steamed on until the look-out atop the foremast could not see the masts of the *Tromp*, and then Captain von Müller turned on a new course, south-east, to draw them further from the Dutch ship's zone, and then due west. They would pass by Bali, the celebrated isle of beauty and beauties, but they would have a chance only to admire from afar, for they were going straight through, into the Indian Ocean, the lair of their enemies.

7

The First Blow

Admiral von Spee lingered for several days in Kwajalein Atoll's spacious harbour, for there was much planning to be done and it was senseless to waste fuel until it was completed. On 22 August he despatched the *Nürnberg* to Honolulu on a most secret mission, made necessary by the destruction of the wireless station at Yap. Under normal conditions the Admiral could have sent messages to the Admiralty from any point in the Pacific, for the Yap station had been powerful enough to reach the German consulate station in San Francisco, which then transmitted messages to New York, whence they were wirelessed to Berlin. Thus even from the beginning, the English destruction of so unimportant a point as a wireless station, created serious difficulties for the beleaguered squadron and pointed up the odds against which Admiral von Spee must operate. But if Admiral von Spee was worried about the difficulties the English caused him, his concern was as nothing compared to the worry he was already causing Whitehall. Very little had happened in the war at sea so far. The German High Seas Fleet was concentrated in the mouth of the Jade River. The English Grand Fleet was clustered at Scapa Flow in the Orkneys, and a squadron was located at Cromarty. Three battle squadrons, making up the Channel Fleet, lay at Portland, and a strong force of light cruisers was based at Harwich. But the Germans had not moved, much to the exasperation of the First Sea Lord of the Admiralty, Admiral Prince Louis of Battenberg. Indeed, shortly after war was declared he made an inflammatory and quite unnaval speech, declaring that if the Germans would not come out and fight the English would dig in after them and rout them out like rats. But they had not; the most spectacular naval effort so far had been that of the *Goeben* and *Breslau*, German heavy and light battle-cruisers, which had bombarded Bone and Philippeville in Algeria and then run through the British Mediterranean Fleet, leaving several English admirals considerably embarrassed. Everyone was expecting a big

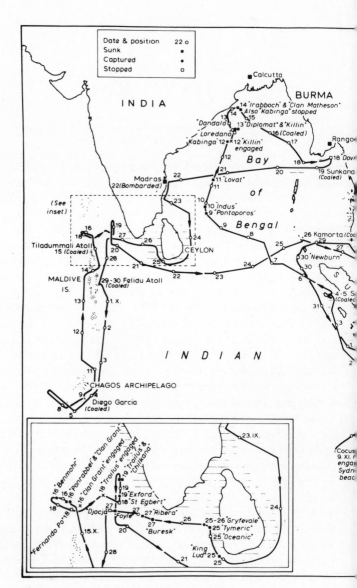

The Route of the *Emden* 1914

CHINA

PENANG

Mousquet

Glenturret

George Town
PULO PENANG

Russian
Lt. Crus.
Schemtschug

South

China

Sea

PHILIPPINE

ISLANDS

set)

AYA

gapore

BORNEO

From Tsingtao,
China

Angaur
19 (Coaled)

18. VIII

21

20

22

23

Sunda Strait

JAVA

28

27

26

24

30

25 (Coaled)

29

Lombok Strait

TIMOR

CEAN

AUSTRALIA

battle in the north, and somehow it did not come off. Consequently the activities of the East Asia Squadron in the Pacific were of more than a little interest in Britain.

On Saturday 22 August, Admiral von Spee sent the *Nürnberg* to Honolulu, to send coded messages to the Admiralty about his plans. The destruction of the Yap wireless station had cemented his decision to move to Latin American waters to operate against British shipping.

He noted that he had sent the *Emden* into the Indian Ocean to harry the enemy, and he intended to send the auxiliary cruisers *Prinz Eitel Friedrich* and the *Kormoran* (the old *Rjasan*) to the Coral Sea and the waters around Australia and New Zealand. He had brought together enough merchant ships to guarantee the squadron 16,000 tons of coal, and he would now travel east, eventually to reach the coast of Chile and work off that area. Chile was chosen because its government had shown pro-German proclivities and he expected to be able to take prizes into Valparaiso and to coal in Chilean ports. He would leave the Marshalls on 23 August and expect to arrive at the Juan Fernandez Islands about 15 October. He had asked Captain von Schönberg (not knowing about Captain Haun's problems) to arrange for 35,000 tons of coal to be delivered by ships from San Francisco. He also wanted some more coal sent from Germany, 5,000 tons to the Juan Fernandez Islands to arrive 15 October and 10,000 tons to be sent to Port Low along with provisions for a thousand men for a month. Ten thousand tons should be laid in at Valparaiso, and another 10,000 tons at various coaling ports along the Chilean coast.

To help *Emden* he had sent another message destined for the German consul at Manila, asking him to send colliers to that point off Timor where *Emden* had stopped. Captain von Müller had planned to return there in a month or two and use that point as an informal base. But of course, the Admiral did not know of *Emden*'s encounter with the *Tromp*, and that von Müller had already abandoned that plan as unworkable.

All this delay and all this misinformation was a direct result of the English destruction of the communications facilities at Yap, a fact the British did not learn at all. *Nürnberg* set out for Honolulu at six o'clock in the morning, followed by the *Staatsekretar Krätke* and the *Gouverneur Jaeschke*, which had been emptied of coal and supplies. If they could resupply at Honolulu they were to return. If their captains could not resupply they were to take whatever action necessary to preserve the vessels and crews.

Shortly after the *Nürnberg* departed, Admiral von Spee told the squadron to make ready for sea. They would move on to Majuro Atoll, since it was not wise to remain too long in one place. They were, of course, to make sure that they left no rubbish floating or any evidence of their presence; that was a standard order, not stated this day by the Admiral but known to all. So the men cleared for sailing, hauled in the buoys to which their boats had been tied during the stay, and raised anchor and began to move. Suddenly, *Scharnhorst*, which was in the lead, slowed and left the line, indicating that the other ships should move out. A few moments later she stopped and the others saw her launch a boat. Fifteen minutes later the boat returned, and the *Scharnhorst* got moving again with a puff of smoke. Then came a message, run up the signal mast:

'*Gneisenau*: I have picked up one of your buoys.'

Captain Maerker flushed and called First Officer Pochhammer to the bridge for a talk. For the rest of that day Pochhammer was not a happy man, living in fear of what the Admiral would do. The Admiral did nothing more. He knew what effect that simple announcement would have.

On 23 and 24 August, Admiral von Spee put the two big cruisers to work at gunnery practice. The next two days were the same. On 25 August, however, the *Titania* got into trouble. She was towing a sleeve target for the cruisers, when she passed too close by the *Gneisenau*'s stern. A rogue wave caught *Titania* and threw her up against the *Gneisenau*'s port quarter; the supply ship's bow anchor caught fluke in one of the cruiser's portholes, and ripped off a long piece of the quarter-deck, then the chain broke, and the anchor hung down from the side of the cruiser, all this under the eyes of the Admiral. The two events did not do much to comfort Admiral von Spee about the quality of seamanship in the squadron, and the training programme for the next few days was increased considerably.

Had it been peacetime, Admiral von Spee would have gone to Jaluit, the seat of German government of the Marshalls. But since the war had been declared, he could anticipate that if the British came looking for him, Jaluit would be the first port of call. So he avoided the place and stopped at the almost deserted Majuro Atoll instead. They moved in quietly, *Titania* scouting for them as they lay around the corner – in case of trouble *Titania* might be mistaken for an innocent merchantman. There was no trouble, and they anchored in the broad lagoon behind the reef, and the men of *Gneisenau* set to putting their quarter-deck to rights once again. Here they waited for *Kormoran*, which had completed its outfitting shortly after *Emden* left port, and was now ready to begin life as a raider. She brought in the merchant ships *O.D.J. Ahlers* and *Göttingen*, which meant more coal for the squadron. She also brought the last news from Tsingtao, which had not yet been attacked by the Japanese although Governor Meyer-Waldeck was waiting. The Japanese ultimatum had been delivered, to be effective 23 August, but Captain Zuckschwerdt had left port before that day so he did not know anything more than that Meyer-Waldeck had vowed to resist to the bitter end. For the next few days the cruisers resupplied from the new merchant ships. Then on 20 August, *Prinz Eitel Friedrich* and *Kormoran* were detached to go raiding off Australia, and the squadron headed due east, bound for South America.

Meanwhile, the *Emden* had slipped through the Strait of Lombok at night, in disguise. It had been First Officer von Mücke's inspiration, when he learned that the captain was worried lest they be sighted and trapped. On the afternoon of 28 August they had steamed slowly, keeping sharp look-out lest any mast-head be sighted. None was, but von Müller was still nervous, and he told von Mücke that the distinctive three funnels and distinctive cut-water bow would make her too easily identified when they passed through the narrow strait. The British might very well be informed and waiting for them just outside. Then why not change the looks of the ship, asked von Mücke, and he explained a way. He would build a fourth funnel. The British light cruisers had four funnels, and in the darkness an observer would hardly note the placement or shape very carefully.

Von Müller approved, and von Mücke had the crew mount a wooden post ahead of the first funnel, and drape it with canvas deck runners, supported by awning poles. It sagged a bit, and from the front was easily recognized as a fake, but from the side at night, it would do very well. So they steamed through the straits that night at ten o'clock. Von Müller's worries were justified; they passed a steamer and several sailing ships, and without knowing, Captain von Müller was sure they were British. Before they completed the passage at midnight the wireless operators reported Radio Batavia's announcement that a 'four-funnel torpedo boat' had passed through the Lombok Strait. Von Müller was much relieved. Next morning when von Mücke asked if they ought not to make the fourth funnel more impressive, the captain recalled that the British cruiser *Yarmouth* carried three round funnels and one oval funnel, and they decided to become a new *Yarmouth*. All day long the seaman laboured, under the critical eye of the captain of *Markomannia*, who conned his ship around the cruiser to examine the handiwork from all angles, and offered bits of advice until he was satisfied that it really did look like a funnel from every view. Finally the funnel was rigged with wire stays that fastened to the foremast and these were marked so that every time the funnel was needed, it would be hoisted into place without difficulty.

During the rest of August, the *Emden* cruised off the coasts of Java and Sumatra, seeing nothing. On the last night of the month he had a narrow escape, although they did not know it. The heavy British cruiser *Hampshire* was also in these waters, and in spite of the story of the four-funnel torpedo boat that had been reported in Lombok Strait, her captain believed there was a German warship about somewhere. Undoubtedly he had the report of the *Tromp*. On this last night of August, the *Hampshire* was very close to *Emden*, having learned (a day late) of her presence (or some presence) off Java. But it was dark that night, and Captain von Müller's ship was blacked out, and *Hampshire* never saw her. The two ships criss-crossed paths in the next few days. On the afternoon of 3 September, von Müller approached the island of Simalur off the coast of Sumatra, intending to go into the harbour of Langini and coal. He arrived off the point very close to dark, and decided against trying to go in that night, so he stayed outside and moved slowly back and forth, then as dawn broke, he moved into the narrow neck of Langini Bay, and behind a small island that protected his ship from being sighted from outside. He never knew it, but on the day before, the *Hampshire* had been in Langini harbour, and while he was steaming off shore that night, she had come out, and anchored round the other side of the point. As he came into Langini Bay in the morning, he had passed within a mile of the British ship, on the other side of the point. And that day, of course, having searched Langini bay the day before, *Hampshire*'s captain saw no reason to run in again, and he moved away from this area.

The *Emden* coaled again from *Markomannia*. This time it was most unpleasant. The ship had very nearly run out of soap, and the men found it hard to get clean. Finally they finished the job, after twenty-five hours in port. Captain von Müller thought they had been unobserved, but at eight o'clock the next morning a pilot boat appeared alongside *Emden* and a white-clad Dutch official stepped up onto the deck, to announce that *Emden* had been in port more than twenty-four hours, had overstayed her leave, and must sail immediately. Captain von Müller said they could not sail until they got up steam, and that this would take two hours. The Dutch official sat in the wardroom drinking whisky and chatting with the officers off watch, and watched and waited. Two hours later he said it was time, and von Müller gave the order to move. The pilot boat followed them out of the harbour, and von Müller steamed for a full hour in the direction opposite that which he intended to travel, with the pilot boat not far behind, watching. Finally, as they moved away from the land, the small boat turned and retreated. Von Müller waited until the boat was out of sight, and then turned slightly to find a heavy layer of low clouds. He steamed through the cloudy area, and made a long sweeping turn, that brought him up on a course to intersect the steamer lane between Sumatra and Ceylon. On the morning of 7 September he reached that lane and turned west to the steamer lane to Colombo.

As he did so, Admiral Jerram was conducting a search for the German East Asia Cruiser Squadron, which had dropped completely out of sight. Jerram had learned from British consul Clive Davies in Honolulu that the *Nürnberg* had arrived there, but Davies could not find out the reason for her visit or where she was going. That was one mystery. Another mystery concerned the British cruiser *Yarmouth*, which had been reported off Singapore and off Bali on the same night a few days earlier. But, Jerram was not looking for the squadron or any part of it deep in the Indian Ocean. He was certain it was lying up somewhere among the German Pacific colonies (which until a few days earlier, had been correct about most of the squadron).

Von Müller sat in the chart room and conferred with Lieutenant Gropius, the navigator. They decided to head for the intersection with the east-west steamer route that led to Singapore. On 8 September they reached this point, but encountered nothing, and when no smoke was seen all day long, von Müller decided to head for the Colombo-Calcutta lane and follow it north toward the Hooghli. They headed north-west, and that night at eleven o'clock the forward look-out reported smoke, and then a light off the starboard bow. Captain von Müller ordered a spurt of speed, and the *Emden* responded, but he was not pleased to see that as she did so, a shower of sparks came up from the smoke-stacks, announcing her presence. Had the ship ahead been a warship she was well warned. But it was not a warship; it was a single-funnelled merchantman travelling away from him, and trying to increase speed. He told the signalman to order the ship to stop, and the signal lamps flickered out the message in Morse code. But the ship did not stop.

He told the gunnery officer, Lieutenant Gaede, to put a shot across her bow, and Gaede did so, one shot, and then another. The lamps flickered again.

'Stop your engines. Don't use your wireless.'

The merchant ship obeyed, and soon Lieutenant Lauterbach and his boarding party, heavily armed, were in the cutter, heading across the narrowing bit of water between the ships. They reached the side of the merchantman. Lauterbach puffed up the rope ladder thrown down to him, and jumped onto a rusty steel deck.

'What ship is this?' he demanded in English.

There was no answer.

This time he spoke in French, repeating the question. The ship's captain fingered a filthy cap and replied.

'Ah, a British cruiser.'

'No,' said Lauterbach in German. 'A German cruiser.'

The captain started. 'This is a Greek ship,' he said. 'It is a neutral ship.'

'We'll see,' said Lieutenant Lauterbach, and demanded the captain's and the ship's papers.

'I have no papers,' said the captain. 'I am bound from Calcutta to Karachi, carrying coal. The papers are going by train. The coal is going to Greece. The papers will meet us in Karachi.'

'Ship's papers, please,' said Lauterbach, fingering the revolver at his hip.

The captain turned and went to his cabin and reappeared with a handful of papers. Lauterbach examined them, then took his signalman aside. In a moment the signal lamp was blinking back to the bridge of the *Emden*.

'Greek ship *Pontoporos*,' said the message. 'Carrying 6,500 tons of coal for the English government, on her way Calcutta–Bombay.'

At first von Müller had groaned with disappointment. A Greek, a neutral. But then with the announcement that she was under charter to the English government, she became an enemy, neutral no longer. It was contraband cargo, and must be confiscated. Here was coal that he needed badly since the *Markomannia*'s bunkers were so depleted. Von Müller signalled back that the *Pontoporos* was a prize of war. The Greek captain protested, and Lauterbach finally brought him over to the *Emden*, where he protested again. There was only one way the captain could keep his ship, said von Müller. If he wished to change his charter and accept German money instead of British, he could sell this coal to the German government.

That was fine, said the Greek captain. German money was every bit as good as British money.

So the deal was struck, but Captain von Müller was not a fool. He sent Lauterbach over to the *Pontoporos* as prize officer, to take command of the ship. Lauterbach and several seamen went back. They found an English newspaper from Calcutta which carried a shipping news column, and Lauterbach hurried back to the *Emden* to read Captain von Müller details of several sailings, times and destinations. On the chart they were able to plot the approximate positions of several merchant ships. So the *Emden* had struck the first blow against British shipping, just as she had struck the first blow against the Russians.

8

Playing Tag

By dividing his forces as he had, Admiral von Spee was enjoying the 'fleet in being' concept to the utmost. That naval term had long ranked high in strategic concepts; the very existence of a body of ships posed a threat to everything within their possible range. Von Spee might be expected to stage a raid on Hong Kong, or Sydney or any point in between, and thus every point had to be protected. By that reasoning, the British were forced to employ ten times as many ships as von Spee had just to protect obvious targets.

When the war began, Australia and New Zealand immediately announced plans to occupy the German colonies near their territory, which they had long coveted. The Australians had sufficient force at their disposal to take German New Guinea but the New Zealanders needed naval assistance to protect their expeditionary force against German Samoa. Admiral Patey, then, had to dispose his forces all around the South Pacific. Admiral Jerram was responsible for East Asian waters, and he had to keep a constant watch on half a dozen points, and still search for the squadron. Such ruses as *Emden*'s creation of the fourth funnel kept him very much in the dark as to what was happening.

On 12 August Admiral Patey set out for the occupation of German Samoa. On 30 August he appeared at Apia in the *Australia*, with a large force that included the French heavy cruiser *Montcalm*, and since the German military presence consisted of a few German police officers and a Samoan constabulary, the resistance was nil. The Australians were next. On 11 September, the expeditionary force arrived at Herbertshöhe and the red, white, and black ensign was hauled down to be replaced by tne Union Jack. There was some fighting at the wireless station, but the Germans could not possibly win, and a few died in vain. Within two weeks the allies occupied German New Guinea, Kaiser Wilhelmsland, Samoa and the Bismarck Archipelago.

In the north, Admiral Jerram was relieved of one major responsibility on 23 August, when the Japanese finally entered the war and began their attack on Tsingtao. Jerram assigned the old *Triumph*, which could not keep up with his cruisers, to the assault on the Germany colony, and in exchange got the assignment by the Japanese of the heavy cruiser *Ibuki* and the light cruiser *Chikuma*, which by his standards was a most victorious trade. The Japanese graciously volunteered to take over the search operations in the Ladrones, the Carolines and the Marshall Islands, and then moved in to seize them as their own. The Japanese Imperial Navy created a new South Sea Command with 1st and 2nd Cruiser Squadrons, and with these began to scour the Pacific.

All this naval activity was directed against two heavy German cruisers, and two light cruisers, one of which was known to be in Honolulu on 1 September. Captain von Schönberg had reached the islands without incident, save a fright from the Japanese battleship *Kongo*, whose wireless transmissions she had caught on 27 August, much too close for comfort. At dusk (by plan) on 1 September, von Schönberg arrived off Pearl Harbour and asked for a pilot. Soon a pilot boat came up, and the little cruiser entered these neutral waters.

Immediately Captain von Schönberg was involved in an argument about coal and neutrality. The rules said that a belligerent warship was not to coal in any neutral port more often than once each three months, and it had not been three months since *Nürnberg* had stopped off at Honolulu on her way from Mexico to join von Spee. Rear-Admiral Moore, the commander at Pearl Harbour was called into the discussion, and he explained the rules to von Schönberg with some asperity. Von Schönberg had called in the German consul to give him moral support, and the consul argued like a sea lawyer that all the Admiral said was true, except that when *Nürnberg* had been in Honolulu last there was no war, and she had not been a belligerent.

The Admiral finally accepted that argument. Von Schönberg demanded 750 tons of coal, enough to take him back to Tsingtao, where he had no intention of going, and by 1 September the Americans knew it. Because of that underlying argument, Admiral Moore said he could have only 550 tons. Later the Admiral relented and gave von Schönberg extra coal. All this discussion took time, and von Schönberg rushed to the coaling dock, for he wanted to be out of the harbour before morning, lest British warships be lurking offshore. In spite of the alacrity with which Honolulu British consul Clive

Davies informed San Francisco of the coming of the cruiser, there were no British warships here, the area having been turned over to the Japanese for policing. And due to failures in communications the *Kongo*, which was responsible, did not receive the message for forty-eight hours, so the *Nürnberg* was never in any danger.

As the ship coaled, von Schönberg began taking on crew, fifty-seven officers and reserve sailors who had been living in the American colony, or came from the North German Lloyd steamer *Pommern*, which had interned here. Von Schönberg did not forget to turn over his vital messages to Consul Rodik, either. Then, the coaling finished, he was ready and eager to get to sea; the *Kongo*, a friendly officer had told him, was only fifty miles away at Molokai. He sailed before dawn, and cleared the islands by sunrise, and then headed towards Christmas Island, where he would meet von Spee and the rest of the squadron.

Admiral von Spee had arrived there earlier and was waiting, steaming slowly and drifting as he waited. *Nürnberg* arrived on 6 September, and Captain von Schönberg went aboard the flagship to report. He took with him bits of gossip from Honolulu, and a number of newspapers, plus all the fresh fruits and vegetables that could be rounded up in their short stay. These were parcelled out among the ships, as von Schönberg conferred with the Admiral. The officers of the cruisers had a hearty laugh over one report: '*Scharnhorst* and *Gneisenau* have been towed into Hong Kong suffering serious injury ...' but some concern over another: '*Rainbow* and *Idzumo* hunt down *Leipzig* ...' The fact was that they had heard nothing from the little cruiser *Leipzig* since her troubles in San Francisco harbour.

That ship had suffered more of the same troubles. When he had reached collier *Mazatlan* and been rebuffed by the Mexican official, Captain Haun had no recourse but to follow the *Mazatlan* into Guaymas harbour to get the coal. He would not do so directly of course. Who knew what sorts of traps his enemies were setting for him? He parted company with the collier and headed for Baja California to hunt for enemy vessels. On 1 September he was cruising off that area, and the men at first were very pleased for finally they were seeing the sun; during the entire time they had been off the American California coast they had only one sunny day. But Captain Haun was faced with a very important decision. He could not operate without either base or colliers. Herr Jebsen, the shipowner, had done his best to evade the neutrality laws, sending *Mazatlan* and the steamer *Marie* out with coal for the cruiser. But *Marie* had also been watched, and in desperation had gone into Mazatlan port, whence she had been destined. Now Captain Haun did not know quite what to do. He was in touch with Jebsen, who sent out a small auxiliary schooner which met them on 7 September, the day after von Spee's rendezvous with *Nürnberg*. The captain had a plan. He would go into Guaymas and fill up with coal from German business firms there. The rail line had been restored and coal was being brought in. He would then come out, and *Marie* would follow him to become *Leipzig*'s collier. This was much safer than going into Guaymas where everyone knew the story of the *Mazatlan*. No one knew anything about the connection between *Leipzig* and *Marie*, even the Mexican government could only suspect. So, as the squadron worried about Captain Haun, it appeared that finally he had solved his coal problem.

On that same day, cruiser *Nürnberg* was finally in action on behalf of the squadron. On his way south to join the squadron, Captain von Schönberg had heard a number of wireless transmissions from the British radio and cable station at Fanning Island. When he arrived at Christmas Island, and told Admiral von Spee about them, this discussion recalled the difficulties that the British had caused the German squadron by destroying the wireless station at Yap, and Admiral von Spee thought it only just that he should do the same for his enemy. So he detached *Nürnberg* that very day (6 September) and on the next day the little ship reached Fanning Island at five o'clock in the morning.

The men on night watch at the wireless station had watched her come up in the morning light, and thought at first that she was a friendly steamer. Then, when they got a view of her profile, they saw that she was a warship, but even that did not disturb them, because British, American, and Japanese warships were sometimes seen here. The distinctive bow and three funnels of the German cruiser were not noticed, probably because there was no one at Fanning with much military knowledge. So they came down to the beach as the *Nürnberg*'s boat moved ashore, and were ready to greet the welcome strangers when the Germans dashed out of the boat, pulled it up on the beach, and next anyone knew, had a machine-gun ashore, pointed at the crowd, and armed riflemen with guns ready. The German boarding officer stepped forward, hand on his pistol.

'Raise your hands,' he said to the Englishmen. 'You are my prisoners.'

Slowly, almost as if they were unable to comprehend, the

Englishmen raised their hands. The Germans searched them for weapons, and finding none, relaxed a little.

'You will take us to the wireless station,' said the officer in charge. 'No tricks.'

The Englishmen led them up the beach to the station and the quarters behind it. The Germans entered the wireless room and made the others prisoner. They broke down the wireless mast and chopped it up so it could not be reassembled. They destroyed the telegraphic equipment. They found the cable station and set fire to it, blowing up the building with hand grenades and breaking up the glass battery jars. They set charges in the water where the Australia-Canada cable could be seen, and in a few minutes they exploded, blowing water, fish, and cable 90 feet in the air. They took all the papers from the station that seemed interesting, 20 rifles and 13,000 cartridges, and about £5,000 in gold bars. The *Nürnberg* had been accompanied by the *Titania*, which carried equipment that made it possible to cut cables. The crew traced the Australia-Canada cable back almost a mile and cut it in several places. All this was accomplished in about three hours, and then the men of *Nürnberg* and *Titania* brought in their boats, and steamed away, headed west, in an attempt to confuse the Englishmen. Only after they were over the horizon from Fanning Island did they adopt their true course, back to Christmas Island.

Admiral von Spee had whiled away the time on one of his naturalist expeditions, leading a number of his officers on a visit to Christmas Island. They left a few marks on this British island to announce their visit, and brought back some coconuts and a few brightly coloured tropical birds which they wanted to adopt.

That evening, Admiral von Spee announced that they would leave shortly to make a raid on Samoa. He was annoyed at the British temerity in attacking the place, and hoped to teach the Englishmen a lesson. When the *Nürnberg* arrived that evening, she was assigned to guard the supply train and escort it to the next rendezvous point, the Marquesas Islands, while Admiral von Spee in *Scharnhorst*, and *Gneisenau* beside her, went off towards Samoa. All spare boats had been put aboard the merchant ships to get them out of the way. All coal was moved into the bunkers so it would not become a fire hazard in battle. The two cruisers crossed the equator on 10 September, and the Admiral was sufficiently relaxed that he allowed the time-honoured initiations into the mystical rites of Neptunus Rex, which involved much horseplay and the ultimate dousing of all the 'pollywogs' in vile pools of oil, rubbish and sea water, to initiate them as 'shellbacks'. On 14 September they approached Samoa, and the engineers took to burning Tsingtao coal, noted for its hardness, which left almost no smoke.

As dawn broke on 14 September the cruisers parted. *Scharnhorst* moved to the north-west of Apia, and *Gneisenau* went around to approach from the north-east. This way they were unlikely to be surprised, no matter what force the enemy might have in the area. The men were ready for battle. That night they had baths in fresh water, and put on clean linen and cotton outer clothing to reduce the chance of infection from injury if they were wounded. Each man was given a red silk ribbon with an identification disc, so his remains might be identified if by no other means. Each was issued a pince-nez – a small wire device that was used to pinch the nostrils together in battle, and reduce the wear and tear of cordite on the lungs – and each man had either a sponge or a rag which he would stuff in his mouth to filter out smoke in case of a smoke attack.

Admiral von Spee had hoped to find enemy ships in the harbour. As they approached he saw lights, but whether they were shore lights or those of ships he could not tell. He reduced speed and waited for dawn to come so he could assess the situation. Obviously the people inside were so confident of their safety that they did not even put out the lights at night.

In the wardrooms of the *Scharnhorst* and the *Gneisenau*, the officers discussed the possibilities excitedly. There ought to be two light cruisers inside, which would have been left over to guard the supply lines after the landing of the 1,500-man expedition force the British were supposed to have brought in here.

At dawn, each ship swung in toward shore, presenting a narrow silhouette which would be almost impossible for the enemy to identify. They moved in then to decide whether to charge in for a torpedo attack or to turn broadside and shell the harbour. As the sun came up, the details of the land began to come forth, and they saw in the harbour the blinking of lights. Who was signalling, and whom were they signalling? Was the *Australia* out there somewhere, getting ready to pounce on the cruisers? Her 12-inch guns completely outclassed their 8.2-inch guns, and she could take them both on with ease, and very little doubt about the outcome of such an engagement.

But *Australia* did not appear. As the light grew brighter, the blue-grey land began to erupt in detail. Behind the Mulinu Peninsula, they saw the town of Apia, white and red in the gathering sun. And behind the town rose Vaea mountain and the long volcanic range that rose

4,000 feet above sea level. But in the middle of the harbour at anchor lay an American three-masted schooner, and further inshore, an even smaller sailing vessel. Otherwise Apia harbour was empty.

The Admiral was so disappointed he did not even stop to destroy the wireless station. There was no point in losing men in battle on the land when there was nothing to be gained. The New Zealanders would bring supplies and rebuild the station almost as soon as he knocked it out. There was not going to be any further German presence in these waters as far as the Admiral knew, until the war was over. So he sailed away, toward the west end of Upolu Island, to get out to sea and decide what he was going to do. At nine o'clock in the morning they were approaching the Strait of Aplima on the west end of the island, when they saw the black, red and white flag of the German Empire suddenly hoisted atop a flag-pole. A launch left the shore and came out to the German ships. They approached the *Scharnhorst* and two men came aboard, planters, who told the story of the occupation by the enemy on 30 August. The French Admiral Huguet had also been there, said the planters, but all the Navy had stayed just one day, and then left the islands on 31 August. The planters wanted Admiral von Spee to help them retake the islands. If he would land a force, they would raise an army of Samoans and within a few days they could wipe out the 1,500 New Zealanders. The idea was tempting, but Admiral von Spee was a realist. How long could they hold out? Was he to lurk in the area, awaiting the coming of the *Australia* and half a dozen cruisers to destroy his force? He could not hope to hold Samoa if he took it, and there was no help anywhere in this hemisphere for him, nor would there be. So, gently, Admiral von Spee told the planters why he could not do as they wished. His advice to them was to make the best of the bad situation, and live with their captors who seemed disinclined to bother their planting activity. The disappointed planters got back into the boat, and steamed off to their island, while Admiral von Spee told Captain Schultz to get up speed. They had to meet the colliers and coal, and then get on with the war.

9

Pressing the English

Aboard the *Emden* after the capture of the Greek ship *Pòntoporos*, Lieutenant Lauterbach combed the English newspapers he had picked up aboard that ship. They were careless in printing the shipping news, but who was to expect that broad English lake, the Indian Ocean, would be invaded by an enemy? Certainly not the proprietors of the *Statesman* or the *Hindu*. The shipping notes were faithful in indicating the movements of ships and their destinations. Since Lauterbach was thoroughly familiar with the routes, it was just a question of finding the Calcutta-Colombo lane and waiting there.

The caravan was slow, for the *Pontoporos* could make only 9 knots and *Emden* was determined to keep her with them. All day long on 9 September they moved toward the steamer lane, but had only reached about half way by the morning of 10 September. No one had much hope of finding a merchant ship in these waters off the major route; why would a ship take a longer trip than necessary? But at nine o'clock on the morning of 10 September a look-out forward spotted a smoke plume, and began shouting. He shouted loud, for Prince Franz Joseph had excitedly offered a bottle of champagne to every man who first sighted a ship. Captain von Müller was not expecting much in this area, but he speeded up the *Emden* and set off after the smoke. All aboard the warship were in fine spirits. First Officer von Mücke even made a joke or two: what the captain needed to do now, he said, was capture a shipload of soap.

In time they came down on the merchant ship and were making ready to speed up in case she suddenly tried to get away. But the captain of the other vessel had no such intention. He was an Englishman, and she was an English ship, the 3,400-ton passenger freighter *Indus*, bound for Bombay from Calcutta, and chartered by the English government to carry men and horses. Eventually she would make her way westward to France, to carry cavalry troops and their mounts, and the stalls for the animals had already been built

8 Captain Karl von Müller, commander of the *Emden*. In a few short months he would terrorize British shipping in half the globe

9 Lieutenant Hellmut von Mücke, First Officer of the *Emden* and leader of the remarkable retreat to Germany

10 The *Emden* on her rampage, without the deceptive 'fourth funnel' that made her look like a British light cruiser

aboard, although just now she was carrying supplies to Bombay, including a large shipment of soap. Since these were English waters, when the captain sighted a warship it seemed certain to him that it must be an English warship, so well out of gun range he ran up the Union Jack, to save the captain of the cruiser the trouble of wasting his coal.

The *Emden* moved on determinedly, until she was in range, and then suddenly ran up the German ensign and Gunnery Officer Gaede sent a warning shot across the bow of the *Indus*. Absolutely astounded, the captain of the merchant ship stopped. Captain von Müller sent Lieutenant von Levetzow over with a boarding party, and from his bridge ordered the English ship to refrain from using her wireless.

'Damned German', said the English captain, quite loudly enough that von Müller could hear his remark across the water, and as the *Indus* drifted a little in the current, she turned, and the far side of the vessel came into view. The men of the *Emden* then could see bits of burning paper in the water and more burning material being thrust from portholes. The British were obviously burning their papers.

Lieutenant von Levetzow had a difficult task. If Lauterbach had not been otherwise occupied with the Greek ship, von Levetzow would not have been selected; for in this case there were complex rules of war to cover, and Captain von Müller intended to obey the letter and spirit of the rules. If the English ship was carrying private goods that belonged to a non-belligerent, the ship might be a prize, but the goods were not. If she was actually British and carrying British cargo, the cargo might be confiscated, but the ship should be sent to a neutral port and sold off. If she was owned by the British government and carrying British cargo, then von Müller could legally do what he wished, take the cargo and sink the ship. These rules seemed complicated, but they represented the thinking of all governments at the beginning of the war: war was a matter between governments, and civilian property was to be treated carefully, even if belonging to enemy nations.

The *Indus*, Lieutenant von Levetzow discovered, was an English ship owned in India, by Englishmen, but chartered to the British government and carrying an official government cargo, so she was liable to the most stringent treatment. As for her cargo, von Müller was delighted, and First Officer von Mücke beamed: here was his soap ship. He wanted to get the *Indus* to some quiet harbour quickly, so they could strip her of her valuables. Von Müller thought that a good idea, until he considered the difficulties. There were no harbours around; he was in mid-ocean. To find a spot on the Ceylon or Burma shore would mean to abandon the Calcutta-Bombay shipping lane and the ships he knew were coming along. Further, this *was* an English lake, and he had best take care. So von Müller overruled himself, and decided to off-load what he could in a little while and then sink the enemy ship.

First, Lieutenant Lauterbach must be brought back from the Greek ship. He was the expert on loading and unloading steamers. But Lauterbach said he was afraid to leave the Greek ship because the captain was a rascal and could be expected to try to escape or to pull some trick at any moment. Captain von Müller searched about, and finally ordered the mate of the *Markomannia* to take over on the *Pontoporos*, so that Lauterbach could attend to the more important duty. He was in a hurry, and when the *Emden*'s cutter delivered him at the base of the *Indus* rope ladder, he began climbing furiously, slipped, fell into the Bay of Bengal, and had to be fished out. But he was a man of immense good humour and he laughed more heartily at himself than anyone else dared. He got to the top, and was immediately all business in mien.

What was the cargo? he asked. When the captain was slow to answer he demanded the papers. They had been burned said the captain with a smirk. Then the captain would make a list of every item in the ship, or he would be shot, said Lauterbach. The English captain blenched, and managed to produce a set of manifests that detailed the cargo. There was enough soap to last the *Emden* for six months; there was fresh meat and flour and fresh vegetables and whisky. The general cargo included pencils and paper in large supply and many other items that the *Emden* could not utilize. But she must be stripped of valuables, and there was no time to play nursemaid to the prisoners. They were loaded off to the *Markomannia* for safe keeping and an armed guard was posted over them there, in spite of the English captain's protests that he should be taken to the *Emden*.

All day long the boats ran back and forth between the *Indus* and her captor. At the end of the day there was still much left that *Emden* might use, but Captain von Müller was eager to be away, so he ordered the ship sunk. A party from the *Emden* then boarded the *Indus*. They took the watertight door off the bulkheads between the boiler rooms and opened the sea-cocks. To speed the process, Lieutenant Gaede was told that he could use the ship for target practice, and he sent four shells into her at the water-line. But she seemed uncommonly difficult to sink; she rode for an hour before she took on a decided list and began shipping water fast. Finally she went down, gurgling. There were several explosions and some debris came up and several boats that had been forgotten tore loose and floated on top of the water, much to the irritation of Captain von Müller, for they were as good as a calling card to say that the *Indus* had been sunk.

Should he stop and destroy the boats? They had drifted and it would take some time. He decided against it; perhaps the British would not come upon them for some time, off the steamer lanes as they were. To go after them would mean to send a boat for each of the *Indus* boats, and chop it open. Firing on a small boat by the ship was extremely wasteful and dreadfully time consuming. So he left, reluctantly, determined to find the steamer route and stay on it until he had definite word that the enemy knew he was in the area. At least his men had learned now, and they should not make the same mistake again.

The prizes began to come more rapidly as they did reach the steamer lane. The *Lovat* was next, an English ship on her way to Bombay to pick up Indian detachments destined for France. The captain was an old friend of Lieutenant Lauterbach's, which dismayed the former and amused the latter. He was sorry, however, to have to ship captain and crew over to the *Markomannia* for the *Lovat* was to be destroyed; von Müller was not taking time to move provisions from this ship. The crews of these English ships could have been set adrift in their boats, but that seemed to Captain von Müller an extremely harsh measure. He had no desire to see any of these men die, and it was his intention to sink several ships and then find one not worth much, which he could load up with the crews of the sunk ships and dispatch to a neutral port. Perhaps he could find a neutral ship with a British cargo, dump the cargo and let the ship go. So the crew was moved, and the sea-cocks of the *Lovat* were opened. Lieutenant Gaede was given permission for a little target practice, even so the ship did not sink properly, and eventually von Müller steamed away, leaving *Lovat* listing badly but still afloat.

The *Lovat* had been carrying some more recent editions of the Calcutta newspapers than the *Indus*, and Captain von Müller scoured them to see if there was any mention of his ship or the squadron. There was nothing. He had not yet been discovered; the ruse off Bali had worked, and it would give him more time.

The captain of the *Markomannia* had some good news the next day, showing how wise it was to entertain your enemies. He had invited the captains of the two English ships up to his quarters for drinks, and after a few they had begun to talk about the war. He learned that three more merchantmen were under charter to the government and following *Indus* and *Lovat*, all heading for Bombay and eventually for France, to carry India's current contribution to the war effort.

The first of these ships turned up at ten o'clock that night, or so von Müller thought. Lieutenant Lauterbach went to board, and soon sent back information that the two captains were wrong, or somebody had got in the way. This ship was the *Kabinga*, an English ship bound for New York with a cargo of jute. This situation posed the sort of problem that could be distressing. If Captain von Müller sank the English ship with its cargo, then Germany would be liable to the American government for the cargo's value. Von Müller did not want to cost his government money. Fortunately at this point he had a use for *Kabinga*. She could take off his unwilling passengers. So the English captains and their crews were moved over to the *Kabinga*, and that ship joined the *Emden*'s train, with a prize crew aboard for the moment. The convoy moved ahead at 9 knots, *Emden* in the van.

Early on the morning of 12 September the *Emden* came upon another British ship, but again it was not one of the promised transports, instead they had a collier. She was the *Killin*, bearing 6,000 tons of coal from Calcutta to Bombay. Von Müller could always use coal – good coal. But this was Indian coal, which was crumbly and smoky. He decided to sink the ship, and the crew was moved to the *Kabinga*. This time, von Müller said, he was going to depend on Lieutenant Gaede to put the ship down after the sea-cocks were open. There was no reason that their gunfire could not be accurate enough to do the task. Gaede took the hint, and indeed, his gunners placed their shots well, and the *Killin* went down in a few minutes. Her funnel broke off, and bobbed around for a time, and von Müller feared he might have to run it down and sink it, but then it sank of its own volition, and he was free to leave.

He was growing more careful. Each ship meant that much more chance for discovery, and when the English became aware that this raider was hunting in their lake, like a poacher on an estate, there would be hell to pay. In the meantime, anything that could be done to delay discovery would be useful.

That day they did not expect any more action and the men off duty took it easy, lolling in hammocks and reading some of Lieutenant Lauterbach's library. Prince Franz Joseph and three other officers were playing bridge, and others were sitting in the wardroom, listening to the gramophone. Then came the word that there came another ship. So used to the procedure had the *Emden*'s men become in a short time, that there was scarcely any excitement. In the beginning, the sight of smoke had sent then to action stations. Now, even though an enemy ship was in sight, there was no need for hurry, since she was not a warship. In a very leisurely fashion, Gaede put a shot across the ship's bow. She stopped and Lieutenant Lauterbach led the boarding party. Soon he came back with the word: she was the *Diplomat*, out of London, carrying a thousand tons of tea in her 7,600-ton bottom.

Captain von Müller decided to destroy her without pause. He was in a hurry, and he did not like the techniques used by the engineers in the past. Too slow. So he assigned Oberleutnant Witthoeft, the torpedo officer, to go aboard with a detachment and blow out the bottom of the ship. Witthoeft and his men opened the sea-cocks, as had the engineers. Then they laid charges at key points, and left the ship. Ten minutes later, the first explosion sounded, followed by several others, and the *Diplomat* went straight to the bottom.

The captures were coming so frequently that Lieutenant Lauterbach was becoming bored, and when Prince Franz Joseph asked if he could not board one vessel, Lauterbach seconded the request with the captain. It was not long before the Prince had his ship. She turned out to be the *Loredano*, an Italian vessel. This posed some interesting questions. Italy was an ally of Germany and Austria in the Triple Alliance, but she had not yet elected to enter the war. If the *Loredano* would take the crews of the various ships sunk into port for him, von Müller could sink the *Kabinga*, and he had about decided not to worry over the American cargo. But the Italian captain of the *Loredano* said he would not do it. Oh? asked Lieutenant Hohenzollern, what if they cast all those people adrift in boats. What would the captain do then? He would pick them up, said the captain. So why not do it without all that trouble, said the Prince. The captain of the *Loredano* apparently saw the point, and it was arranged.

But the Prince returned to the ship and told Captain von Müller that the Italian captain seemed most untrustworthy. Von Müller decided not to go ahead with the plan, and to confuse this Italian. They parted with expressions of goodwill, the Italian ship steaming toward Calcutta, while *Emden* moved off due south – as long as the Italian ship was in sight. Von Müller did not trust the Italian one whit. He sailed south but only as far as the Madras-Calcutta steamer lane, and then he turned onto that, having covered his tracks. That night they encountered another Italian ship, and with this adventure behind them, they did not even stop to talk, but simply exchanged hails, and stayed on their course. When the Italian was out of sight they changed course and moved off the steamer lane, then back at a different point. They ran into heavy weather that night, and the next morning the officer of the watch spotted a superstructure on the horizon. They steamed toward it, only to discover that it was not a ship as they had believed, but the tower of the temple of Puri, and that they had moved off course and were in danger of becoming stuck in the mudflats off this Indian city. Captain von Müller reversed course, and took them back into deep water, away from the shore.

On this day, von Müller decided it was time to lighten his load. One reason the navigation had become confused was that they had to spend so much time rounding up their charges who kept getting lost. *Kabinga*, in particular, was a nuisance, so von Müller said it was time to let her go. He knew that once she reached port, his days of secret operations would end. The British would start a great ship hunt in these waters for the cruiser, and he would have somehow to elude them. So that day, the prize crew was withdrawn from the *Kabinga*, and her captain was given his position and told to sail for an Indian port. Soon the *Kabinga* was gone.

The *Emden* took the *Trabbock* that day, another English collier, but she was in ballast so there was nothing but military gain in sinking her. She did, however, make a fine spectacle, for when the charges exploded in her bottom, they ignited the coal dust that had been gathering there in nooks and crannies for years, and the ship blew up in a magnificent series of fireworks. Since it was growing dark the sight was most impressive.

The *Emden* moved quickly away since von Müller did not want to risk being pinned by an English warship against the light. It seemed that her luck would never cease, for in running, she came across another ship, the *Clan Matheson, en route* to Calcutta from Southampton.

'What nationality? English?' demanded Captain von Müller from his bridge.

'No. British,' said the captain, who was a loyal Scotsman.

The sinking of the *Clan Matheson* tore at many a heart aboard the *Emden*. She was carrying typewriters, and office equipment, and railroad locomotives, all possible instruments of war for the enemy. She was also carrying several Rolls Royce automobiles, the finest in the world, and Prince Franz Joseph and his friends shook their heads to see the terrible waste of war. She also carried a magnificent racing stallion, destined for the Calcutta Racing Club, and Lauterbach, who knew of such matters, said this horse was the favourite in the coming Calcutta Sweepstakes. No longer. The thoroughbred was shot as an act of mercy, as the demolition crew got to work. It took only forty-five minutes to clear the ship of the crew, set the charges and blow *Clan Matheson* to kingdom-come. The Germans were becoming very efficient destroyers.

That night von Müller began to grow testy, and First Officer von Mücke knew from experience that the captain was worrying about their fuel supply. It was always this way. Sure enough, late that night the captain ordered the navigator to set a course due south, well away from the steamer lanes. He wanted privacy. There were no deserted islands in the area – a safe little bay was what he really wanted – so he could coal at sea.

Von Müller's timing could not have been better. Early in the morning the wireless operators intercepted a message that had been sent in the clear by the Calcutta lightship. It identified the *Emden*, and reported that the German ship had sunk the *Diplomat*, the *Kabinga*, and the *Pontoporos*. It gave the position last reported: 86°24′E 18°1′N. The reporter was the treacherous Italian captain of *Loredano* who had professed eternal friendship for Germany to Prince Franz Joseph. The Prince was furious and wished he had shot the captain out of hand. Captain von Müller, more experienced in the ways of allies was not surprised, but he was annoyed because the captain had given his word of honour that he would not identify or embarrass the *Emden*, and to von Müller a word of honour was not a matter for trifling. The next Italian they might encounter would not get off so easily, but as von Müller knew, it really did not make that much difference to his operations that he had been betrayed, since the *Kabinga* would arrive in port by the next day anyhow. She did arrive, the official news came out that the *Emden* was raiding in British waters, and the balloon went up, as they said in Whitehall. The naval base at Colombo was told to put out every available search ship. The Hong Kong base was notified and Admiral Jerram was ordered to send several cruisers into the Indian Ocean. Admiral Patey was informed, and told to watch all the south-western edges of the Indian Ocean. The loss of these ships was not a laughing matter. The Admiralty did not know about several of the *Emden*'s captures. In one week she had taken seven ships.

For two days Captain von Müller steamed south and then in a circle in a deserted region south of Calcutta, off the travel lanes but not so far that he would waste a good deal of valuable coal in getting back. On 16 September the weather was as calm as a lake at evening, and von Müller decided to coal. He had *Pontoporos* brought up along-side, and fenders rigged between the ships. There were not enough fenders, so some were improvised from boards and hemp matting. The merchant ship tied up and stopped her engines. *Emden* maintained way on her starboard screw.

No one had actually examined the Greek ship's holds, so it was a disappointing surprise to learn that the coal she carried was dusty and slack. One look and the engineering officers knew they were in for a bad time from the bridge with that coal, which would burn slowly and smokily. Further, the coaling was particularly obnoxious, because of the great amount of dust. After thirteen hours, the *Emden* had managed to secure only 450 tons, which filled her bunkers about half-way. This amount was not satisfactory, but the men were exhausted, the ship filthy, and von Müller felt the urge to disengage and get out of this area before someone came along.

Von Müller felt that he had been very lucky to take so many prizes so quickly, when hampered by the presence of the poky Greek collier, so he decided to send her away. He chose a rendezvous point at Simalur Island, and sent the merchant ship there under her armed guard. She would wait, as the *Emden* and *Markomannia* continued their adventures. *Pontoporos* steamed away in one direction and the *Emden* in another. An hour after they were out of sight, the black gang dug into the new coal, and Captain von Müller was furious. It was even worse than he had expected after the engineer's reports. It burned with a greasy smoke that could not be entirely eliminated as was the case with the Shantung and Manchurian coal that the *Emden* usually burned. But there was nothing to be done at the moment except suffer the difficulty, so von Müller headed into the Bay of Bengal. His luck seemed to have changed; he found nothing on the Madras-Rangoon steamer lane, and nothing on the Calcutta-Singapore route. He met only one ship, and when Lieutenant Lauterbach boarded her she turned out to be a Norwegian named the *Dovre*, a neutral that must be released. Captain von Müller at least managed to get rid of the crew of *Clan Matheson*, and he gained one important bit of intelligence. The captain of the Norwegian ship told him that the night before they had been approached by a warship that did not identify itself, but had played its searchlight all over the merchant vessel until the captain was satisfied that she was what she seemed to be. Then, without a single word, the other had steamed away. This ignoble treatment had annoyed the captain, so he volunteered the information that he had just come from Penang and that the French cruisers *Montcalm* and *Dupleix* were moored in that harbour. He also secured several English language newspapers from Penang and Singapore that reported on some of the exploits of the *Emden*. The reporter had checked with the Royal Navy, and predicted that the German cruiser would be sunk within the next few days by the British squadron that was massing for a search of the area.

The officers of the *Emden* had some good laughs as they read the newspaper, but Captain von Müller's sense of danger was aroused. It was intensified that night when the wireless operators of the cruiser reported that the British were searching for him industriously. They heard many calls from a ship that signed herself QMD, and a shore station inadvertently spilled the beans, telling another vessel that QMD was the British cruiser *Hampshire*.

So Captain von Müller knew that his enemies were after him with a vengeance. That was to be expected. Now he must strike swiftly, move swiftly and plan the most audacious manoeuvres possible if he were to survive.

10

A Britain Paralysed

As Captain von Müller prepared one audacious action and Admiral von Spee prepared another in that second week of September, 1914, the British Admiralty was seriously worried. Admiral Jerram was shocked on 14 September to learn that *Emden* had appeared in the Bay of Bengal and was sinking British ships. He had lain his plans as carefully as possible to prevent just such a situation, and until this day he had been positive that the wide net he had spread would entrap any German raider trying to get into the Indian Ocean. But suddenly the Germans seemed all about, endangering Britain's lifeline, her shipping. On the same day that Jerram reported to Whitehall that *Emden* had escaped his net, Admiral Patey had to report that Admiral von Spee had appeared off Apia with *two* cruisers, not five. The seers of naval intelligence had reported confidently that *Scharnhorst, Gneisenau, Nürnberg*, and *Emden* were obviously on their way to South American waters, and that the *Leipzig*, having left San Francisco and encountered difficulties off Guaymas, was going to join them. Suddenly, these reports confounded the experts, who expected that the first to be heard of von Spee would be an end run around Cape Horn to try to reach Germany. It appeared now that the British assessment of von Spee's plans was totally in error. The idea of a squadron split up, with the cruisers conducting themselves as individual raiders, sent shudders down the spines of merchant captains and insurers everywhere. The light cruiser *Dresden*, not a part of the squadron, was operating off the east coast of South America and had sunk several vessels. Now, in this second September week, came the news that *Leipzig* was still in Mexican water, and apparently had no intention of seeking the rest of the squadron, and that *Nürnberg* had destroyed the wireless station at Fanning Island, apparently operating independently.

Then came worse news: the German cruiser *Königsberg* had appeared off East Africa. Where would the Germans strike next? Not knowing, the Admiralty took desperate measures. Australian and New Zealand convoys to England were suddenly cancelled until further notice. Expeditionary forces heading for German New Guinea were stopped, lest the *Gneisenau*, or the *Scharnhorst*, or both of them, suddenly appear and disrupt the operations. The cruisers of the Australian force and those of the China squadron had to be completely rearranged, to make a new net to catch these elusive warships. Believing that von Spee was heading for South America, the Admiralty had strengthened defences on the west coast there and was planning to do more. Rear-Admiral Sir Christopher Cradock was promised more ships, but this new development denied them to him; there were not enough ships to plug all the holes that suddenly appeared in the net. The battleship *Defence* had been destined for Cradock, but it was stopped at Malta after voyaging from the Dardanelles. New instructions were issued to Jerram and Patey, telling them that destruction of the German squadron was their first priority. Mining, ship traffic, military convoys would all have to wait until this dangerous force was destroyed. Thus three British squadrons, plus a score of lesser units were immobilized by five German ships.

As for Admiral von Spee, he had last been seen by his enemies steaming north-west from Samoa. Of course this sighting had been expected and on the evening of 14 September he had turned due east, to meet the collier *Ahlers* at a rendezvous at Suvarov Island, to coal. But when he got to Suvarov and met the merchant ship, he discovered there was no suitable harbour, so the coaling must wait. He would strike a blow first, a blow at the French for their temerity in sending the *Montcalm* to help the British in stealing German territory. He would strike the Society Islands, he would seize all the coal that should be there to supply the French warships, resupply his vessels with meat and fruit and vegetables, and take whatever shipping he could use, destroying the rest.

As they moved, von Spee sent messages to the *Gneisenau* in code, outlining the plan. They would steam to Papeete, on the north-west coast of Tahiti Island, the capital city, which was located on a long harbour inside a coral reef. They would stand outside and send in a boat, if they did not encounter warships, and demand the surrender of the colony. The *Gneisenau* would ready herself to sweep for mines and then both ships would enter. If the authorities had surrendered, no one would get hurt. If not, they would go in shooting.

The *Scharnhorst* led the three-ship flotilla to the island of Bora

Bora, one of the Tahiti group, and they approached the lagoon of the harbour and anchored offshore. Almost immediately a war canoe put out from the shore, bearing a dozen native paddlers and two Europeans in white suits and topees. As they came alongside the *Scharnhorst*, the two Europeans stood up perilously in the canoe to salute. In a few minutes they came aboard the ship, and identified themselves: one was a brigadier of *gendarmerie*, he said, proudly, and the other was a businessman. Admiral von Spee had not flown any flags as he came in to Bora Bora, and the names of his ships had been removed from bow and stern. He appeared now on the quarter-deck, resplendent in his high-collared white uniform trimmed with gold braid. To a naval man, his uniform cap with the German Imperial Eagle, would have identified him immediately. But the near-sighted brigadier had not seen many warships in his day, nor many admirals, and he took this naval force to be British.

'I am the representative of the French government here,' the brigadier said proudly, with a little bow. And then he made a sweeping gesture to the horizon. 'I now place myself at the disposal of the Admiral ...'

Admiral von Spee found it hard to repress the smile that wanted to come. Obviously this was the glorious mistake for which he had hoped.

'What news of the war?' he asked carelessly.

'Sadly, none,' said the brigadier. 'We learned from one of your British ships that you have declared war on *les sale Boches*, but we do not even know what *La Belle France* is doing. We are forgotten here, I must say.'

That much was apparent. Bora Bora, one of the Society Islands, belonged to the Petites Iles Sous-le-Vent, a hundred and twenty miles north-west of Tahiti. It was obvious that if they did not even have a motor launch, these people would not know much about current affairs. As the Admiral suspected, they had no wireless here, and their usual contact with Papeete was the monthly mail sloop.

'France marches at our side against Germany,' said von Spee, hoping the Kaiser would forgive his lies. 'But I fear that the German fleet has captured Tahiti, and now we are afraid to go there to coal. Have you heard anything?'

'My goodness, no,' said the brigadier. 'Is there a German fleet in these waters? Well, if they did attack Tahiti, it would not be long before they had it.'

'Why is that? The island has her defences ...'

'Not now she hasn't,' said the brigadier. 'There has not been a warship in Papeete for a year. All we have is the gunboat *Zelee*, and she is so old that her guns have been taken off and mounted on the land. Firing them from the deck might knock out her bottom.'

'What about the garrison; surely it is strong?'

'Twenty-five soldiers and their lieutenant. Of course there are the twenty gendarmes, but what does that add up to? It is nothing, Nothing.'

Admiral von Spee was inclined to agree gratefully, but he did not. Instead he brought out champagne, and the French looked admiringly at the bottles, as the corks popped.

'*Salut.*'

'Confusion to our enemies,' said the admiral, who had brought a bit of it himself. He meant every word of that toast.

After a few more glasses of champagne, the brigadier and his civilian friend were only too eager to go ashore and find supplies that von Spee needed. Alongside the two ships came canoes full of fish, pigs, and cattle, fruits and yams. The butchers set to work and soon had the hanging lockers of the cruisers filled with carcasses. It was time to coal, then, and the *Ahlers* was brought into position between the *Scharnhorst* and the *Gneisenau*. In these protected waters, the two cruisers could both coal at the same time, and the process was much speeded by this manoeuvre.

Admiral von Spee added to the illusion of alliance by paying the brigadier for all this provision in English sovereigns, part of the fortune captured from the British wireless station at Fanning Island. He was generous and all the suppliers were pleased with the benevolence of their friends. At four o'clock in the afternoon the coaling was finished and all the provisions had been stored away. The ships set out to sea once again. As they passed the cape that marked the entrance to Bora Bora harbour, a tricolour was raised on the mast on the land and dipped in salute. The officers who had gone ashore had made sure that indeed there was no wireless station at Bora Bora, so the Admiral yielded to his sense of irony, and raised and dipped the great red, white and black naval ensign of Imperial Germany. He would have given much to see the face of the French brigadier at that moment.

Von Spee set course for Papeete then, intending to arrive at dawn, on 22 September but when the sky began to lighten they discovered that in the night, which had been squally, they had been carried westward by the current further than expected. By the light of the fading stars they corrected the navigation, but by the time they reached Papeete harbour, their presence had been advertised. Whatever value the element of surprise would bring was lost.

Ashore, Lieutenant de Vaisseau Destremau, and his fifty stout defenders were prepared to die bravely. His men were scattered around the island — their main task was maintenance of order. Destremau got on the telephone excitedly and warned every post of the coming of two unknown warships. They might be friends, but then they might be enemies. It was known from the Australian broadcasts that the *Scharnhorst* and the *Gneisenau* were out in the Pacific, and no one quite knew where. As the silhouettes of the ships grew, Destremau ordered the firing of the old bronze cannon in the harbour three times to signal an emergency.

At 6.30 the two ships suddenly appeared close enough for recognition, and Lieutenant Destremau's heart sank, for he recognized them immediately as the *Scharnhorst* and *Gneisenau* — two equal masts, four medium funnels, that cut-water bow built for ramming, all meant they could not be English but were the enemy.

The lieutenant ordered the immediate destruction of the harbour entrance buoys. Perhaps, he hoped fervently, one or both of the enemy ships would run aground. He ordered the coal in the fuel dump set afire: they would get no pleasure from his supplies. He ordered the poor old disarmed *Zelee* taken into mid-harbour, burned and sunk. The *Boches* might find some use for her, they were that diabolical, but he would prevent it.

Lieutenant Destremau then spoke to his second in command, Ensign Charron. 'Open fire in slow salvoes on the leading cruiser,' he said. 'Cease fire when she shows her colours.' A shot or two went out from shore, but the distance was too great, so Destremau told Charron to hold fire for the moment. The French defenders watched, then, as the two cruisers bore down on them, 2,000 yards off shore, coming toward the channel through the reef.

As they came within range, Admiral von Spee stood on the command bridge of the *Scharnhorst*, glasses trained on the shore. He grunted.

'Ah, Fielitz,' he said to his Chief of Staff. 'They have recognized us. Look there.' He pointed to the plume of black smoke at the edge of the harbour. 'They are burning their coal.'

As he moved the glasses along the port, he saw the quay crowded with people, and the gunboat burning in the middle of the harbour. Just then puffs of white smoke broke out in the hills behind the town, and three salvoes of shells fell around the two ships. There were no hits. 'What impudence,' said Captain Fielitz.

Von Spee ordered the ships turned athwart the island, so all turrets could fire, and opened fire on the coastal batteries. Soon they were silent. And as the German ships began shooting, the people fled the quay and the town, to go back into the hills. Von Spee was annoyed by the temerity of the defenders. Somebody might have been hurt by those popguns. He brought the ships across the neck of the harbour, and the 8.2-inch guns opened up on the installations. The *Zelee* was still afloat, and they fired into her until she capsized. They saw a freighter in the harbour, flying a huge French ensign and they fired on it. (Later von Spee learned that she was the German collier *Walküre*, which had been interned at Papeete at the outbreak of war, and then called a French prize.)

After the ships had used 90 rounds of 8.2 ammunition, the Admiral ordered the firing to end. He then considered the idea of going into the harbour to see what other damage might be done, and what supplies he might find. But Lieutenant Destremau's ready defence indicated that the French must have taken all actions to make his life miserable; there very well might be mines in that harbour, and he could see that there were no marker buoys to show him the inner channel. Also, he had been in sight for about three hours, and the French probably had wirelessed the outside world. Australia and New Zealand were not so far away; Samoa was even closer; what if the British had come to Apia following his visit and divined that he might hit Tahiti? No, it was time to be gone. So Admiral von Spee turned the two cruisers and left Papeete to its own devices, and Lieutenant de Vaisseau Destremau to the admiring gratitude of his countrymen for saving the city and the colony from the rapacious enemy. Soon the land was out of sight, as the cruisers sailed their usual false course to confuse watchers, and then turned north and east, toward the Marquesa Islands, where they had made arrangements to meet the *Nürnberg* and the supply train.

Soon the news of the German attack on Tahiti reached Whitehall, and added to the worries of First Lord Winston Churchill and his officers. The Germans simply could not be allowed to ravage the Pacific in this manner. Patey had the word; he must stop them, and Jerram must bring the Indian Ocean under control. But saying was not quite doing, and nobody in Whitehall was able to give either English Admiral a clue as to what von Spee and his irritating – no, devastating – squadron would do next.

11

'...And Destroy the German Cruisers'

As the days went by and the German cruisers seemed able to move at will everywhere in the world, British shippers and merchant captains became thoroughly frightened. Von Spee was known to be roving the Pacific with those two heavy cruisers that moved like ghosts. The *Emden* had sunk seven ships in the Indian Ocean with the greatest of ease. Captain Max Looft's *Königsberg* had won the honour of capturing the first British steamer taken by a German man of war, the *City of Winchester*, which carried the best of the Ceylon tea crop of 1913-14. Her loss had panicked the London tea market. Whitehall first declared that the shipping sunk in the eastern end of the Indian Ocean had been the work of *Königsberg*, and she was given credit for them. Admiral Jerram was still certain that no one could have run his gauntlet successfully from the east, and he had embraced the theory that *Königsberg*, coming from the German colony of East Africa, had been doing the dirty work. But it was all terribly mysterious. How could *Königsberg*, seen off Madagascar at the outbreak of war, have made her way to the area off Rangoon? All these speculations were suddenly brought to an end on 21 September, when *Königsberg* turned up at Zanzibar, and destroyed the old British cruiser *Pegasus*. For a month Rear-Admiral King-Hall of the Cape squadron had been searching for *Königsberg*, with several ships, until Whitehall had assured him that Captain Loof had managed somehow to get into the other end of the Indian Ocean and that King-Hall should separate the old cruisers *Pegasus* and *Astrea*, which as a team, were a match for the German ship. The destruction of *Pegasus* just in the manner that Admiral King-Hall had warned about made the Admiralty even more touchy and more worried, and all the Admirals entrusted with defences of the corners of the Empire felt the irritation emerging from London. It was somehow as if all of them were at fault.

By this time the German cruisers had engaged the imagination of the whole world, and von Spee, and his captains had acquired

11 The burning of the British oil tanks at Madras. The *Emden*'s destructive capacities seemed just then to know no bounds

12 Three of von Spee's captains at the races in Tsingtao during the regatta with the British East Asia Squadron

13 After the *Sydney* finally ceased firing, this wreckage was what was left of the proud little cruiser *Emden*

14 Lieutenant von Mücke, centre, knee bent, takes stock of his position after the *Emden* sailed away to battle that fateful day

mystical qualities, largely because of the many inaccurate reports. Had these been true, the ships must have had wings to move so rapidly about the oceans. But move they did, enough to cause fear and flurry, and paralyse British shipping in Burma, India, Australia, New Zealand, Hong Kong, South Africa and the area south of the Red Sea, and along the eastern coast of South America.

The whole system of supply from the British colonies was threatened. Just now it was disrupted and would remain that way until the safety of the seas could be assured by the destruction of these ships. But where to look? As the reports came in of sightings in the South Pacific, two ends of the Indian Ocean and both shores of South America, the task seemed herculean. By the third week of September naval intelligence had the following estimates:

Von Spee: Somewhere in the South Pacific with an unknown number of ships.
Scharnhorst and *Gneisenau* were definitely travelling together.
Nürnberg flitted about like a humming bird, apparently from North Pacific to South and back again.
Emden was presumed still to be with the squadron.
Leipzig: Somewhere off Mexico or Central America.

Those estimates accounted for the squadron as it had been organized, but there were other German cruisers to be taken into account:

Dresden: somewhere off the east coast of South or Central America.
Königsberg: In the Red Sea, off Madagascar, or off Rangoon. No one seemed quite sure. That meant *Köngisberg* was somewhere within a circle of several million square miles.
Karlsruhe: somewhere off the east coast of South America.

It seemed conceivable, given the new British assessment of Admiral von Spee's audacity, that the Admiral might be bringing all these ships together. Or was he keeping them all apart? Whatever, the mystery put the entire British maritime industry and Royal Navy on edge, and to raise questions within the cabinet (although not yet in Parliament) as to what was being done to put an end to this threat.

At that moment, the *Dresden*, sister ship to the *Emden*, was already on the Pacific side of the South American continent, following orders from Berlin to join up with *Leipzig* and raid, and then wait for the coming of von Spee. Similar orders went out to the *Karlsruhe*, and the *Leipzig*. So the worst fears of Whitehall seemed to be coming to fruition that week.

Dresden had already done far more damage than London realized,

and given the nature of her captain, more than Berlin might have
expected. For Captain Fritz von Lüdecke, the commander of *Dresden*
was not really regarded as one of Germany's first line fighting men.
He had actually become involved in the war on this level by mistake.
In July 1914, von Lüdecke had been assigned to take the new
Karlsruhe out to the Pacific and turn her over to Captain Erich
Kohler, one of Berlin's brightest young stars. Von Lüdecke was then
to bring the *Dresden* back for a much-needed refit, and then would be
sloughed off into some other job. But as it turned out, a few days after
the ships met at Port au Prince, Haiti, and exchanged captains, the
war broke, and Captain von Lüdecke found himself ordered to go
raiding allied ships along the coast of the Americas. 'Carry out
Kreuzerkrieg,' said the orders, and Captain von Lüdecke began
studying his handbooks.

He was ordered into Zone III, which meant the South Atlantic
along the South American coast, and he eluded the British very
neatly, although they assigned the heavy cruisers *Suffolk* and *Berwick*
and the light cruiser *Bristol* to find him. The trouble was that the
London planners expected him to move north and fish the waters off the
United States, and when he went south, there simply were not enough
British forces to search for him.

She became part of this enormous mystery of the German cruisers,
that baffled London. One day in July she was reported off Port au
Prince, having met the *Karlsruhe* on some mysterious mission.
(Perhaps one trouble with naval intelligence was its excessive
imagination.) The next day she was gone, and was not heard of until 4
August, the day Admiral Cradock learned authoritatively that
Dresden was off New York harbour (when actually she was steaming
steadily southward toward her new station). On 4 August that report
had come from the wireless station at Newfoundland. The *Karlsruhe*
was up there too, said the Newfoundland station. With this news the
English and Canadian ships in the St Lawrence were thrown into a
panic and Whitehall did not help a great deal by ordering all ships in
North American ports to remain in port until Admiral Cradock could
arrive from the Caribbean with his cruisers. (It was a wonder that
Cradock did not run into *Dresden* and *Karlsruhe* going the other
way.)

All sorts of rumours confused London. The Canadian Navy
department at Ottawa decided that the Germans were going to seize
the French islands of St Pierre and Miquelon, and turn them into
naval bases to harry Canadian shipping. Nobody in Berlin had

thought of that! All Canadian ports were closed to shipping, and for two weeks *Dresden* held Canada enthralled although she was thousands of miles away.

On 6 August she had taken the English steamer *Drumcliffe*, travelling in ballast from Buenos Aires to New York. She was off the Amazon River at the moment. *Dresden* was lucky, for although the *Drumcliffe* carried a wireless station, the captain had little faith in it, and when the German cruiser appeared, it did not occur to him to send off a distress signal. So a chance of placing one of the cruisers at its proper point was lost.

Captain von Lüdecke showed his mettle in this capture. Here was his first enemy ship, a perfectly fine 4,000-ton merchantman – and he let her go. The reason was that when the prize crew boarded, and the captain had surrendered his ship, he asked mildly: 'What are you going to do with my wife and child?'

'Wife and child? *Mutter und Kinder. Donner und Blitzen!*' Captain von Lüdecke had not the slightest idea of what to do with a wife and child, and the handbook said nothing. So he let the ship go. At least he had the presence of mind to take her wireless station, and he forced the captain and crew members all to sign a statement that they would not engage in war against Germany. Then feeling that he had done his duty magnificently, Captain von Lüdecke released the freighter. What Berlin would have said about that, or von Spee, for that matter, Captain von Lüdecke never discovered.

That very same day, an hour later in fact, the *Dresden* encountered another English freighter, the *Lynton Grange*, on her way from La Plata to New Port News. And as they were boarding *Lynton Grange*, up came *Hostilius*, a third English ship on her way from La Plata to Cuba. Von Lüdecke let them all go! They were not carrying war materials, he said. Of course, less than a week later *Hostilius* arrived at Barbados and *Drumcliffe* at Jamaica, and the *Dresden* was definitely placed. So, mistakenly, was *Karlsruhe* (the captains' identifications were so different that Admiral Cradock thought two cruisers were involved) and so single-handedly Captain von Lüdecke had undone all that the English rumour mill had done for the *Admiralstab* in those first days of war.

Had Berlin been aware of this, and von Lüdecke available, that captain would undoubtedly have finished the war running a ferry to Sweden.

The *Dresden*'s war was quite unlike any other German cruiser's. She had no trouble getting coal; all she had to do was send a message to Berlin, and *presto*, a collier appeared to do her bidding. This was because Berlin was busily laying in colliers along the South American routes, for her cruiser warriors, and had managed to get a number out of the North Sea before the war began. In the second week of August the *Dresden* coaled from the German collier *Corrientes* in a little inlet on the Brazilian coast, and no one bothered them. But how von Lüdecke survived is a tribute to blind luck. He came upon the British steamer *Dunstan*. They were close enough for the British captain to identify the German cruiser, yet von Lüdecke let the *Dunstan* go, and of course the captain immediately reported her position. A few days later he sighted the Brazilian steamer *Bahia* and did not bother to stop her or check her wireless; she immediately gave the world an accurate fix on the warship.

While von Lüdecke was wondering what to do with himself, he was called up by the German collier *Baden*, which was eager to give him some more coal. He decided that was a good idea and they met at the Rocas Islands. Why, no-one in his right mind could understand; their meeting place was just under the Brazilian lighthouse, and here von Lüdecke, chose to coal. The lighthouse keeper watched all this activity with unfeigned interest and even came out to the ship to observe. 'Ah, a German warship', he said. He was glad to see them.

'German?' said von Lüdecke in tones of surprise. 'Why this is a Swedish warship, the *Fylgia*.'

'Of course,' said the lighthouse keeper. 'What a stupid mistake.' And he went back to his lighthouse wondering how stupid the German captain really believed he was. A Swedish warship indeed, with all the crew speaking German. And he supposed she was on her way to the Antarctic to look for whales, too. In a short time the news reached Admiral Cradock that a German light cruiser had coaled at the Rocas Islands, and the collier was identified. Captain von Lüdecke had decided to keep the *Baden* with him because she was modern and clean and made 12 knots and carried her own wireless station. The British now were beginning to assemble quite a dossier on *Dresden*'s war activity – and the cruiser still had not struck a single blow in anger. But finally, even Captain von Lüdecke was stirred to action, on 14 August, when she encountered a man as wrong-headed as himself. He was the captain of the British freighter *Hyades* which was carrying a cargo of corn for England. *Hyades* had been stopped the day before by the British warship HMS *Glasgow*, and warned of the presence in these waters of *Dresden* and *Karlsruhe*. Of course, said the captain of the *Hyades*, who had heard enough of these wild stories already, and did not believe a word of what the officers from *Glasgow* said. He stopped in Pernambuco, and was again warned. He ought to make a wide sweep out into the Atlantic to avoid the Germans, said both warnings. Of course, said the captain of *Hyades*, and he went right on his way, following the shortest distance between two points. So he was on the Buenos Aires-London steamer run when he was sighted by *Dresden*, and even Captain von Lüdecke could not think of a good reason not to sink the ship. So he did, after transferring the crew to the collier *Prussia*, which had joined him. Von Lüdecke had a truly ludicrous amount of coal at his disposal. The reason was that at the outbreak of war fifty-four German and Austrian ships were in mid-Atlantic, and all of them were directed by the *Admiralstab* to make themselves available to German warships. Since there were only two German warships in the area, the result was sheer luxury for both.

On the day after sinking *Hyades*, the *Dresden* encountered yet another British merchantman, the *Siamese Prince*. But she was carrying British merchandise from London to La Plata. Since Argentina was neutral, by Captain von Lüdecke's reasoning, this was neutral cargo in a British bottom – and he let the ship go on by. Small wonder then that by this time the confidence of British shippers about the South American run was beginning to return. With *Dresden* on duty, it appeared that the English had little to fear.

Von Lüdecke gave every impression of being an outright fool. He sent the *Prussia* in to Rio de Janeiro, carrying the officers and men of the *Hyades*. Of course, when the *Hyades* docked, immediately the Englishmen went to the consulate and told everything they knew; and had a British cruiser or two been present there, the *Dresden* might not have lived much longer to tell any stories of her exploits. To date these had not been very impressive. The most remarkable aspect of the *Dresden*'s career was the ease with which she met friends. She went off to Trinidad Rocks, not to be confused with the island of Trinidad. There she met half a dozen German freighters and the old gunboat *Eber*, which was wheezing along, trying to get home. Captain von Lüdecke then did strike what might have been his most important blow for Germany. He ordered the *Cap Trafalgar*, a fast German liner, to take over the guns and ammunition of *Eber*, and made of her an auxiliary cruiser. This, of course, was not his own idea, but Berlin's. Captain Julius Wirth of the *Eber* would take over the liner, and make a raider of her. So saying, Captain von Lüdecke steamed away, ostensibly to hunt British ships and strike blows against the enemy. A few days before the end of August, off the River Plate, the

Dresden came across the British freighter *Holmwood*, carrying a cargo of Welsh coal, which her captain said was the best in the world. But so replete was Captain von Lüdecke that he did not think about keeping the *Holmwood* as a collier, but took off the crew and sank her. A few hours later von Lüdecke came upon the steamer *Katherine Park*, another English steamer, but carrying a cargo bound for New York. Von Lüdecke let her go too, on the same old basis that she was carrying neutral cargo.

Perhaps suspecting that something was amiss with this captain, Berlin ordered him to find the *Leipzig* and put himself under her command. That way, perhaps Berlin might get a little action from this cruiser. So von Lüdecke rounded the southern tip of South America, and went into Orange Bay on the Pacific side of Cape Horn. So relaxed was this captain, that the mood was transferred to the crew. When they had a few hours of liberty in Orange Bay, they went ashore to walk a bit, and most of the crewmen followed the age old custom in these parts of marking their names, the dates of their visit and the name of their ship on everything in sight. When they went back to the ship, one of the junior officers remarked to the captain that this was probably a foolish idea – to have let them go ashore and thus identify the ship and its travels. Captain von Lüdecke suddenly realized what he had done, and sent the men back to the shore to erase all evidence of their presence. But who could remember where every man had trod and where he had carved on a tree? The *Dresden* seemed determined to ignore the war that raged around it.

As the other German cruisers chalked up victories under most difficult conditions, Captain von Lüdecke loafed along, doing very little. On 16 September he sailed again from Orange Bay, and two days later sighted the English steamer *Ortega* bound for Southampton from Valparaiso. Captain von Lüdecke began a desultory chase; the English captain decided he would not be caught and headed into Nelson's Strait, below Hanover Island. This was uncharted water, dangerous for any ocean-going ship of the 1914 period, but Captain D.R. Kinneir felt it was better to risk a wreck than certain capture by the much faster cruiser. (He did not know his enemy or he might have bluffed it out and escaped.) So Captain Kinneir went into danger, and Captain von Lüdecke declined the gambit. *Ortega* moved into Smyth's channel safely, and then into the Atlantic Ocean, and *Dresden* turned away to do nothing in particular, it seemed, save coal and take on supplies from that amazing fleet of supply ships, and wait for the *Leipzig*. As far as the *Admiralstab*'s concept of cruiser warfare was concerned, the *Dresden* was an almost total disappointment, to date.

Leipzig's career had been even more disappointing, but for an entirely different reason. Captain Haun had not captured or sunk a single enemy vessel in six weeks of warfare, but unlike Captain von Lüdecke, Haun had a very good reason: he had been told to stay on the American station, and he had found nothing but difficulty there, due to the American insistence on real neutrality.

On 8 September, Haun had brought the *Leipzig* into Guaymas to take advantage of some of that coal aboard the *Mazatlan*, which he could not get otherwise. He had twenty-four hours in which to coal and get out, and Herr Jebsen had made sure that there would be no delays. The coal was waiting for them on the quay. They took the ship directly into the dock rather than waste time and effort with barges and boats. In short order Captain Haun learned that although Washington and Mexico City might be strong on neutrality the authorities of Guaymas were more lenient (greased by the generosity of Herr Jebsen). Posting a twenty-four-hour wireless watch to keep track of the emissions of his enemies, Captain Haun risked a longer stay, and was entertained royally by Herr Jebsen, Consul Moeller and other members of the German community. While he toasted, his men toiled in the ship, but at the end of a day and a half they had taken on more than 900 tons of coal, and Haun no longer felt desolate about the future. On the night of 9 September he was ready to head out to sea; he had made arrangements for a collier now, and he had plenty of coal for the moment. The *Leipzig*'s war could begin. Cautiously he sent the collier *Marie* out ahead lights blazing, and followed her to lurk along the shore, the *Leipzig*'s dark shadow hardly noticeable against the profile of the land. No one was out there, so he set a course for Panama, and prepared to sink enemy shipping.

Two days went by, without event, but on the third day, 11 September, the *Leipzig* overhauled a steamer and ordered her to stop. She did not, so Captain Haun ordered a shot across the other ship's bow, and that stopped her immediately. Oberleutnant Jahnke, the boarding officer, soon reported that this ship was the British tanker *Elsinore*, travelling under ballast back to Central America, having just delivered a cargo of fuel oil to San Francisco. Lieutenant Jahnke searched the ship but found little that would help the *Leipzig*. The English captain came aboard the *Leipzig* chiding Captain Haun for firing on him. He would have stopped at the hail, he said, except that his helmsman had misunderstood orders. Captain Haun was no von Lüdecke, and the Englishman's arguments left him unmoved; Haun sent the crew of the tanker to the *Marie*, and told the gunnery officer that he could use the ship for target practice. The 4-inch guns of the cruiser began firing, and at 5.30 that afternoon the *Elsinore* sank.

In Guaymas, Captain Haun had finally received a message that had been long delayed. The trouble was that Germany had few friends in the northern half of the western hemisphere, and so the message, which had first reached Santiago had been sent on to San Francisco, and finally Vice-Consul von Schack had entrusted it to Herr Jebsen, who delivered it to Haun. The collier that Haun had asked for weeks ago, had finally been sent, not to Mexico, but to Freshwater Bay in the Galapagos Islands. She would wait there for five days, from 15 September. Captain Haun knew that time was short, so he hastened onward that evening. At daylight on 18 September he reached the Galapagos group. When he came to Freshwater Bay on Indefatigable Island (Isla Isabella) he found the 8,000-ton freighter *Amasis* waiting for him, carrying uniforms, fresh food, wines, beer, soap and 3,000 tons of coal. For two days the men of the *Leipzig* transferred supplies to the cruiser. Then Captain Haun went ashore, while his men took on fresh water and negotiated with a local ranchero for fresh beef.

Unlike Captain von Lüdecke, Captain Haun had a strong sense of survival. He knew it would be helpful if he could get rid of the crew of *Elsinore* in a way that would take the British a long time to discover what had happened to the ship. He made arrangements with the local Ecuadorean government officials to accept the Englishmen as refugees without making any fuss about it over the wireless. Then he sent the *Leipzig* off to Tagus Bay on the west side of Albemarle Island, where *Marie* was waiting out of sight. That had to be done because she carried no wireless, and the prisoners were aboard, waiting. The prisoners were carried back to the big island and unloaded, and on 22 September, the *Leipzig* set out for the Bay of Guayaquil, followed by her two supply ships, while the captain of the *Elsinore* fumed and insisted fruitlessly that the Ecuadorean officials wireless Guayaquil immediately and tell the British consul what had happened. It was several weeks before an English ship happened to call in at the Galapagos Islands, and the story of the sinking of *Elsinore* came out.

Meanwhile on 25 September the *Leipzig* captured the British steamer *Bankfields*, which was carrying 5,000 tons of sugar-cane from Peru, destined for England. She also had a treasure aboard: a flock of chickens and a pen full of Yorkshire pigs. The men of the *Leipzig* took the animals off with the crew, and loaded them all aboard the *Marie*. Then they sank the *Bankfields*, and went off to enjoy fresh eggs and an enormous roast pork dinner on Sunday.

Captain Haun was extremely conscious of the need for readiness and security. On 27 September he decided to top off his bunkers again to be ready for emergency, and went into a tiny anchorage at the guano island of Lobos de Tierra. He sent the *Marie* around to the other side of the island, to watch out for ships while he coaled from the *Amasis*. Actually his reason for despatching the collier to a point out of sight was to be sure the English prisoners did not see anything that might help the enemy's cause, and to keep the *Marie* hidden from any curious persons on the guano island. His precautions taken, Captain Haun then moved in to coal. In the harbour he saw a four-masted barque which was loading with guano and on the morning of 28 September a pair of scruffy ruffians appeared alongside the *Leipzig*, and were invited on deck. One said he was a Peruvian official. (This was Peruvian territory.) The other said he was the captain of the barque, an American. Haun was so suspicious of the pair of them that he hustled them off his ship in short order, promising not to harm the American ship. Two days later, when he left the island, and rejoined *Marie* outside, the wireless operator picked up a broadcast from Radio Callao: 'the *Leipzig* and two auxiliary cruisers are raiding up and down the coast of Peru ...' Haun's two ruffians had been more effective than he thought; they had discovered the name of the ship and the existence of the *Marie*, in spite of his precautions.

However, the misadventure had its bright side. On 30 September, when *Leipzig* was cruising off Callao, the German consulate's wireless radio station informed the ship that the British had stationed a powerful squadron in the area. This was Admiral Cradock's force, which consisted of the heavy cruisers *Good Hope*, and *Monmouth*, the light cruiser *Glasgow*, and the auxiliary cruiser *Otranto*. They were searching for the *Leipzig*. A second message was more encouraging; the *Leipzig* was to find the *Dresden*, which should be cruising along the Chilean coast, and Captain Haun was to direct a joint effort against the enemy.

At that very moment, Admiral Cradock was hot on the trail of the *Dresden*, another object of his assigned search. He had been promised a superior force, consisting of the ships at hand and the old battleship *Canopus* and the *Defence*. This would make him more than a match for all the German cruisers known to be loose in three oceans, if they teamed up, as the Admiralty believed they would. 'As soon as you have superior force,' said Admiral Cradock's latest orders, 'search the Magellan Strait with the squadron, being ready to return and cover the

River Plate, or according to information, search north as far as Valparaiso, break up German trade, and destroy the German cruisers ...'

When Admiral Cradock would have that superior force was another matter. For with the discovery of *Emden*'s foray into the Bay of Bengal and von Spee's adventures in the South Pacific the movement of *Defence* had been stopped and she had not been started again. That reduced Admiral Cradock's superiority to nothing, for *Defence* was a modern battleship, but *Canopus* was an old wheezer that had virtually no value against anything larger than a destroyer. But he was to continue anyhow, and do the best he could. On 22 September he had begun searching the southern waters, looking for *Dresden, Leipzig,* and *Karlsruhe,* which might have joined up. That day the Admiral was informed of Captain Kinneir's narrow escape in Nelson Straits from a German cruiser. Admiral Cradock turned that way with his flagship *Good Hope,* the *Monmouth* and the *Glasgow* and *Otranto.* They found nothing but they began searching about the area for signs of the cruisers, and they stopped off in Orange Bay. A shore party went into the land to see if there was any sign, and they found one of the telltale boards on which a seaman of the *Dresden* had carefully written his name, home town, the date, and the name of his ship. So now, courtesy of Captain von Lüdecke's woeful inexperience and judgement, Admiral Cradock had identified one of the ships for which he was searching and located her in place and time. Cradock leapt to another conclusion: the *Dresden* must be an advance agent for the von Spee squadron. It was important that he keep track of her and capture her if possible, and as soon as possible. That judgement caused Admiral Cradock to make some extraordinary efforts. On 28 September he called on the British consul at Punta Arenas and learned that the Germans had recently sent the German merchant ship *Santa Isabel* into that port from Orange Bay, and that some of the German seamen had got drunk and begun bragging about the big base that von Spee was going to put up there. The consul also informed Admiral Cradock that several German merchant ships were moving around the area, and that one of them had sailed a few days earlier loaded with fresh provisions and had returned empty. Had these gone to Admiral von Spee? Was he then, actually in the area, although his last reported sighting was at Tahiti?

Admiral Cradock took some precautions. It was well known that the Chileans, particularly the Chilean Navy, were extremely pro-German. On 28 September Admiral Cradock made it a special point to call on the Chilean Admiral at Punta Arenas, complain about the elusive Germans, and announce that he was heading for Valparaiso to search them out. And, good as his word, that evening he sailed the squadron. But once outside the harbour, the ships blacked out carefully, and turned in the opposite direction, heading for Cockburn Channel. That water had not been charted since 1820, when a few feet one way or another did not make so much difference. But unlike Captain von Lüdecke, Admiral Cradock was willing to chance a lost ship to secure the advantage of surprise. This night the squadron travelled through snowstorms, in waters almost unknown, marked by tricky currents, planning the voyage so as to arrive off Orange Bay, where the Admiral hoped he might this time find the *Dresden, Leipzig,* and *Karlsruhe,* setting up the base for the Admiral von Spee. At sunrise on 30 September the British squadron reached the entrance to Orange Bay, and at a signal, all four ships sped inside, guns ready.

But the bay was empty. Disappointed, Admiral Cradock sat down to think. Here in Orange Bay he felt the presence of the Germans, and he knew intuitively that very soon he would meet his enemies.

12

Coronel Beckons

While Admiral Cradock was hurrying to Orange Bay to meet his disappointment, Admiral von Spee was thousands of miles away in the French owned Marquesas Islands, taking on coal and provisions again. They put in at Controleur Bay on the south side of Nuku Hiva Island, and when the coaling was finished the Admiral declared a holiday for the flagship. Not so for the *Gneisenau*; she was sent to Hiwaoa, the seat of government, to capture the town, and particularly to seize the liquid assets of the Bank of France there. The Admiral believed in fair treatment for the ranchers, farmers, and suppliers he met along his way, be they neutrals or Germans or even enemy nationals, but he was running out of cash. The money taken from the British wireless station at Fanning Island was nearly gone, so he needed to replenish his coffers. What better way than to make his country's enemies pay in gold? When he reached Chile, he would be able to use the German government's credit, through the embassy but until then he wanted to pay his way and leave no unnecessary enemies behind.

The *Scharnhorst* docked at Anne-Marie Port, the ship was released from war status for the moment, and a period of leisure began. All the men who wanted it could have shore leave, and all did. Some work had to be done, and of this by far the most pleasant duty was the provisioning. The Admiral soon learned that the German trading house of Scharf and Kayser had been closed down at the outbreak of hostilities. But instead of usurping the inventory, the French had locked the doors of the warehouse. Von Spee had them unlocked and the sailors began trundling carts full of wine, beer, tinned milk, sardines, vegetables, sugar, tobacco – everything a ship might need, including cloth and needles and a sewing machine. For weeks the men had been improvising; after they ran out of soap, they used sand and soda to scrub; after they ran out of matches, an engineer invented an electric cigar lighter which was hung in the wardroom. But now all these needs were met. Adversity had taught the men of the squadron some new tricks, and they did not miss the usual ship's supplies such as fenders because they had learned to make better ones than could be bought by unravelling hawsers and winding them into balls. So with the reprovisioning in the Marquesas (*Gneisenau* unlatched the doors of the Scharf and Kayser branch in Hiwaoa) the ships were as fit as they could expect to be, having spent three months continually at sea. On the night of 30 September, as Admiral Cradock's officers shivered in the wardroom of the *Good Hope*, and the Admiral pored over charts amid the glaciers of Cockburn Channel's islands, Admiral von Spee and his officers enjoyed a hearty feast, thanks to Scharf and Kayser, and the perhaps unwilling hospitality of their French hosts. The wardroom table groaned with fresh yams, bananas, pawpaws, mangoes and pineapples, and from the warehouse stores came Dutch cheeses, sausages and caviar. There was fresh meat and fresh fish, and plenty of wine and beer. This was the way to fight a war!

The next day, the *Gneisenau* arrived at Hiwaoa, and not knowing what would be found at this seat of government, Captain Maerker came in like a warrior, guns ready, decks cleared for action. First officer Pochhammer led the landing party, in clean white uniform with epaulets and a pistol and cutlass, and his armed cutter led several of the ship's boats, each packed with sailors fully armed. Inside the harbour, they approached the stone seawall, whose steps led up to the quay. The cutter moved up and down in the swell, and Commander Pochhammer poised himself on the gunwale, waiting for the proper moment to leap onto the slippery hand-hewn steps. A large crowd of civilians, many of them girls and women, stood at the top, and as they saw the hesitation of the Germans, they began to giggle. Finally a French gendarme saw their plight and hurried down the steps to give Pochhammer a hand up. The German officer took the outstretched hand gladly, came ashore, then suddenly realized he was overclose to an enemy, and dropped the hand as if it were afire. The poor gendarme was surrounded by stern sailors, rifles fixed with bayonets, and he was ordered to take Commander Pochhammer to the officer in charge.

The officer led the party across a small tongue of land, and Pochhammer suddenly saw why they had so much trouble, and the quay seemed so small. The boat had come in at the wrong landing, in the wrong bay. They passed by the police station and Pochhammer suddenly stopped them in mid-stride. He sent a pair of men there to find the official safe, and guard it so the French could not remove the money inside. They headed then for the governor's house and as they arrived that gentleman appeared, in full dress uniform, his hair still wet from the comb, and his buttons half undone, but he was wearing boots and spurs, and if he had been ready for them he would have been quite resplendent. The governor was also the doctor, and he was not much used to official calls from foreigners. He was somewhat taken aback then, when Commander Pochhammer put on his most official demeanour and warned that the Germans had captured this place and would tolerate no resistance. Anyone who caused trouble would be shot, he said. He intended to seize everything of value that belonged to the French government, so the governor might as well begin by showing him the valuables right away.

Valuables? What valuables? asked the governor. Well, the gold hoard, to begin with. There was no gold hoard, said the governor.

Pochhammer did not believe this, so the hunt began. The police station was also the centre of government, and here the Germans found the only safe on the island. It was opened, and inside was found the money hoard: about £2,500, including coins from the First Republic, from Napoleon's consulate, from Napoleon's Imperial days.

Pochhammer took it all, including postage stamps and postal money orders, although how he believed the French government would honour money orders drawn by Admiral von Spee against Paris was more than the governor could understand.

The governor was then asked – nay ordered – to the *Gneisenau*, so that Captain Maerker could pay his respects. The poor man apparently expected to be murdered, but once aboard the captain was quick to allay his fears, give him a drink, and apologize for the dreadful exigencies of war. One drink led to another, as Pochhammer ashore supervised the stripping of the Scharf and Kayser warehouse here, and after the third the governor decided these were jolly good fellows after all, and expansively invited Maerker and his officers on a pig hunt. Maerker was very pleased. A little later some of his enthusiasm died when he learned that these were not wild hogs, but local pigs let loose to run wild until wanted for the table. But a pig hunt was a pig hunt, and dear to every Prussian heart. They went out, with guns, but found that the pigs came when called. Indeed they did. Large pigs came with small pigs, and white pigs came with black pigs. Fat pigs came with thin pigs and noisy pigs came with quiet pigs. Soon the officers gave up and adjourned to the governor's mansion for French drinks to match the German drinks, and the torpedo room crew and the black gang were given the honour of finishing the pig hunt. By evening they had brought aboard the *Gneisenau* so many pigs that the sty built hurriedly by the men aboard had to be enlarged, and the port foredeck became a pig haven.

The governor decided that it was a matter of French honour to be sure that his guests (enemies no longer) were sent off loaded with the provenance of the island. He suggested that next day they should have a cattle round-up to supply the ship with an adequate amount of beef. So they did; actually the cattle were German anyhow, the property of the Scharf and Kayser manager, who lived in lonely isolation, a pariah, on the edge of the town until the coming of the *Gneisenau*, when suddenly he changed into the best of fellows. Eight cows were herded up and taken back to the ship, one escaped just before loading and made her way out of town. She alone survived the round-up; the butchers were waiting at the gangway, and the other seven beasts were soon hanging in the ship's meat locker.

All this was accomplished by the evening of 2 October, and then the *Gneisenau* sailed away, leaving the governor to explain his strange behaviour in the face of the enemy to his constituents, many of whom had fled into the countryside to conduct guerilla warfare against *les Boches*. As they steamed out of the harbour, Captain Maerker had a message from the Admiral. The squadron was leaving the Marquesas, said von Spee, and gave Maerker a rendezvous point. The Admiral was in a hurry to get to Easter Island, and thence to South America. So they all left the French territory, and had not been gone many hours, before the wireless stations began to send out the word of their unwelcome visit.

The *Titania* went straight on to Easter Island to check out the area, in case of trouble. The freighters *Yorck* and *Göttingen* followed the squadron, bearing their precious burdens of coal. Stripped of their coal, the *Holsatia* and *Ahlers* were sent to Honolulu to intern themselves, since there was no way they could really hope to get back to Germany. They carried messages from the Admiral to Berlin; he would be at Easter Island until 25 October, and then go to the southern tip of South America and assemble all the cruisers. That meant he would have *Leipzig, Dresden*, and *Karlsruhe*, if all went well. The squadron would number six ships, and should offer the enemy plenty to think about. The large number of colliers in South American waters, and the friendliness of the people of Argentina and Chile might make it possible for the squadron to operate here for some time. All these things remained to be seen.

On the night of 3 October, perhaps aided by freak atmospheric conditions, the flagship made contact with *Dresden* at the remarkable distance of 3,500 miles. Admiral von Spee used this opportunity to give his orders for the light cruisers to assemble and told Captain von Lüdecke to superintend the arrangements. *Dresden* called up *Leipzig*, found her that night, and transmitted the order to appear at Easter Island. The next night, encouraged by success, Admiral von Spee sent a long message to the *Dresden* giving some details of his plans, and to make sure it was all received, it was repeated. The wireless operators of *Good Hope* intercepted the message, and although Admiral Cradock's intelligence officers could not read it, they knew it must be from some German warship, and they suspected it was from von Spee. They transmitted the message as received to London for possible decoding. When it arrived, it was decoded promptly, for the Admiralty had broken the German naval code. So in the first week of October London knew what to expect: Admiral von Spee was heading for the west coast of South America, to conduct cruiser warfare against British merchant shipping. Admiral Cradock was going to have to stop him, since he was the only one in the area with a force even theoretically capable of doing so.

The intelligence game did not go all Britain's way in this sector of the world, however. The many friends of Germany in Chile and Argentina had kept the German consulates informed about the movements of the British squadron, and the consulates had passed this information along to Captain von Lüdecke. So that night, von Lüdecke informed Admiral von Spee that Cradock was in the area, although he did not know quite where. He did know the squadron's strength: *Good Hope, Monmouth, Glasgow*, and *Otranto*, and when von Spee learned this much, he knew he had nothing to fear, unless Cradock was reinforced. His two big cruisers were more powerful and modern than anything Cradock had, and the combination of *Nürnberg*, plus two or three other light cruisers meant that he would outgun Cradock if the British admiral was so foolish as to seek him out to do battle.

The light cruiser *Glasgow*, Admiral Cradock decided, could help him ascertain the whereabouts of the enemy by visiting the Falklands Islands. This British possession would be a likely stopping point for the German squadron on its way because there were many fjord-like inlets in the misty hills that could be used for coaling. Anyhow, Cradock wanted to warn the governor that the Germans might turn up, if they had not already, and to make sure that if that happened he would be informed.

The trouble, of course, was that there was no wireless at the Falklands, no telephones, no communication with the outside world except by chance or the regular monthly mail vessel. The *Glasgow* sailed into Port Edgar to coal, along with the *Monmouth*. *Glasgow*'s intelligence officer, Commander Lloyd Hirst, was despatched to Fox Bay, where the governor was located, in order to pass the messages from the Admiral. He hiked across the rugged hills in a snowstorm and made his way to Fox Bay, only to find that the governor had already left this place, and there was no one there but the manager of the sheep station and a few shepherds. Commander Hirst arranged for the shipment of some sheep to the squadron. The first chore was to find able-bodied men to drive the sheep, since most of the young men had enlisted in the armed forces and were gone. Then he headed across the bay to the settlement on the other side, where the governor was supposed to be. For this voyage the sheep station manager lent him a boat with an outboard motor. He reached the shore, found the governor gone, and returned. On the way back the outboard motor broke down during the middle of a snowstorm on the bay. Poor Hirst and his guide had to row back a full mile into the wind, pelted by snow and sleet.

He then headed back toward the ships, accompanied by several shepherds, a band of sheep, and a number of sheep dogs. Someone had found horses for the trip, and Commander Hirst rode ahead to the top of a hill, where he lit a brush fire and made signals, Red Indian style with smoke, to ask the ships for boats and a work crew to load them. Just as he finished his message the darkness of evening lowered, and it began to snow again. The snow stopped as night came, and the moon came out, bright and cold. Hirst had to ride down to the shore, find the boats and then direct the shepherds to the proper place. He found the 'boats' but there was only one of them. The big steam cutter could not get into shore at this shallow place, so the only boat that came in was an oared cutter, commanded by a fifteen-year-old naval cadet. He would supervise the loading.

By this time it was pitch dark. Forty-five sheep were baaing their way down the steep hill. In the nick of time Commander Hirst found that the kitchen garden of an abandoned farmhouse would do for a corral, and the fence was repaired. Three large brush fires were lighted to direct the shepherds to the right place, and when they arrived, the sheep were wrestled down and hogtied by Commander Hirst and two Falkland Islanders, while the cadet put the finishing touches on the ropes, and his sailors stood around the perimeter where the fence was weak, yelling like banshees to keep the sheep from breaking through the rotten fence. One old ram broke through anyhow, bowled over a blue jacket, and disappeared into the night, with a toss of his head. But by eleven o'clock that night the sheep were all tied down, and the sailors began carrying them to the boat. They loaded the whaleboat, and then found that the weight had grounded it, so they had to get out and wade in the icy water. Several sheep jumped, or wriggled overboard, and had to be rescued. They may have gone into the water at forty pounds, but fleece soaking wet, they came out at more like a hundred and fifty. Finally, the waders led the boat to deeper water, and trans-shipped the first load to the steam launch, and went back for a second. By midnight all the sheep, sailors and cadet and Commander Hirst were back aboard the ship, and the Falkland Islanders had vanished into the gloom. Commander Hirst reported to the quarter-deck.

'Have a nice outing?' asked the officer of the deck. Commander Hirst was still pondering the question as he drank down a hot toddy, changed his socks and reported to Captain Luce on his walk of twelve miles, boating excursion of six miles, including row of one mile, ride of fifteen miles, and his athletic deployment with the sheep. From the morning, when he left the steam launch and waded ashore in below-freezing weather, he had been wet from the waist down, but he hardly believed the captain would be interested in that.

'How was the trip?' asked Captain Luce.

'The governor was gone,' said Commander Hirst.

'Oh,' said Captain Luce. 'A pity.'

'Yes,' said Commander Hirst.

'Well. Perhaps you had best turn in. Some of the chaps would like to do a bit of shooting tomorrow, and since you know all about the place ... They say the early morning shooting is best. Five o'clock then?'

'Of course,' said Commander Hirst. 'Delightful.'

13

The Hunter

As the hunt intensified for Admiral von Spee in the nether regions of South America, London grew a little more queasy about the presence of that other, unknown German cruiser somewhere in the Indian Ocean. All the odds seemed to indicate that this was *Königsberg*, which had been 'lost' for sometime. But *Königsberg*'s appearance at Zanzibar on 19 September to destroy the old *Pegasus* had scotched that theory. So Admiral Jerram had to come to the conclusion that the ship in the Indian Ocean was one of von Spee's. Aboard the *Emden*, Captain von Müller was just then taking action to be sure that the British were under no further apprehensions about his existence. He had decided on the most daring of manoeuvres, he would appear at a major British port to see what destruction he might cause. He headed for Madras. As the *Emden* travelled, the officers and men were treated to a whole series of news reports from various wireless stations in the area. The German cruiser in the Indian Ocean had been found and sunk, said the reports. Sunk indeed! The English would soon see, said von Müller's men.

The captain had chosen Madras because it was a long way from Rangoon, and he had been last seen off Rangoon. To appear completely across the Bay of Bengal on the Coromandel coast ought really to confuse the experts of the Admiralty. Just how many cruisers did the Germans have in the area, would be the question, and that is precisely the reaction that von Müller wanted to achieve. Another factor persuading him to choose Madras for attack was its layout, with port installations close to the sea, which meant no problems about mines. The final factor was the information given to von Müller that one of the crew had once worked in the port at Madras and could describe the area from memory, oil storage tanks of the Burma Oil Company in particular. They would make a lovely inferno. The man also remembered the old guns that guarded the port, dating back to

1880 and excellent for sinking sailing ships. Von Müller had little to fear from Fort St George above the harbour.

For several days the cruiser steamed across the wide bay, which in another area would have been called a sea. Lieutenant Gaede held gunnery practice one day, but the duty was generally light. On 22 September von Müller ordered the ship slowed. He wanted to arrive at night, and as evening approached the *Markomannia* was detached and sent to a rendezvous point to get her out of the way. As darkness fell the 'fourth funnel' was set up, to help confuse the enemy.

Captain von Müller had not used it since entering the Bay of Bengal, which had also added to the confusion already: a four-funnelled ship had come in past Bali, and a three-funnelled ship had captured all those English vessels. What was anyone to think? With the fake funnel von Müller expected to be able to move right up on the city without detection. Anyone who saw the profile of the ship would recognize another British light cruiser.

Although the *Emden* had London concerned, the worry about enemies had not trickled down to Madras, it seemed. As the ship came up on Madras light, the light went on, bright as ever, a beacon to any enemy in the area. Of course the British had not a thought in the world about an enemy in the middle of Indian waters; such an idea was unthinkable, and that was apparent as the *Emden* came along the beach. For the city spread sixteen miles along that beach and extended eight miles inland, and every bit of Madras was lighted up as it had always been. The harbour lights burned brightly, beckoning the *Emden* to the red and white tanks of the Burma Oil Company. At nine o'clock the ship went to battle stations, and headed in at 17 knots. Forty-five minutes later she was in close enough to turn on the searchlights and they were focused on the oil tanks. The first salvo boomed out into the night, missing the oil tanks, but (unknown to von Müller) knocking out one of the guns of the battery at Fort St George. But soon Gaede had the range. The guns fired into a steamer and set it afire. They worked over the harbour installation and in a few minutes the oil tanks were blazing brightly, and obscuring the city behind them. A few shots were fired at the *Emden* but so few that most of the men did not even know they were under attack. The reason was simple enough: all the officials and officers of the garrison were in town at the Madras club that evening, celebrating the news that the Royal Navy had just sunk the one threat to India's prosperity, the German raider *Emden*. The happy colonials were in the dining-room, toasting good fortune when an Indian servant padded in to call their attention to the fires blazing in the harbour.

The wind was blowing offshore that night, and so the fires from the oil tanks did not spread across the city as they might have done. But *Emden* expended 125 rounds of 4-inch ammunition, and burned a number of installations besides the oil tanks. When Captain von Müller decided it was time to go, and turned north, the fires were burning very nicely. As the ship steamed away, the Germans could see the burning of Madras for many hours. Then they turned south, and put the past behind them. They were going to move to the ship lanes off the Ceylonese port of Colombo.

From this point on, Captain von Müller was in deadly danger and he knew it very well. Admiral Jerram had verified the cruiser's presence in the Indian Ocean on 16 September when the treacherous Italian captain of the *Loredano* had appeared in Calcutta. Jerram had then sent the heavy cruiser *Hampshire* and a Japanese cruiser to the Indian Ocean. They were circling all around *Emden* at this point. They had set rendezvous off Madras three days before *Emden* got there, and then sailed for Akyab, chasing a false rumour that *Emden* was there. The Japanese cruiser had searched around Colombo, and then departed. It was, after all, a very large ocean.

Von Müller's immediate problems were to find victims and to find coal. One should bring the other, and this time it must be good hard coal, for the engineers were complaining that the ship's boilers would soon be fouled if they did not stop burning that atrocious Indian dust. *Markomannia* still held some good Shantung coal, but not much.

On 24 September the *Emden* had a narrow escape when the Japanese cruiser passed within sixty miles of the ship in its searches. The transmissions between that ship and *Hampshire* were clear, since much had to be sent in the open. The officers in the wardroom told Chief Engineer Ellenbroek that they were really afraid because of his smoke. And it was true, although they jested: the coal from *Pontoporos* burned with such gaseous presence that von Müller said he was sure they could see the ship fifty or sixty miles away. Finally von Müller could stand it no longer and ordered Ellenbroek to turn to his diminished supply of Shantung coal. On 25 September just twenty miles off the southern shore of Ceylon, the *Emden* overhauled the 3,600-ton merchant ship *King Lud*. Lieutenant Lauterbach went out to board in high spirits. He wanted newspapers, to tell of their exploits. He wanted coal, good coal. But when he got to the *King Lud*, he found that she was travelling in ballast from Suez to Calcutta, and she had no newspapers late enough to tell of *Emden*'s doings, nor enough coal to make the transfer worthwhile, nor any supplies they might want save a store of potatoes. So *King Lud* was sunk with dispatch and *Emden* went on.

The ship moved back toward Colombo, and that night von Müller lay just thirty miles off the port, and the watch could see the searchlights stabbing out to sea from the harbour. That night they saw running lights, and overhauled a ship. Captain von Müller had cautioned them not to betray their presence immediately, so they hailed the ship in English and did not identify themselves. She was a Norwegian, so they let her go, and all her captain could say when he entered Colombo port, was that he had been stopped by a warship and questioned in English. Since *Hampshire* and other vessels were out searching for *Emden*, that incident did not even arouse the authorities of Colombo.

Later that night the careful watch off the harbour was rewarded. They saw a merchant ship sail from Colombo, and they waited for her just off the island of Minicoy, which shielded them from the shore.

When the ship was well outside they hailed her. This was an English vessel, the *Tymeric*, carrying a cargo of sugar to England. Lieutenant Lauterbach took Prince Franz Joseph with him on this boarding party. They had decided to leave a large crew aboard, because they wanted to take the *Tymeric* along for a hundred miles or so, to be well outside British waters when they sank her. But when the captain of *Tymeric* learned of their plan, he flatly refused to have anything more to do with his own ship. He would be damned if he would navigate, or even con the ship. His chief engineer refused to return below. And, said the captain, 'I'll tell my men not to obey any orders from any damned Germans.'

Captain Tulloch of the *Tymeric* was a choleric man and with some reason, that night. Just two hours earlier he had been sitting in the office of the port captain at Colombo, getting his sailing instructions.

'Any danger?' he had asked.

'Not a bit. The sea is clear.'

'What about that German cruiser?'

'She is at least a thousand miles away. There's nothing to bother you from here to Aden ...'

So the *Tymeric* had sailed, and *immediately* been overhauled. Captain Tulloch's anger was not just against the Germans. He had pulled in at Colombo for only one reason: to ascertain the whereabouts of the *Emden*. Had he not gone inside he would have moved right on by, and been a hundred miles away when *Emden* came to Colombo to call.

Lieutenant Lauterbach was sympathetic as one old merchant skipper to another, and he tried to calm the captain down. But the more he spoke of 'the fortunes of war' and the need for a little co-operation for a while, the more Captain Tulloch raged. Lauterbach, too, was a choleric man and he began to lose his temper. He also watched Captain Tulloch closely, and when he caught sight of the captain saying a few terse words to his chief engineer with a meaningful look on his face, Lauterbach knew instinctively that they were hatching a plot to do something to the ship. Any delay would endanger the *Emden*, and they knew it. So Lauterbach berated them, and then sent a message to Captain von Müller, advising that the *Tymeric* be sunk immediately. Nor should they take these trouble-some Englishmen aboard, as had been their custom. Captain Tulloch and his men would go into the boats, and make their own way back to Colombo if they could. But first, Captain von Müller would deal with the English captain. Captain Tulloch and his chief engineer were taken aboard the *Emden* under heavy guard, with Lauterbach warning that they probably would be shot for their plot against the ship.

Tulloch boarded the ship with a cigarette drooping from his lower lip. When he reached the quarter-deck, he did not remove it in the presence of Captain von Müller. First Officer von Mücke snatched the cigarette from the Englishman's lip and began to upbraid him. Captain von Müller put an end to the tirade; he could understand his officers' behaviour because they were under pressure and worried more than a little about their position so close to the British base. Von Müller chided the Englishmen and sent them to the port side of the quarter-deck under guard to contemplate their sins. Later they were moved to the ship's brig to consider the dangers of defiance. The crew were after all brought aboard, because von Müller did not like abandoning people at sea.

But the *Tymeric*, despite all the trouble, brought welcome news to Captain von Müller and his men. Lauterbach found a number of English newspapers, including that very day's editions of the Colombo papers, and several stories of the exploits of the *Emden*, plus an account of the mysterious bombardment that had destroyed much of Madras' port facility.

The German cruiser *Emden* appeared before Madras last night (Sept 22) at nine o'clock and shelled the city. As a result of the first two salvos the gasoline storage tanks of the Burma Oil Company were set afire. Then the cruiser fired several more salvos, damaging a number of houses. The telegraph office was hit. A shore battery responded after the third salvo, and the *Emden* ceased its fire then and retired. Two policemen on duty near the oil tanks were wounded. The steamer *Chapra* of the British India Company was in the battle zone and eight of her crew were wounded. The principal result of this incident has been to stop the return of confidence of the shipping men, of which the signs are already visible ...

That meant that von Müller had indeed succeeded in what he set out to do. That attack on Madras has been staged for just this effect, to frighten the shipping men and delay Britain's acquisition of supplies and soldiers from this area of the globe.

There were little stories to buttress the official account, and these made most enjoyable reading for the Germans. One told how the *Emden* had struck such terror into the Indian population that they began to desert the city, fearful that the *Emden* would return again at night and kill them. So Madras was thoroughly frightened and confused. So much the better for Germany.

In fact, the whole of the Bay of Bengal was almost equally disturbed. For two solid weeks (and von Müller did not know this) not a single ship had entered or left Rangoon harbour. Instead of comforting Rangoon to learn that the *Emden* was on the other side of the bay, the news of the Madras attack struck new terror, and shipping was again delayed.

As the officers read the stories and chuckled over them, their irritation with the adamant Captain Tulloch and his engineer vanished. They could afford to be generous with their enemies, and although they kept the captain in confinement because they were really afraid that he might try to damage the *Emden*, they allowed him playing-cards to while away the time until the crew of the *Tymeric* would eventually be sent away.

Quite when that would be nobody knew. It depended on the number of ships the *Emden* might take. And how many that would be seemed debatable, unless, Engineer Ellenbroek said, they could capture him some good hard coal. Otherwise, the prospects seemed dim. They did capture another ship on the morning of 26 September, the 4,000-ton merchantman *Gryfevale*, on her way to Colombo from the Red Sea, again in ballast. Again she had consumed most of her coal, and was of little use. She was a rustbucket, and not of much value to anyone. Captain von Müller decided he would use her to unload the crews of *Tymeric* and *King Lud*, so he put aboard a prize crew and they tagged after *Markomannia*.

That day they passed a Dutch freighter and later in the day the wireless operators heard a conversation between that ship and an English warship. The Englishman asked the Dutchman if he had seen the *Emden*.

'For reasons of neutrality, the answer is refused,' was the Dutch ship's reply, and although it was technically quite correct, it certainly let the Englishman know that *Emden* was in this area. Von Müller would have to be even more careful now.

The next day, after the Dutch incident, the *Emden* came across her coal ship, to the delight of Engineer Ellenbroek. She was the *Buresk*, a collier laden with fine Cardiff coal. The engineer was happy with his gift from the sea, and von Müller was even happier because this ship was under contract to the Royal Navy, and the coal the *Emden* was about to use had been intended for Admiral Jerram. What was needed now was a little peace and quiet to get some of that aboard the *Emden*.

First they had to get rid of all the unhappy guests. For several hours the boats moved between vessels, taking all the English crews aboard *Gryfevale*. Lieutenant Lauterbach, who had discovered a treasure trove of beer, wine, and liquor aboard that ship, had it moved over to the wardroom lockers of the *Emden*. The generous Lauterbach also told the captains of the English ships that they might have some of the drink to get them back to port. But once the locker was opened, some of the English seamen got into it, and soon were dead drunk. A fight broke out in the mess deck, and the Germans had to bring out their guns and threaten to shoot, before the ship was quieted down. When Captain von Müller learned the cause of the incident, he dressed Lieutenant Lauterbach down thoroughly. The lieutenant took it sheepishly and promised never again. The drink was retrieved and moved – every bottle of it – aboard the *Emden*.

All this commotion had delayed the transfers, and so the *Gryfevale* continued in the train. That afternoon the *Emden* captured her thirteenth ship in less than three weeks. She was the *Ribera*, another vessel in ballast. She would be just about the last for a while, said her captain. He had just learned of a port embargo on all shipping in the Bay of Bengal, to last until the *Emden* was eliminated, the authorities said. They indicated this would happen in a matter of days.

But that night the *Emden* captured the steamer *Foyle*, and that crew, too, was added to all the others aboard the *Gryfevale*. Lieutenant Lauterbach reported that it would be impossible to squeeze another man aboard that vessel, so that night von Müller despatched her to Cochin. To be sure that her captain did as he was told, von Müller gave him specific sailing instructions and told him to keep on course, lest he be torpedoed by German submarines or another raider. The implication was that the Bay of Bengal was alive with German shipping, and most of these Britons were willing to believe it by this time. So *Gryfevale* sailed away, and von Müller made a point of changing his course several times to throw off any pursuit. As the English ship departed, the men of *Emden* heard three loud cheers given for them by their enemies, and they were very pleased. For the *Emden* had achieved a reputation in these three weeks that was admired by all. The newspapers aboard the *Tymeric* had indicated the British admiration for the chivalry of their enemies. For not a single person had been hurt intentionally in all these captures, and every crew had been sent homeward, treated as well as was humanly possible. It was a remarkable record. How long it would last was a growing worry for Captain von Müller. He had the feeling that his enemies were closing in on him, and so he decided to remove himself entirely from his current scene of operations. The *Emden* began moving on a course for the Maldive Islands, far across the Indian Ocean. Here von Müller would re-group and prepare for a new start in a different direction. The Maldives were far off the beaten path and he would not expect his enemies even to think he might head there. A little time was what he needed. Engineer Ellenbroek was already talking about losing speed through a fouled bottom. He wanted to get somewhere to careen the ship and scrape her. That was no substitute for a dockyard job, but they were not going to have any dockyard jobs in the Indian Ocean, and anything would help.

Adjutant von Guerard, who was in charge of the wireless station, heard so many messages from English warships that he set up a twenty-four-hour monitoring system. Next day Guerard reported that not fewer than sixteen ships were obviously in the Indian Ocean, searching for the *Emden*. Captain von Müller had not moved a moment too soon to escape the 'heat' generated around the Bay of Bengal. The news was no surprise to von Müller, but it did make him a bit philosophical, and he confided to First Officer von Mücke that he really did not expect the ship to survive many more weeks. Already they had struck the most important blow of any German unit against the British enemy, and had demoralized British shipping across the world. But it could not last forever. This sobering assessment caused von Mücke, a man in his middle thirties, to contemplate his own death for the first time, and he waxed equally philosophical in the wardroom.

So that day was one of sober reflection for the officers of *Emden*, who could be proud of their ship and its record, but who must feel a little gloomy about the prospects. They would have felt much better had they known just how their little ship had incommoded the whole British naval war effort already, and it certainly had done just that.

Britain wanted action from her navy. Late in August a plan had been devised to intercept German destroyers off Heligoland, using two light cruisers and two destroyer flotillas, and several submarines. Three battle-cruisers were added to the force at the last minute, and the First Light Cruiser Squadron as well. Altogether it was a strangely made operation, with the Admiralty informed after the fact of the detachment of the ships, and the original destroyer-cruiser-submarine combination knew nothing of the coming of the support ships. As it turned out, the support ships saved the day, for the Germans spotted the submarine-destroyer combination and sent out all available light cruisers. The destroyer force found itself on 28 August in a hornet's nest, with light cruisers all around them, wearing the wrong sort of flags. Admiral Beatty, leading his cruiser force, rushed to the rescue, knocked out two German light cruisers and retired. In all, the Germans lost three light cruisers, one destroyer, and suffered serious damage to three other light cruisers with 1,200 casualties. The British lost no ships, and suffered some damage to the cruiser *Arethusa* and three destroyers. The British hailed a great naval victory, which depressed the Germans mightily, so the adventures of the *Emden* in the Indian Ocean did much to raise German morale in early September. Later that month, the British sent a cruiser force off the Dutch coast, and lost three old armoured cruisers, *Cressy, Hogue* and *Aboukir*, to German submarines, and Winston Churchill, who had been riding high, suddenly began to feel the pressure of public displeasure. The adventures of *Emden* in the last days of September did nothing to strengthen his position.

Having continued the depredation of the British ocean for weeks, suddenly the *Emden* disappeared at the end of September, which made the British more uneasy than ever. Von Müller reached the Maldives on 29 September, and immediately took on fuel. He sent the *Markomannia* back to find *Pontoporos*, which had been diverted to a rendezvous, and take off her coal. *Markomannia* would then go into the Dutch East Indies and buy whatever provisions were available. It seemed unlikely that even *Tromp* would recall the name of the collier that had been with *Emden* when she came through the strait. It all seemed so long ago. After leaving *Markomannia*, von Müller steamed to the Chagos Archipelago, a group of islands so deserted that most sea captains forgot they were on the charts. Here he set about doing what could be done at sea to put the ship into its best fighting trim. She was cleaned, and canted in the harbour so her plates could be scraped. The tubes in all her boilers were changed for new ones. Half the boilers were shut down at all times, and they were thoroughly cleaned, and the condensers were overhauled.

All this was occurring in the first week of October, as the British searched high and low (in all the wrong places) for the *Emden*, and as Admiral von Spee made ready to begin his destructions along the Pacific coast of South America. The German cruisers were very much on British minds. Their elusiveness gave them a mystique that could not be denied.

14

Coronel

The *Monmouth*'s shoot was not precisely a success. The geese were there all right, and the gunners were skilful enough. By all rights a good goose should stay near the water, and this is where the gunners lurked, along the shallows of the bay. They shot two dozen geese, until a curious shepherd wandered down from his hill and asked them what they wanted them for.

'Geese,' said a young lieutenant from *Monmouth*. 'One eats them.'

'Kelp geese?' asked the islander in his rustic tones. 'Never heard of a man eating a kelp goose. Pigs won't touch 'em.' So the huntsmen learned that they had been at the wrong place at the wrong time. 'Up there,' said the shepherd, pointing to a flattish hill a mile or so away, 'they's upland geese up there. That's what you want.'

However, duty called, and the hunters returned to the ships empty-handed and chastened with experience. They found that *Good Hope* was expected at any moment from her excursion into Orange Bay, and that the squadron would sail. It was 3 October and Admiral Cradock had new orders from London. He was to patrol between Punta Arenas and Valparaiso.

Admiral Cradock still had Orange Bay on his mind, and on 5 October he organized another foray into that water, but again found the bay empty. When that fruitless mission ended, he turned north-ward. The Admiralty's decoding of the long German message had just come through, and now he knew that von Spee was in the area, and that action might not be far off. Cradock hoped for some reinforcements, but instead of sending him more ships, the Admiralty decided to create a whole new search force under Rear-Admiral Archibald Stoddart. It would do Cradock no good to argue that the ships assigned to him could scarcely defeat von Spee without a miracle. *Canopus*, his 'battleship' was fit for nothing but port guard duty, and his two armoured cruisers and light cruiser, and auxiliary cruiser were no match for the German guns. He had already warned

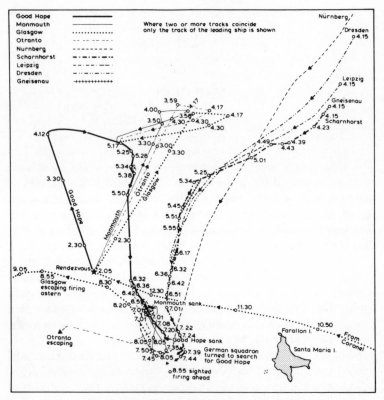

The Battle of Coronel, 1 November 1914

London about *Canopus* and London, in its enigmatic way, had not replied. That was his answer. So, he must make do.

For the next week, Admiral Cradock searched the nooks and crannies of the Tierra del Fuego, duty that was dangerous enough without having to think about a powerful enemy. Here Cradock located a coaling base that he marked down for the future, but that was all the squadron got out of the excursion. *Good Hope* then went back to the Falklands so that the Admiral could find the governor. The other ships of the squadron went up to Coronel. *Monmouth's* look-outs saw smoke on 13 October and chased a ship for three hours before coming up to discover that it was a Frenchman. They saw nothing else but the fleet of German colliers and freighters anchored in Coronel's bay, and thus immune to them, within the safety of neutral waters.

Admiral Cradock was quite put out with the Chileans and particularly the Chilean Navy. The sentiment here for the Germans was unmistakable; even so it was more than an insult when the wireless stations tracked the British squadron and then made reports about its whereabouts and strength each day that could not help but get to von Spee's ears. Cradock complained to the Chilean naval authorities. The Chileans replied that their messages were meant for their own forces. Then why were they sent in the clear, asked Admiral Cradock. The Chilean admiral apologized. He had to send messages in the clear, he said, because every time the Navy developed a new cipher and turned it over to the wireless stations ashore, they sold the cipher to Argentina's Navy (Chile's natural enemy) and so it was no use trying to use a cipher. If the explanation was logical, in a South American sort of way, it still did not help Admiral Cradock out, but he continued his unrelenting search for the enemy.

Had Cradock encountered von Spee at this juncture the results of the action would have been very even. For von Spee was heading across the two thousand miles from the Marquesas to Easter Island, with only his two heavy cruisers and the *Nürnberg* and his supply ships tagging along behind. On 12 October they had arrived at Easter Island, as Admiral Cradock searched around the unfriendly waters of Cape Horn. And here they met the *Dresden* and the *Leipzig*, and the German strength suddenly shot up remarkably. *Karlsruhe* was half expected to join up but nothing had been heard from her, so the others would move along. The German squadron assembled then, a thousand miles from the Chilean coast. When the Germans arrived they found that the people of Easter Island, unencumbered by wireless sets, knew nothing about the war. Admiral von Spee did not enlighten them, since this place was Chilean territory, and legally he should only remain for twenty-four hours. Actually it suited his purpose to stay much longer, so he let sleeping dogs lie.

The squadron remained at Easter Island for a week. At the very beginning of the stay, *Nürnberg* collided with a collier, the *Baden*, and her port propeller was bent. The Admiral ordered immediate repairs, which meant the little cruiser had to be run into shallow water and at low tide canted over at least fifteen degrees to starboard. The other ships took on supplies in a leisurely fashion. Admiral von Spee had half a dozen supply ships in his train, and many more holed up along the Chilean coast waiting for him. It was a very pleasant feeling, but von Spee could not linger too long here. His purpose was to get into the Atlantic, where it was conceivable that he could cruise between

South America and Africa, cutting the British lifelines, and with all these supply ships, last an indefinite time, and then dash back to Germany.

Even as von Spee prepared carefully for his coming run around South America, and faced the prospects of meeting at least one British squadron, the pressure in London was so great that Cradock, who had been working around the Falklands, was ordered to take his squadron into the Pacific. Admiral Stoddart would take over the Atlantic search, with a far more formidable squadron, consisting of the *Carnarvon, Cornwall* and *Bristol*, all cruisers, the auxiliary cruisers *Macedonia* and *Orama*, and the battle-cruiser *Defence* which had originally been assigned to Cradock. Why Cradock was not simply reinforced, rather than supplanted, was one of the mysteries of the day. Its answer lay in the hysteria in London; those German cruisers simply must be wiped out and so every bit of force had to be used. But not knowing where the cruisers were, the Admiralty wanted to patrol the greatest possible area. So the forces were spread thin. Cradock had only his ships at hand, and the promise of the *Canopus*. But that vessel's value to the squadron was indicated on 15 October, the day that she was supposed to arrive at the Falklands to join Cradock. The end of the day came, and no *Canopus*. The 16th went by and she did not show up, and the same was true on 17 October. She finally came wheezing in on the night of 18 October, in such dreadful shape from her short sea voyage that three more days were needed to make her as ready for sea as she would ever be. London had her listed at 17 knots, which might have been her speed on the day she was commissioned. But in October 1914, *Canopus* barely made 12 knots under optimum conditions. The dreadful condition of the ship caused Cradock to inform London that as long as he had *Canopus* with him, he could make only 12 knots. London's attention was elsewhere; there were too many fish to be fried just then, and Cradock's very sensible warning that he could not hope to defeat von Spee under the circumstances, went right over London's head.

On 18 October Admiral von Spee was almost ready to sail from Easter Island. The *Nürnberg*'s propeller had been straightened out. The English cattle rancher at Easter Island, from whom they had bought beef and mutton, had been paid off in French gold from the Marquesas, and old Mrs Routledge, who had relatives in England had written them all over the past few days, and handed the letters to Admiral von Spee personally to post for her when he reached his next port. He was very jolly about it and she quite expected that. It was not often that a civilized ship called at Easter, and the mere fact that this squadron was German was hardly a consideration at all. It was not as if they were at war or anything like that, said Mrs Routledge. Quite so, said Admiral von Spee. He was pleased to oblige the lady. A few live animals were taken aboard the warships to augment the beef the butchers had been dressing for a week, and the emptied colliers were sent off to Chilean ports to fill up their bunkers and given rendezvous points. That afternoon of 18 October, the squadron sailed for the Juan Fernandez Islands just off South America, fifteen hundred miles away.

On 22 October the squadron celebrated the birthday of the Empress at sea, with an inspection and extra rations of beer for the men. Prince Franz Joseph broke out champagne to drink his aunt's good health. Spirits were high; although the more sober-minded among the officers took the occasion to assess their personal chances of survival for the next few weeks or months, they were anything but downcast. Not so the British. Admiral Cradock was appalled at the condition of *Canopus* and as he set out to obey his orders and move to the west coast, he again told London what he could to secure some assistance. He was going 'around the Horn', but would send *Canopus* to make her way through the Straits of Magellan, because he was not sure she would survive the Horn journey if the weather roughened. Having said that, he asked once more that *Defence* be sent on to him, as promised. But London reacted with a deaf ear to the plea: 'DEFENCE IS TO REMAIN ON THE EAST COAST UNDER ORDERS OF STODDART. THIS WILL LEAVE SUFFICIENT FORCE ON EACH SIDE IN CASE THE HOSTILE CRUISERS APPEAR ...'

London still believed, against all evidence, that the Cradock squadron could somehow match up to von Spee's in strength, and Winston Churchill kept mentioning *Canopus* as if she were really still a fighting ship.

The Germans arrived at Mas a Fuera, a rocky islet in the Juan Fernandez group. There they coaled on 26 October, in the shadow of the 3,000-foot mountain, and made their last preparations for the run along the Chilean coast. They were about four hundred miles west of Valparaiso. The British squadron, just then, was assembling three hundred miles north of Valparaiso on the Chilean coast. That day, Admiral Cradock sent the *Glasgow* down to Coronel, the port of Concepción, with despatches for the British consul. He had access to a powerful wireless transmitter and could reach London quickly, and at the consulate they maintained a complete file of all Admiralty telegrams for Cradock. London was to be told that the squadron was now on the look-out for von Spee.

So *Glasgow* headed south. When she was opposite Valparaiso she picked up the signals of a German warship not more than a hundred and fifty miles away. It was actually *Leipzig*. That same day, as Admiral von Spee coaled at Mas a Fuera, Admiral Cradock informed the plodding old *Canopus* of his plans. He would wait for the return of *Glasgow* from delivering her messages, and then all ships would assemble at Mas a Fuera for coaling.

On the night of 29 October, von Spee was moving off Valparaiso, close enough that the men of the ships could see the lights of the city. But he was not nearly so much interested in what he could see as what he could hear. All night long the air waves hummed with messages from German shore stations. The German espionage network on this coast was excellent, and they had the British pin-pointed. In the morning, when Admiral Cradock stood off the roads at Vallenar, Admiral von Spee knew. A few minutes after *Glasgow* appeared at Coronel, Admiral von Spee knew. The British were not asleep. *Glasgow* had collected German cipher wireless transmissions all the way down the coast, but these had to be sent to London for decoding, and could not be expected back for several days. So while *Glasgow* had in hand all the information needed about the movements of von Spee there was no way to read it. Commander Hirst, the squadron's assistant intelligence officer, was aboard *Glasgow*, and he noted the heavy German traffic in a message to Admiral Cradock. Cradock then began a search for the Germans, and the squadron's ships moved apart to search. *Glasgow* searched the coast around Coronel but found nothing. *Otranto* cruised to Puerto Monte, but there met Chileans so fiercely pro-German that her officers could get no information at all. But *Otranto* did find the German squadron. At one o'clock on the morning of 31 October she located the call sign of the *Leipzig* at a point very close to Coronel.

As these events were occurring in South American waters, there was more than a little excitement in London. On 28 October Prince Louis of Battenberg had resigned as First Sea Lord, prompted by a public campaign against him because he was related to the ruling German Hohenzollern family. But if the reasoning was wrong, there were grounds to believe that the shake-up was still right; Battenberg was anything but a strong figure, and with him in command, Winston Churchill was running every phase of naval operations. Churchill could be a brilliant strategist. He also could be stubborn and determined, even when wrong, as in the case of the attitude he had taken toward Admiral Cradock and the chase of von Spee. Actually, at the end of October, London was not at all sure that von Spee was going to turn up right away. 'The situation on the west seems safe,' was one appreciation of the situation, 'because a Japanese battleship (*Idzumo*) and cruiser (*Hizen*) and a British light cruiser (*Newcastle*) are moving across the northern Pacific ....' These were supposed to be on the west coast of South America soon, and it was indicated they would somehow help Cradock out. Actually the *Hizen* was at Honolulu, probably prompted there by the two appearances of *Nürnberg* in recent weeks, and the *Idzumo* was far north of Cradock. The Admiralty continued to deny Cradock the use of the *Defence*, and apparently the *Canopus* was not quite so badly off as Cradock had been led to believe, for she was making 16.5 knots. But Cradock had already decided he could not work with her and had left her behind.

A message was sent by the 'new brooms' to Cradock to comfort him and assure him that he would not be expected to act without *Canopus*, or until an adequate replacement for that ship could be assigned. But the message never reached Admiral Cradock for he had grown weary of arguing with London and sailed on the evening of 21 October. When the *Leipzig* was located close to Coronel, Cradock decided the time had come to act. He knew, and his officers knew, that by choosing to fight the enemy they were going to almost certain doom. The statistics told the story:

Ship	Class	Built	Tonnage	Speed	Guns
		British Squadron			
Good Hope	Armoured Cruiser	1907	11,000	24	8 8.2-inch 6 5.9-inch
Monmouth	Armoured Cruiser	1903	9,800	22	14 6-inch
Glasgow	Light Cruiser	1911	4,800	25	2 6-inch 10 4-inch
Otranto	Armed Merchantman	not reported	not reported	17	4 4.7-inch
		German Squadron			
Scharnhorst	Armoured Cruiser	1907	11,000	24	8 8.2-inch 6 5.9-inch
Gneisenau	Armoured Cruiser	1907	11,000	24	8 8.2-inch 6 5.9-inch
Nürnberg	Light Cruiser	1908	3,400	23	10 4.1-inch
Leipzig	Light Cruiser	1906	3,200	23	10 4.1-inch
Dresden	Light Cruiser	1909	3,500	24.5	10 4.1-inch

The comparison did not show all the differences. The Germans ships were more modern, better armoured, and better equipped. They had been at sea for two years, and their crews were well trained. The British squadron's *Good Hope* and *Monmouth* had been mobilized at the outbreak of the war, and their crews were new and untried. The Admiralty had taken a stern attitude toward 'waste' of ammunition, so Cradock had not fired their guns once in all the time since the outbreak of war. Further, though it was not known at the moment, the German gunnery was superior and their ammunition was better. The British armour-piercing shells of *Monmouth* and *Good Hope* were incapable of piercing the armour of *Gneisenau* and *Scharnhorst*; the ammunition was obsolete, and so were the fuses of the 4-inch and 6-inch guns.

Admiral Cradock was very upset by London's attitude toward him. Winston Churchill had practically indicated that Cradock did not have the courage to seek out and engage the enemy, and that his continued requests, for more strength were unwarranted and possibly cowardly. The Admiral (Troubridge) who had let the *Goeben* and the *Breslau* slip through the British Mediterranean fleet had been tried by court martial, and although he was acquitted as he most certainly ought to have been, the stain of it remained. Cradock had observed all this behaviour in London, and he had written to a friend just a few days before: 'I will take care I do not suffer the fate of poor Troubridge.'

So now, faced with the certain information that if *Leipzig* was off Coronel, so must von Spee be there, Admiral Cradock decided to go after the enemy with his vastly inferior force. And if that final wire from the Admiralty, telling him to wait for help ever reached him (which seems doubtful) then it was too late and he was committed already in his mind.

Admiral Cradock ordered *Glasgow* to meet him fifty miles west of Coronel at noon on the next day, and he began sailing to that point. *Glasgow*, before she headed out, delivered the last messages to the consul at Coronel, and then sailed. When the consul sent the message that Cradock was going out to engage the enemy, and it reached London, the new Admiralty Board read, checked the message file, and expressed shock that Cradock had been denied the use of the *Defence*, when he obviously needed her. That order was rescinded, and the *Defence* was ordered to Cradock. But it was all done on 3 November, much too late. At noon on 1 November Admiral Cradock reached the rendezvous point, and the four ships of the squadron soon joined up.

Cradock formed the squadron into a broad line to travel along the coast, covering a front of forty-five miles, and began moving northward, hoping to find the *Leipzig*. The search had just begun when *Glasgow*, which was closest to the Chilean coast, noted a blur of smoke on the horizon. Captain Luce turned, signalled and began speeding towards the smoke. The rest of the squadron followed.

The Germans for whom they were looking had been busy that morning. On the day before they had hoped to bottle up *Glasgow* in Coronel harbour but they had arrived too late. So this morning they were searching, although it was Sunday and the ships were generally more relaxed this morning than usual. *Titania* had an adventure of her own — she captured a Norwegian sailing barque single-handed. She had stopped the ship for a routine investigation because it was lying low in the water, and sure enough found the Norwegian was carrying a cargo of coal for Admiral Cradock's ships. So she was taken in tow by *Titania*, which was then ordered to the Juan Fernandez Islands to await the return of the squadron's fighting ships.

The cruisers stopped several ships this morning, too, for the area was busy with traffic. But they all turned out to be neutrals, carrying neutral cargoes, and the same was true in the afternoon. At four o'clock in the afternoon the men began to make the ship ready for night. The decks were scrubbed again, and all the debris of a Sunday was carefully put away for disposal later.

Suddenly the bugle blew and the drums were beaten, calling the men to action — but everyone knew it was the routine nightly call, which meant to go to their battle stations, check their guns and equipment and make sure all was shipshape for the night. The gunners oiled their guns and made sure the covers were on to protect them from dampness. The engineers toured the engine rooms to make sure no cotton waste was lying about, and that the stokers had not slopped coal around the decks. The torpedo men checked their 'fish', those weapons so prized by cruisers in this period. The deck officers checked the upper works, and the boats, to be sure they were seaworthy and had all their emergency equipment. The medical officers checked their supplies. And at the end, the first officer of each ship reported to his captain that the ship was clear, ready for action, and battened down.

All this activity had taken a scant quarter hour, so well trained were the German crews. The men stood poised at their battle stations, waiting for the usual order to dismiss that would enable those off watch to go below. But the order did not come, for just as the first officers were reporting, the foremast look-out of the *Scharnhorst* sang out: 'Two clouds of smoke on the horizon ...'

A moment later came the word that the two clouds had become three clouds. On his bridge, Admiral von Spee strained to peer through his binoculars, but the ships were too far away and he could see nothing. Still, the chances were very strong that these were the British. What other ships would be travelling three together? So instead of the all clear, the battle stations order was repeated and the call to clear the ship for action rang through the *Scharnhorst*, and almost immediately afterwards, through the other German cruisers. At 4.20 the drums were rolling and the battle flags were rising to the tops. Five minutes later Admiral von Spee had his first glimpse of the enemy; two ships suddenly appeared on his horizon, and he identified them as enemy warships.

'Full speed ahead,' he called to Captain Schultz, without taking his eyes from the eyepiece of his glasses. He recognized the *Monmouth* and the *Glasgow*. The signal bells clanged and the wireless operators began calling the other ships, transmitting every order of the Admiral in seconds. The *Gneisenau* was back a number of miles, and two of her boilers had been taken down for cleaning, but that was immediately put to rights, and she prepared for the action that was coming. Her stokers speeded the pace of their shovelling, and soon she came in sight of the thick cloud of smoke pouring from the funnels of *Scharnhorst*. The Admiral did not care who saw him now, for he was ready for battle.

Up ahead, the look-outs of *Glasgow* had spotted the Germans just three minutes after *Scharnhorst* was alerted. They had altered course to the south-east to run toward the enemy, and soon Admiral Cradock heard from Captain Luce that *Scharnhorst*, *Gneisenau*, and one light cruiser were in sight. Then Luce saw *Scharnhorst* turn toward his ship, to put himself between the land and that British ship. *Glasgow* had no wish to be cut off from the rest, so she turned, and went back to join *Good Hope*.

Von Spee turned for two reasons, one to keep the British away from the neutral waters of Chile, in case any of them should run for safety; and the more important reason, for he did not expect his enemies to avoid battle, was to seek the lee position, so that the wind would blow the smoke of his ships away, and the light would be behind him, and not in his eyes as the sun set. It was a distinct advantage of position.

At 4.30 the air was crackling with messages from both sides, including messages from Admiral Cradock to *Canopus* in case she should be coming up as she ought to be. But *Canopus* was two hundred and fifty miles back, and could not possibly arrive in time to weight the battle. Indeed, she could not arrive for a whole day. Even so, Admiral von Spee sensed that Admiral Cradock was signalling to the British command somewhere, and he tried to jam the messages.

By five o'clock, *Scharnhorst* was making 20 knots, although half an hour earlier not all her boilers had been in operation. He still thought he was facing three British ships, for *Good Hope* still had not come in sight. The British steered a course that gradually forced the Germans to look into the sun, but as the day came to an end, this would cease to be a disadvantage, and the Germans would be masked against the high range of the Cordillera mountains, while the English would be silhouetted against the last rays of light on the seaward horizon.

The two squadrons moved southward, each commander assembling his ships and making sure they were battle ready.

At 5.47 *Good Hope* returned and the other ships formed a line of battle behind her, *Monmouth*, then *Glasgow*, then *Otranto*. Admiral Cradock turned south-east, trying to wrest the lee position from the Germans, but with the wind against him, he could not manage it. *Otranto* could not take the buffeting of the rising seas and maintain the speed necessary to cut in. She was making 16 knots and that was virtually her maximum. When Admiral Cradock had satisfied himself that this was the case, and he could not take the lee, he turned south.

Admiral von Spee was trying to get his ships into position for an action at sunset. Until then he was content to stay away from the enemy, for *Nürnberg* and *Dresden* still had not caught up with the rest of the squadron. But at 6.18, Admiral Cradock forced the action. The battle flags of the British ships went up, and he increased his speed to 17 knots telling *Otranto* she *must* keep up. He sent another message to *Canopus*, giving his position and asking hers. *Canopus* replied: she had turned inland, and was now further away than ever. So there was no hope from that quarter. With his smaller force, and smaller guns, Admiral Cradock's one chance might be to outmanoeuvre the enemy, and strike with the light in the eyes of the Germans. This was precisely what he wanted to do, von Spee told himself, and he would not permit it to make any difference. Von Spee was totally confident, as well he might be. For although *Good Hope* was larger than the two big German cruisers, the more modern German ships had far more effective guns, and as for *Monmouth*, she was outclassed by both cruisers. The *Glasgow* was bigger than any of the German light cruisers, but she was only one and the German guns were as good as hers. Three German cruisers were more than a match for her, obviously. As for *Otranto*, she was more or less in the class of *Titania*, which Admiral von Spee had sent away. *Otranto* carried four 4.7-inch guns, and might even hold her own against a destroyer, but not against a light cruiser. Altogether the British force was completely outclassed, and this meant in the training of the men as well as the number and condition of the ships. For, as Admiral Cradock knew very well, his men were scarcely more than reserve-trained. Three months earlier the vast majority of his officers and men had been selling bonds in the City, or working steamers across the seven seas, or fishing in the north country. *Otranto* had been running the Atlantic as a liner, and *Good Hope* and *Monmouth* were both in the 'mothball' fleet. Only *Glasgow* was manned by regulars, and it was the only ship whose guns and gunners had been tested thoroughly. The German East Asia Squadron, on the other hand, had a long tradition of seamanship; for the last few years one of its ships had either won or come in second in the competition for the Kaiser's gunnery cup. Half the officers and men were old hands at their job, while the other half had been licked into shape since coming 'out east' in the spring.

Still, Cradock was risking all on the desperate chance that he could close and take advantage of the sun. But Admiral von Spee was not falling into the trap. When he saw the British ships turning toward him in a battle line, he ordered the German cruisers to run, *Dresden* still had not joined up; the sun had not set but was in the Germans' eyes. The range was 18,000 yards, and would close rapidly if von Spee did not turn, but he turned away, just enough to keep the range as it was, and he watched carefully.

The wind was freshening, and the ship plunged into the water with the underslung cutwater, sending up heavy spray that reached back to von Spee's bridge. The seas were heavy enough to give von Spee pause, for they would interfere with the aiming of the small cruisers in particular. But there was nothing to be done about that. Even aboard the *Scharnhorst*, the men were getting a soaking; the sea plunged through the forward turret on one particularly heavy dip, and soaked the men even in the magazine below it.

The day was fast waning. Finally, at a few minutes before a quarter to seven, von Spee was ready. The sun was setting and in a minute or two would no longer interfere with his gunners. The British ships were outlined clearly against the setting sun and would stay outlined against the orange and purple that would hang on in the sky. Behind the German squadron were the mountains, covered by a heavy layer of cloud that dulled the outlines of the cruisers. Admiral von Spee gave the order to move toward the enemy. As he did so, Admiral Cradock took pity on the *Otranto*. She had no business among this crowd, and she was certain to be destroyed without giving much advantage to the British — unless letting her be used as a target would be called an advantage, and all that might do would be to prolong the battle. She could not possibly affect the outcome otherwise. So *Otranto* turned away, and then there were three British cruisers facing the five German ships.

As the sun began to fall below the horizon, Admiral von Spee manoeuvred until he was 12,000 yards from the enemy. Then as the sun dropped, the squadrons were just over 11,000 yards apart, and von Spee gave the order to open fire. In a purist's sense, he was hardly ready. His ships were straggling, not in a neat line, and *Dresden* had just managed to come up to a point seven cables behind *Leipzig*. But the Admiral was impatient. This next hour, in the waning daylight, would give him every advantage. If the battle were prolonged into the darkness, no one knew what might occur; the moon could give good enough light, but there were various rain squalls forming over the mountains, and they might move out to sea, and the British might yet escape him, or even worse, might be in a position to do serious damage to his squadron if the weather changed.

Without some such interference even an armchair student could have predicted the course of the battle. The German squadron could fire a total broadside of 4,750 pounds, as compared to the British squadron's 2,100 pounds. Or, in the terms of the battle: the *Scharnhorst* could fire 2,200 pounds of shells against *Good Hope*'s 1,200; *Gneisenau*, which would address herself to the *Monmouth*, could fire 2,200 pounds against the English cruiser's 600 pounds; and *Leipzig*, *Nürnberg* and *Dresden*, could each fire 186 pounds against *Glasgow*'s 325. *Glasgow*, alone among the English ships, had enough power to cause her smaller enemies to be wary for it was conceivable that she could knock one or two of them out.

Scharnhorst fired the first salvo, which landed 500 yards short of the *Good Hope*. Her second salvo bracketed the British flagship, and the third struck squarely on the forward turret, a flash of flame rose up, and the 9.2-inch gun of that turret was knocked out, right then. The *Gneisenau* was only moments behind the flagship in opening fire, and in three minutes the *Monmouth* was on fire in the forecastle and the 8.2-inch guns of the *Gneisenau* were booming with the accuracy that had won her the Kaiser Cup in 1913, just the spring before. The

Leipzig and the *Dresden* opened fire on the *Glasgow*, too, but the range was too great. *Nürnberg* was out of position, and did not fire at all in the beginning. All the British ships began firing rapidly, but the light was now dreadful for them. The Germans could see the shell splashes in the water but the British could not see theirs because the German ships were almost lost against the darkness of the mountains and the storm that hung above them. They did not know if they were undershooting or overshooting. In fact they were overshooting, by such a margin, that the men of the *Scharnhorst* did not know they were under fire.

Captain Edwards of the *Otranto* flatly disobeyed his orders to remove himself from the battle. Seeing how things were going from the beginning, he turned about, and zigzagged towards the Germans, offering his ship as a target and trying to confuse the enemy gunners, and give the British cruisers time. But the *Gneisenau* ended that attempt by stopping its punishment of the *Monmouth* for a few moments and placing one salvo 50 yards off *Otranto*'s starboard bow, and a second one 25 yards astern. Captain Edwards knew that the third salvo would do dreadful damage to his ship, and he took *Otranto* out of an action in which it did not belong, as he knew very well.

Seven minutes after the battle began, *Leipzig* had moved in close enough, despite *Glasgow*'s fire, to begin straddling the lightest of the three English cruisers, and *Dresden* was also firing and coming close.

Sea and wind were serving the Germans well. In the beginning the smoke from *Scharnhorst* had drifted back and obscured the vision of the gunners of the *Gneisenau*, but when Admiral von Spee saw that, he ordered the *Scharnhorst* to change her relative position by a few yards, and the smoke stopped troubling the other cruisers. The wind blew the smoke down the line, far enough away not to bother the German gunners, but sometimes obscuring the smaller cruisers completely from the view of the British. And the British were further bothered by their inexperience. The Germans had learned to adjust to firing in heavy weather, but their enemies had not, and from the beginning the battle was more uneven than even the disparity in forces and guns would suggest. The *Leipzig* put one shell against the conning-tower support, which was in the sea cabin of the captain of the *Glasgow*, but Captain Luce was on the bridge and escaped the direct blow, and the shell did little other damage since it did not explode.

The fires soon broke out aboard *Good Hope* and spread. *Monmouth* took a shell in her forward turret and a long tongue of flame shot forth. The turret was silent. *Monmouth* sheered off to starboard and never did get back into position. But she continued to fight, and put one shell below the armoured deck of the *Gneisenau*, damaging the structure of one 8.2-inch turret, and blowing up the master storeroom. Water was coming in but when the damage control parties went below, they discovered the water was not from below the water-line, but came from the decks – water that had been shipped in the heavy seas, and come through the holes made by the shell.

But then the *Monmouth*'s gunners found their target again, and the cry went up: 'Fire in the after battery.' Commander Pochhammer, whose major battle function was damage control, led a crew back quickly to the battery. The danger was great, for if the fire reached the cordite in the battery it would burn and then blow, and the magazine would probably follow. Then the ship might be in serious trouble.

Pochhammer arrived in a cloud of smoke, and could see virtually nothing inside the turret. Ten minutes went by before he discovered that the shell had smashed the sheet iron around the turret, and then plunged through the deck, starting fires below. This was serious, but not as serious as if the turret had been knocked out. For although it was apparent that the Germans would win this encounter, the loss of a turret was a matter that could never be rectified at sea, and *Gneisenau* might never get home if enough damage was incurred today.

By this time the British ships were in difficulty. Von Spee's luck in getting the mountains at his back made the ships of the German squadron nearly invisible to the British gunners except when the enemy guns flashed. *Monmouth* had fires fore and aft. The fire forward was extinguished by the damage control party there, but immediately the ship was hit again the fire broke out once more.

Glasgow, having lost touch with the two light German cruisers, *Leipzig* and *Dresden*, was firing with her forward turret at *Scharnhorst* and with her after turret on *Gneisenau*, but her 6-inch shells were not very effective against the heavy armour plate of the big cruisers.

At 7.35 the distance had closed until a little over three miles separated the British and German flagships. Von Spee estimated that *Good Hope* had already been hit thirty times, and the ship was on fire in several places. As the Admiral peered through his glasses, he saw the *Good Hope* altering course, to make a torpedo run on her enemy, so he altered course as well, to be ready to dodge torpedoes. He looked over at the *Monmouth*, and saw that her whole forward section seemed to be ringed with a rosy glow that indicated dreadful fires below. Both ships were still firing their guns, but it was apparent that both of them were virtually destroyed already, while the German heavy cruisers were still barely hurt. The *Gneisenau*'s after turret had been brought back into action when a lieutenant seized a fire axe and chopped away the sheet-iron plating that had bent around her swivelling mechanism. The fires aboard both ships were under control, or had been extinguished.

The moon began to rise, further assisting the Germans by bringing the sharp silhouettes of the British ships into focus. The *Glasgow* was firing at *Dresden* when she could see her, and *Dresden* was firing back. One 4.1-inch shell struck the British light cruiser at the water-line just below the seamen's mess deck, above the port screws. The explosion stove in the side, with a hole that measured about six square feet.

Then the darkness began to close in, as the moon was obscured by the clouds drifting over from the land. Rain began to fall in sudden squalls. Through the murk Admiral von Spee could see the *Good Hope* from time to time. Then the ship was obscured by a squall for several minutes, and through the darkness came a brilliant flash of explosion and the noise following. The *Good Hope* had blown up – a shell had struck one of her magazines. When the clouds cleared away, at the point where *Good Hope* had been there was nothing to be seen. Captain Schultz ordered the *Scharnhorst* to cease fire.

Admiral von Spee took this respite to check on the condition of the other ships in his squadron. Not a man had been injured aboard the *Scharnhorst*, but what about the others? The reports were demanded and soon came: *Dresden*, no hits, no injuries. *Leipzig*, no injuries. *Gneisenau*, several hits from the guns of *Monmouth*, but only two men slightly injured. One stoker had been at his battle station forward when the six-inch shell hit there, and he had suffered several flesh wounds. A helmsman on the upper bridge had been struck by shrapnel from a shell that hit the foretop and exploded, and he had a gash in the back of one hand.

'Man the searchlight', came the order, but anyone who thought Admiral von Spee was going to rescue the survivors of the enemy flagship was wrong. The searchlights were trained on the *Monmouth*, and the guns of the *Scharnhorst* began to fire on her from one side, as those of the *Gneisenau* fired from the other. Another squall broke out, and the *Monmouth* disappeared from the Germans' view. When the squall broke, and the clouds cleared, there was again nothing to be seen where she had been.

The wind was rising and so was the sea. Admiral von Spee had the searchlights trained around in the three hundred and sixty-degree search pattern for a few minutes, but no one could see in the dark. The British ships were gone, so the order came to clear the guns and go to the alert condition for the night.

Further inshore, the *Glasgow* continued to fight the two German light cruisers that came into view occasionally, as long as anything could be seen. But finally darkness made it impossible to fight, and the *Glasgow* turned away to the north.

Admiral von Spee issued his night orders. The three light cruisers were to comb the area for sight of the enemy and report immediately. He did not know precisely what damage he had inflicted, for although he had seen the enormous explosion aboard the *Good Hope*, even if dimly, strange things happened in battle, and the British flagship might have survived and escaped. All von Spee knew was that the ship had been badly damaged and did not seem to be capable of continued fight. As for the *Monmouth*, he simply did not know, nor did anyone else, and the *Good Hope* apparently had escaped.

Actually, the *Monmouth* was badly hit. Just before Captain Luce turned north, he warned the bigger cruiser to head north-west, and thus possibly to avoid the Germans. *Monmouth* was listing badly and taking water, and most of her guns were out of action, but she was still moving, as *Glasgow* moved away and Captain Luce secured an estimate of his own damage. Only six shells had actually struck the ship, and most of these had hit in the hull in the bunker area, and were dissipated by the coal. So *Glasgow* was still in good shape.

The *Leipzig* and the *Dresden* headed out in search from the point where they had received the Admiral's orders. Von Spee took the heavy cruisers on a great circle course, to try to find any surviving ships, but *Glasgow* eluded the net; and steamed away, with *Otranto* right behind her.

The *Leipzig* soon came across a point in the ocean which was littered with debris, and the men could see British corpses in the water. They saw no survivors, or so they said. They were moving fast – 18 knots – and the Admiral had said nothing about picking up enemy survivors.

Captain von Schönberg had completely missed the action, but

Nürnberg did come across the *Dresden* and the *Leipzig*, and she was directed south to try to intercept the enemy. At about 8.30 that night a look-out spotted a warship on the port bow, and the gunnery officer wanted to open fire. Captain von Schönberg halted him: first they must identify the ship. It might be one of their own. So he waited, and the *Nürnberg* moved up on the other vessel. It soon became apparent that the other ship was listing badly, but that meant nothing to von Schönberg because he did not know what had happened in the battle. He ordered the signalmen to send recognition signals to the other ship. They were sent, once, twice, three times, but were not answered. By this time the *Nürnberg* was so close to the other ship that von Schönberg could turn on his searchlight, and when he did, he saw the white British naval ensign. Even von Schönberg was convinced that this was the enemy.

It was indeed the *Monmouth*, and she was listing so badly that she could not bring the guns of her port side to bear any longer. So von Schönberg moved the *Nürnberg* around to the port side and began firing. 'To me,' said Lieutenant Otto von Spee, son of the Admiral, 'it was dreadful to have to fire on the poor devil no longer able to defend herself, but her flag was still flying.'

The captain of the *Monmouth* tried to reach the shore, hoping at least to beach his ship. But the *Nürnberg* swept past again and again, firing at point-blank range. Finally, the *Monmouth* turned toward her enemy, and von Schönberg knew that the captain of the *Monmouth* was going to try to ram him as he came by. He moved cautiously away, and continued to fire for another fifteen minutes, as fast as the 4.1-inch guns of the little cruiser could be operated. *Monmouth* shuddered, and the shells continued to find their marks, until finally she rolled over to port and capsized. From the *Nürnberg* men could be seen sliding down the red paint of her bottom and into the sea. But nothing could be done for them. As a precautionary measure, the German cruiser's crew had filled the ship's boats with water, and they were useless. But Captain von Schönberg had no orders to rescue enemy seamen either, and so he made no attempt. *Monmouth* soon sank, and down with her went most of the crew of five hundred and forty officers and men. The survivors struggled in the high seas for perhaps a few hours, but these waters were always cold, and man's chances of survival were not great. None came back from *Monmouth*, nor any of the 900 officers and men of *Good Hope*.

The *Nürnberg* moved away from the scene. After half an hour smoke was seen to the south-east, and von Schönberg worried. But it was only the two big German armoured cruisers. Von Schönberg broke radio silence at 9.15 to report.

'I have sunk an enemy armoured cruiser,' he said.

'Bravo,' said Admiral von Spee. No one in the squadron knew whether the Admiral was being ironic or not.

15

The Hunted

Nearly halfway across the world from South America, the *Emden* had spent ten days in the Chagos Archipelago in October, and then gone back out to maraud. Her raiding was so successful that it is hard to tell whether *Emden* or the rest of the squadron caused the British more misery in the month of October, 1914. For several days she played hide-and-seek with the British heavy cruiser *Hampshire*, which arrived at the Maldives two days after von Müller sailed from Diego Garcia. The ship captured the *Clan Grant*, carrying cattle, the Blue Funnel liner *Troilus*, carrying metal and rubber for England, and the *St Egbert*, within a few days. Then came the *Chilkana*, owned by the British India Company, and the *Exford*, a collier. All but the *St Egbert* were sunk, and that ship was used to transport the crews of the others to safety. Von Müller continued to show himself every inch a gentleman of the old school.

At the end of October, as Admiral von Spee was working his way east to South America, Captain von Müller was planning a coup that would again shake London. He was going to attack the harbour of Penang on the Malay Peninsula. On 27 October he sailed for that port, and arrived just offshore at night. He waited until 4.30 in the morning, and then took *Emden* dashing into the harbour at full speed. Inside he saw the Russian light cruiser *Yemtschuk*, just as a small boat pulled away from her side: the cookboat bearing the petty officers and cooks on their way to the Penang market to shop for the day's fresh groceries. The *Emden* moved in to within 300 yards of the enemy, and torpedoed the *Yemtschuk* twice, raked her with the 4.1-inch guns, and then fought a short battle with the French destroyer *d'Iberville*, which was partially screened from the *Emden* by other ships, before rushing back out of the harbour as the city came awake. *Yemtschuk* was sunk, her back broken. Outside the harbour, *Emden* was engaged by the French destroyer *Mousquet*, and the German cruiser sank the French ship too. Unlike his comrades off South America, von Müller put

15 The British battle-cruiser *Inflexible* in 1915 one of the most powerful warships in the world

16 HMS *Invincible*

17 His Majesty King George V and Admiral Sir F. C. Doveton
Sturdee

boats overboard and sent his doctors to help rescue the survivors of the sunken French ship, but the Frenchmen swam away, preferring to risk the dangers of the sea rather than trust a German. However the French wounded were in no condition to swim, and thirty-six of them were picked up and saved, at least for a time. Several of the French sailors were badly injured and in spite of the efforts of the surgeons, they could not be saved.

Emden again made a clear getaway from the scene of the action, although this time the airwaves chattered for days, and the hunt was redoubled. The pressure from London was now unremitting: the *Emden* must be destroyed, and she must be destroyed as soon as possible no matter what the cost to Admiral Jerram and Admiral Patey.

But even as she was hunted, the *Emden* continued her raiding. She took the freighter *Newburn* on 30 October, and instead of sinking the ship, sent it into Khota Raj, on neutral Dutch Sumatra, to carry the French survivors, for no other reason than that the German doctors said they could not give the wounded adequate attention on board the *Emden*, and some would die if they were not brought ashore.

By this time Captain von Müller had been out for three months. His ship had sunk or captured twenty-three merchantmen and had terrorized two cities, sunk an enemy cruiser and an enemy destroyer, and the men had travelled aboard the *Emden* for thirty thousand miles, most of it in the heart of enemy territory, with their hunters all around them. This one little cruiser had inflicted many millions of pounds in damage to the allied cause, physically, and this said nothing of the losses to that cause by the interruption of shipping, which was virtually paralysed in the whole region. Captain von Müller was the object of a stream of messages from the admiralties of England, France, Russia, and Japan, and as the single four-ship squadron of Admiral Cradock hunted for Admiral von Spee off the South American coast, no fewer than seventy-eight allied warships were engaged in the search for the *Emden*!

On the 2 November, as Admirals Cradock and von Spee moved on converging courses off Coronel, Captain von Müller took stock. From recent captures and from the newspapers aboard the ships, he had learned that the *Pontoporos* which he had sent off to a rendezvous point, had been captured. The *Markomannia*, his own collier, had been sent off a month ago and had not been heard from since. He was depending on two other colliers, the *Buresk* and the *Exford*, both of them captured ships, which had been sent to other rendezvous points.

His problem was coal, and the signs of wear of the ship itself, which by rights was due for a major dockyard overhaul. It was simply a matter of time until something broke down, but as long as time held out, Captain von Müller was determined to cause Britain more damage. One way he could do that, and perhaps relieve some of the pressure on himself, was to wipe out the British cable and wireless station at Direction Island. At this point two sets of cables crossed. One set travelled from Australia to Zanzibar and Africa, the other set went from Australia to India. By cutting them and destroying enough of the material to delay communications for weeks, he might enlarge his own scope. So he put that plan in motion, as Admiral von Spee was destroying Admiral Cradock's squadron, and the *Emden* turned toward Direction Island on the western end of the Indian Ocean.

16

Interlude

On the night of 2 November, the sole surviving warship of the British squadron, the cruiser *Glasgow*, headed south to meet the old battleship *Canopus*, and warn her of the change in England's fortunes. As they moved away, from the bridge of the *Glasgow*, the officers could count the shells fired into *Monmouth* by *Nürnberg*: they counted seventy-five flashes before the unequal struggle ended. That was the end of the battle for them, and they began to assess the damage to their ship. She had been under fire for nearly an hour by at least three German ships, and still she had scarcely been hit. Only four of her men were wounded. As for *Otranto*, she had watched the battle helplessly, and then Captain Edwards had sailed for Montevideo to await new orders, while *Glasgow* went to Port Stanley in the Falkland Islands, still trying to find *Canopus*.

The Germans, meanwhile, had spent the night cleaning ships from the stink of cordite and the minor damage of the battle. Next morning, Admiral von Spee ran into Valparaiso, ostensibly to see if *Good Hope* had taken shelter there. Actually, he had come to trumpet his important victory, and he was furious to discover by wireless from the Chilean city that the British Admiralty, and its first lord, Winston Churchill, were denying that any battle had taken place in the sea off Coronel. Churchill of course was in the dark, until *Glasgow* reached the Falklands and reported the story of the disaster. Then, the headlines stunned all England, and much of the rest of the world. The *Emden*'s foray against Penang and the von Spee victory in the Pacific indicated a power and a determination that gave a new lift to German sailors everywhere. The propaganda value of these victories by a handful of ships was enormous, coming as it did at a time when the Battle of Ypres was proving that the contest on the Western Front was likely to be long and arduous. The submarine successes and the remarkable exploits of Admiral von Spee's tiny fleet had become wonders of the world.

The German squadron entered the Bay of Valparaiso at daybreak on 3 November. A Chilean torpedo boat came out to investigate the strange warships, identified them at long range, turned and went back inside. Soon a pilot boat appeared and at eleven that morning the *Scharnhorst, Gneisenau* and *Nürnberg* were all anchored in the harbour. The *Leipzig, Dresden,* and the colliers stayed outside because neutrality rules stipulated that only three belligerent warships of one nation might be in one port at one time.

The von Spee squadron was greeted with joy by the German community, and particularly the maritime community, for nearly a dozen German freighters were in the harbour, tied down there by the presence of the British outside. Now that Admiral Cradock had been defeated, they hope to regain the freedom of the seas.

The moment the German squadron came in sight, the British authorities in Valparaiso began making protests, but in the atmosphere of that day, no one listened to them. However, the British soon informed the Chilean authorities that von Spee had spent a week at Easter Island, in direct violation of Chilean neutrality laws, a fact they had learned when a British warship called at the island. This matter was serious, for it was raised officially with the Chilean government and could not be ignored. Admiral von Spee was called upon by Minister von Eckert to give him some plausible story, and the Admiral pleaded grave difficulties with his fleet after the long voyage across the Pacific, and was so utterly charming about it that the Chileans said no more. After all, von Spee did have the strongest fleet in South American waters at the moment.

The Admiral's prime reason for coming in to Valparaiso was to be in touch with Berlin. The long weeks at sea had taken toll of his ships, and the experience gained had shown him that the original German plan for cruiser warfare was sound only on a temporary basis. He could not hope to survive long in these waters using colliers that sneaked in and out of neutral ports, while the British built an ever greater force against him. He knew his enemies would do just that, although he did not know that even as he planned the force was being built on an emergency basis. The Admiral was lucky in one sense. He could remain in Valparaiso for only twenty-four hours. He could inform Berlin and tell them his plans. Berlin could hardly get back to him with a return message before he sailed.

So the Admiral went ashore to a hero's welcome staged by the German colony. He was met at dockside by newspapermen and photographers, who snapped and questioned and tagged after the party until von Spee had made his courtesy call on the Chilean naval authorities and entered the German embassy. Members of the German colony came out to see the ships and were royally entertained. The senior officers of the squadron went to the Deutsche Klub of Valparaiso and were treated as honoured guests. Later in the day the junior officers and men were given leave, in watches, and the Chileans and the Germans greeted and entertained them. The German language newspapers in Valparaiso were given a complete account of the battle (as much as von Spee wanted to give out without assisting his enemies) and this was copied by the Spanish language newspapers that day. When the brief leave ended, the ships put back out to sea, the squadron augmented by several dozen reserve officers and men from the merchant ships in the harbour.

Actually, before Admiral von Spee had gone into Valparaiso he had not known the full extent of his victory. He suspected that the *Good Hope* had eluded him. But he learned from the Chileans, who had it from the British, who had it from the *Glasgow*'s report that day on reaching safe waters, that the *Good Hope* was not reported, and obviously had sunk. Admiral von Spee refused to join in the general rejoicing that the enemy had been trounced. For although he had won a victory, he realized better than any other why he had won, and that the odds for his survival were now less than they might have been before, had he only been able to avoid the enemy. For he knew his British cousins, and that their wrath would be enormous, and their determination to destroy his squadron would be greater than ever. Indeed, a sense of *weltschmerz* seemed to settle over the flagship as it left Valparaiso harbour. Captain Schultz felt it and so did the other senior officers. A sense of impending disaster went with them as they steamed out of this neutral port.

Admiral von Spee set course for Mas a Fuera. Here he had made rendezvous with the other cruisers and the supply ships. When he arrived, he found the *Leipzig* there already, with a prize, the four-masted French barque *Valentine*, which was carrying a cargo of Cardiff coal, again for the English. The French captain had been so slow to surrender that Captain Haun had almost sunk her before even boarding, but finally she had stopped, and the difficulty was explained. The French ship had been at sea since long before the war began, and her captain knew nothing about it. When the Germans informed him that they were about to capture Paris (wishful thinking) the captain was desolated, and subsided into total silence. That ship's coal was welcome, and next day, 6 November, *Dresden* came into the harbour, escorting the steamer *San Sacramento*. But she was not a prize, rather a gift. She had been chartered by the German government at San Francisco, to bring 7,000 tons of coal to the squadron, and 1,000 tons of much needed tinned foodstuffs. On 9 November one would have thought Mas a Fuera was a German possession, not Chilean. There were thirteen German ships and their prizes in the harbour that day, and they were all busy either coaling or shifting cargo. *Gneisenau* was assigned to empty the two sailing ships of coal, which was a most difficult task because the yards got in the way and the sailing ships lay so low in the water that the gangways rigged between vessels seemed to go straight up. The weather grew rough at midday, and by afternoon the sailing ships had to be moved away lest they crash against the sides of the cruiser and do serious damage to the warship. The *Valentine*, nearly new, one of the last of the Cape Horn sailers, was destroyed before they left Mas a Fuera. The *Prinz Eitel Friedrich* which had been in Admiral von Spee's entourage for too long, was prepared to go out on her own as a raider now. Admiral von Spee found her a nuisance, neither good stout collier nor a fighting ship that could hold her own in battle. She had her place, but it was a lonely one, out on the sea, searching for unwary enemy shipping. And as her captain and crew knew very well, her life as a raider could scarcely be a long one unless she had more luck than anyone expected. For while the raider could stand up against such a ship as *Otranto* perhaps, she would fall beneath the guns of any real warship, and as everyone knew the British must soon strengthen their presence in these waters.

These days of respite were spent making the squadron as sleek and strong as possible under the conditions that existed. No one was under any illusions that the passage around the Horn and across the Atlantic was going to be an easy one.

17

The End of the *Emden*

On the night of 8 November, as the officers of the flagship were invited to dine aboard the *Prinz Eitel Friedrich* in Mas a Fuera harbour, and sample the fine supply of French and German wines that this luxurious liner still carried, aboard the little cruiser *Emden*, in the Indian Ocean, Captain von Müller was making preparations for his assault next day on Direction Island (one of the Cocos Islands). He expected a serious defence here, since it was only logical that such an important communications point would be protected. He decided to send Kapitänleutnant von Mücke, so important did he consider the missions, and with von Mücke would go two officers, Leutnant Gyssling, and Leutnant Schmidt, thirty seamen, fifteen technicians and two wireless operators, to make sure that all was destroyed in a proper manner.

That night the little cruiser stood off the island, fifty miles out so that she would not alert her enemies. In the morning the fourth funnel was raised again, for all during this voyage Captain von Müller had noted that it worked wonders in allaying any fears that his enemies had as he came near. It should work again. Well before dawn the ship began to move. First Officer von Mücke made sure his men's guns were oiled and ready, and he commandeered all four of the ship's light machine-guns for the task ahead. At six o'clock von Mücke reported to the bridge in his white uniform and topee, and the ship stopped to put the two boats and the steam launch over the side. The launch would tow the boats in through the reef, two miles, to the harbour. The men got into the boats and the steam launch took its tow. In half an hour they were ashore.

The Germans' worries about British defences were needless. Only a few dozen civilians manned the wireless and cable station, and in the face of arms there was no point in trying to conceal anything; the Germans would have found it anyhow. So they told their enemies where the cables were located. Director D.A.G. de H. Farrant, the director of the Eastern Extension Telegraph Company's offices here, was called from his bungalow, and when he came down he delivered the keys to all the buildings, and the congratulations of the staff to von Mücke. For what, asked the Germans? For winning the Iron Cross, said Farrant, with a grin. Didn't they know? Berlin had broadcast an announcement that every man of the *Emden* had been awarded the Iron Cross for the ship's performance.

Von Mücke was not overburdened by a sense of humour so he did not laugh at the thought of his enemies informing him of his good (and their bad) luck. He busied himself with the task at hand, destruction of the communications equipment and it was done quickly in a thorough Teutonic fashion.

An hour went by, and another. The tasks of destruction took longer than von Mücke had anticipated. Nor did he know that the real reason for the smile on the face of Director Farrant was not the Iron Cross awards but the fact that he had managed to send off a message before the Germans landed. Before six o'clock, as *Emden* was making her way to the point of departure, she had been observed by a Chinese cook at the station, who had informed the wireless men. One of the wireless men had climbed to the top of the wireless building and looked out over the entrance to the harbour. He had seen the ship with four funnels and deduced that it was HMS *Minotaur*, a British cruiser which had been in this area for some time. But he had gone off to the director's house to report. He had met the station doctor *en route* and the doctor had brought out his glasses and taken a look. He had seen then that the fourth funnel was fake, and that the ship was not flying any flag, as a self-respecting British man-of-war was certain to be doing here. The two took this information to Director Farrant, who was just struggling into his clothes, and he ordered them to send a message: 'S.O.S. Strange ship in entrance to harbour.'

It was done, sent several times with the station's signature before the transmission was suddenly jammed. Then Director Farrant was positive that he was dealing with the *Emden*. He changed frequencies and sent one last message: S.O.S. *EMDEN* HERE. That message was sent continuously in spite of jamming from the ship, until the moment that von Mücke's men entered the wireless station and ordered the men to stay away from the keys.

Aboard the *Emden*, Captain von Müller was annoyed with the British for sending out messages, and relieved when the last one suddenly stopped in mid-sentence. Von Mücke had done his work, but not knowing that the enemy had been sending furiously for nearly half an hour, he continued to work in a leisurely fashion to do the job of destruction properly. Meanwhile, Captain von Müller looked at his watch and fretted. He never liked to be at the mercy of someone else, waiting for a subordinate to return. He was not worried, he had satisfied himself in the past two days that no enemy vessels were within two hundred and fifty miles of him. That estimate had been made by the wireless operators after two nights of constant watch. So von Müller was not nervous, he was just impatient.

At about 7.30 the explosions began, and von Müller was pleased. He saw the tall radio mast slowly topple and fall. At about that time Adjutant von Guerard came to the bridge with a note from the operators: they had picked up a message from an unknown ship that was calling the wireless station. But the ship was two hundred and fifty miles away, or more, and so von Müller paid little attention.

An hour later he was growing more impatient. Von Mücke should be leaving the island now, but there was no sign of his men at the landing. Fifteen minutes went by, and still no von Mücke. At nine o'clock a look-out reported a smoke cloud on the horizon. That should be the collier *Buresk*, reporting as ordered. Von Müller did not worry. A few minutes later the look-out identified the single funnel and two masts. It was the *Buresk*. But the look-out then reported that there was *another* smoke plume behind that of the *Buresk*, one much larger. Well, perhaps another victim was drawing near, to fall into the *Emden*'s net. That thought persisted for fifteen minutes. Then the ship beyond *Buresk* changed course, and the look-outs could see that she was a warship, a big warship. And at that moment the wind caught her stern ensign and showed plainly the whiteness, and on it the cross of St George.

It was 9.15. First Officer von Mücke had exceeded his time limit by fifteen minutes. Normally it would not have made much difference, but now it made all the difference in the world. The *Emden* was in deep trouble. Captain von Müller ordered the siren blown to warn von Mücke that they were moving away, the anchor weighed, and the ship brought to full fighting capability. It was an astounding order, given the state of relaxation that existed aboard the ship, but the men went to battle stations, and turned to engage the enemy.

That enemy was HMAS *Sydney*, an armoured cruiser which was about twice as large as the *Emden*. She displaced 5,400 tons, could make 26 knots, and was armed with eight 6-inch guns, as opposed to *Emden*'s ten 4.1-inch guns. The smaller guns would have a hard time competing, because the deck and hull and gun positions of the

Australian ship were all armoured. Only the luckiest of shots would do much damage, and Captain von Müller knew this, but he had no recourse. The enemy had come to him and he would fight.

She had come almost by accident. *Sydney* was engaged just then in the escort of a convoy. In a way, the *Emden* had herself to blame, for convoy escort was not normally duty for a heavy cruiser, but the fear of the *Emden* in these waters was so great by November, 1914, that very little in the maritime world was normal. *Sydney*'s convoy was travelling slowly, and was less than fifty miles from Direction Island when the convoy commander had been informed of the message from the shore station. Immediately he had released the *Sydney*, and now, just after nine o'clock, here she was, moving in. By 9.30 she was six miles off Direction Island, heading south, and seeing this, Captain von Müller steered due north. He was fighting for time, he needed half an hour to get up full steam in the boilers. But Captain Glossop of the *Sydney* understood only too well what von Müller was doing, and he gave the German ship no advantage. Seeing *Emden* turn north, Sydney turned hard to starboard and headed directly at the smaller vessel. By 9.40 the ships were only about four miles apart.

Von Müller opened fire at 5,600 yards. The first three salvos from the *Emden*'s 4.1-inch guns bracketed the Australian ship and the fourth salvo hit home. A bright yellow flash came from the centre of the ship. In spite of the armour, one shell at least had done some damage, and von Müller complimented his gunnery officer, Lieutenant Gaede. He would have been even more complimentary had he known the damage actually inflicted. That one shell had struck in the fire control room of the Australian cruiser, and damaged the automatic gun aiming equipment. *Sydney*'s men now must return to the old and less accurate system of manual operation of the guns. But in spite of the disadvantage, *Sydney* was the more powerful ship. Captain Glossop moved her back, out of range of the German guns, but within the range of his own 6-inch guns. And from 7,000 yards, where the *Emden*'s guns could not reach, his gunners began firing methodically.

That was the beginning of the end, for ten minutes later the Sydney's guns found the *Emden* and put a shell near the bridge. Lieutenant Gaede was wounded and so was Torpedo officer Withoeft. Captain Müller was wounded too, but so great was his concentration on the unequal battle that he did not even know it.

What was von Müller to do? He could run, but the *Sydney* was 6 knots faster and perhaps even more since *Emden*'s bottom had been fouled by months at sea, so to run would simply be to prolong the agony. All he could do was try to close with the enemy and hope for the best. But the *Emden*'s luck was running out. A shell struck home behind the crow's nest of the mainmast, and blew down the look-outs. Another fell in the mounting of one of the after guns and destroyed both gun and guncrew.

At ten o'clock Captain von Müller noticed the slowing of *Emden*'s rate of fire against the enemy. He called Gaede to inquire.

'The range is too great,' said the gunnery officer. 'Why waste ammunition?'

Captain von Müller tried to close. He swung to starboard; Glossop swung to port to keep the distance and his great advantage. Soon a direct hit on the fire control centre put that gun control system out of action and the *Emden*'s gunners were reduced to manual fire. Lieutenant Zimmerman, the officer in charge, was unhurt, but all the men around him were dead.

Torpedo officer Withoeft asked von Müller to get in close enough so that he could launch a torpedo attack, but Captain Glossop would not let them close. The shooting went on. The *Emden* had not got up to full steam when one shell penetrated below decks and broke several steam pipes. Live steam began spouting in the area. A second hit killed every man in the No. 1 gun crew and a third hit in that area struck directly into the ready ammunition of the port No. 4 gun. Then the ship took several hits aft and began to blaze. The steering was knocked out, and then the internal communication system broke down. Captain von Müller could communicate with his officers only by megaphone and runners. A hit on the deck smashed the torpedo flat, and filled it full of gas.

At 10.25, Captain von Müller managed, by a series of brilliant manoeuvres, to close the gap but by this time most of the *Emden*'s guns were silenced. Von Müller asked Gaede why the rate of fire was so slight, and Gaede replied somberly that most of the ammunition handlers had been killed. In the torpedo flat emergency repairs were made and Lieutenant, the Prince von Hohenzollern was ready to fire a torpedo from the port side. But then the *Sydney* moved away again and the range was too great.

Von Müller's only hope now was to continue to zigzag, to spar, to evade, and hope that a lucky shot would penetrate a magazine aboard the *Sydney* and put her out of action.

At 10.45 a shot hit the foremast, where Lieutenant von Guerard was stationed, and as it toppled he and several men fell to their deaths. Ten minutes later a shot from the *Sydney* pierced the deck and the water-line, making a new hole in the torpedo flat that enlarged the old to 16 inches. Water began pouring in so quickly that the Prince and his men abandoned the flat. Gunnery Officer Gaede, making the rounds of the fighting guns, was hit by shrapnel and lay dying. The deck was a shambles. The men could not get from ammunition ready rooms to the guns to deliver ammunition, except by crawling over jagged pieces of wreckage. All three funnels were hit, two were totally demolished and the third canted at a crazy angle across the buckled deck. The foremast lay across the port side, its tip dragging under-water. The surgeons and first aid men moved about the deck, stopping every few feet to help the wounded. They ran out of bandages and morphia, and had to go back to the surgery for more.

At eleven o'clock the electrical system of the ship was completely unworkable. She was being steered from the steering flat aft. Since the funnels were destroyed the fires burned badly and the *Emden* began to slow. On the deck, most men were wounded. One boatswain's mate had taken over direction of a gun when his officer was killed. His arm was shot off but he stood there, doggedly, directing fire.

A shell carried away the captain's bridge. Luckily von Müller was just then on the main deck inspecting the damage. In von Mücke's absence he had to estimate damage himself and take charge of damage control. From this point on directions to the steering flat were passed from man to man, down to the helmsman, and directions to the engine room were also passed, down the engine room skylight.

When Captain von Müller had finished his inspection and saw that only two guns were operable, that the torpedo system was damaged beyond use, and his men were wounded and dying he decided to run the ship aground on the coral reef of North Keeling Island. Thus, he reasoned, he would prevent the enemy from ever using her, and he would also save the lives of many wounded who would inevitably die if the ship sank.

As von Müller turned toward the reef, Captain Glossop anticipated what the German commander intended to do, and he increased the rate of fire, trying to sink the *Emden* before she could beach. But at 11.15 von Müller ran her aground on the south coast of the island. She was firmly stuck. Then the fires were put out and the sea-cocks opened to make sure she settled tightly on the reef.

All this while the ship was under fire. Captain von Müller had not run down his battle flag and the *Sydney* continued to shoot. But when Captain Glossop saw that the ship was stopped and aground, he ceased fire, and went off to chase after the *Buresk*, which had fled north.

Von Müller then heard the silence descend on the ship and the loudest noises were cries of the wounded. He toured the deck, gave permission to any man who wished, to jump overboard and swim for the island itself, possibly there to evade capture. He found the Prince, and ordered him to destroy the secret books in the wireless room and the captain's cabin. He organized another party to destroy the guns and any useful equipment. But the destruction party could not move aft of the engine room hatch, because the metal in that whole area was red hot from fires started by the *Sydney*'s shells. After finishing his work forward, the Prince tried to get aft, by creeping between decks. Lieutenant Gropius and his men were aft, and might need help. The going was slow, and when the Prince reached the laundry a pitiful sight unfolded. The Chinese laundrymen, who had been promised so much, were there, all dead. A shell had come into the laundry and killed them all as they stood at their tubs.

The Prince and his companions tried several times to reach the after portion of the ship but without success. The metal amidships was just too hot. So they retreated to join the main party on the main deck, under the broken foremast on the forecastle. This was the least damaged part of the ship, and the wounded were all brought here.

At midday the captain discovered that all the water tanks above the main deck had been destroyed and those below were underneath the torpedo flat which had been flooded with sea water. The only drinking water on the ship was what had been left in the pipes, and when these were drained there was barely enough liquid to wet the lips of the wounded. So more men were asked to volunteer to go to the island, where there might be fresh water and where there certainly were fresh coconuts which would slake thirst. But the men on the ship were unable to pass a line ashore, so that attempt failed.

All during the afternoon the survivors remained under blazing sun. The *Sydney* finally reappeared towing two boats. These were the boats of the *Buresk*; when the warship had overtaken her, the German crew had thrown papers overboard and opened the sea-cocks. The *Buresk* sank in deep water, and these were the boats of the crew. The *Sydney* approached the *Emden* and to the *Emden* survivors this immediately meant salvation, if their saviours would send them to a prison camp. But as *Sydney* came up, and stopped two miles off the *Emden*'s stern, she sent up a signal. Von Müller had ordered the signal and code books destroyed and no one could read the signal, so he had his signalman send up flags that read in Morse: No signal-book. But the Australian captain paid no heed and *opened fire again* on the wrecked hulk.

Captain Glossop certainly did not share Captain von Müller's attitude toward warfare, that much was certain. But the gesture, inhumane as it might be, also represented a compliment to the men of the *Emden* (even if it was one they might have preferred to pass). So thoroughly had the *Emden* frightened the British and all who sailed for Britain, that the dismasted hulk of what had been a warship still seemed dangerous enough to destroy. As the 6-inch shells began arriving on the foredeck, men began to fall, dead and wounded. Many men jumped overboard and tried to make it to the island. The Prince jumped over with a plank, but soon found that he was joined by half a dozen men and all the plank was good for was support, as they drifted and watched the *Sydney* batter their ship with new blows that started fires and killed more men. The shelling continued for half an hour until even Captain Glossop must have realized that it was nothing less than slaughter. The guns stopped, finally, and a boat came to the *Emden*. But the boat did not hold a doctor, or a responsible officer of the *Sydney*. Not at all. It was a *Buresk* boat and the officer in charge was Lieutenant Fikentscher. The *Sydney* then sped off to Direction Island, bent on the capture of Commander von Mücke and the *Emden* landing party. That was the situation of the men of the *Emden* as darkness fell. They were huddled together on their wreck, with no water, the wounded suffering, and the officers wondering what to make of the inexplicable behaviour of an enemy that showed no mercy. The night passed without event, except that a few of the wounded died.

Next morning at dawn the officers and able-bodied men hoisted the flag of the *Emden* upside down, to show distress. They had given up expecting any succour from the *Sydney*, but hoped that a steamer might come by and save them. But just after midday the *Sydney* did appear, gingerly. Two cutters were sent to the *Emden* filled with armed men and one stood off with its men waiting, ready to rescue their friends from these dangerous Germans. One officer came aboard to bargain with Captain von Müller. If the captain would guarantee the conduct of his men, and only if he would do so, would the *Sydney* take them off the wreck. Von Müller was puzzled, not recognizing yet that he and his men had created a legend in the southern oceans of an unbeatable crew that could move mountains. The men of the *Sydney* were obviously afraid of them even yet. Captain von Müller found it quite easy to promise that his men would not try to seize the *Sydney* and he would be responsible. Then the Australians began to give a little attention to the wounded.

The cutters began to take the men of *Emden* aboard, and one went over to the island to rescue those who had swum ashore. Von Müller remained on his ship, and was in the end the last man off. He had spent his last hour there, while waiting in trying to build fires near the magazines so that the ship would blow up and could never be reclaimed by his enemies. The fires went out however, and the ship remained, and for many years afterwards those who came by this spot could see the hulk of the *Emden* on its reef.

Taken to the captain's quarters of the *Sydney*, von Müller was given a drink and praised for his brave conduct during the unequal battle. He held his tongue about the treatment accorded his crew by the Australians, full knowing that anyone who would so behave would not respond kindly to criticism of his gentility in so doing. But he did venture one question. Why, he asked Captain Glossop, had the *Sydney* come back and shelled the *Emden* for half an hour the second time, when there had been not the slightest indication of belligerent behaviour aboard the hulk?

'Why,' asked Captain Glossop rhetorically. Why, because von Müller had not lowered his battle flags. Captain Glossop had never thought that perhaps the captain could not reach the after portion of the ship to lower them. He had only known that this was the most dangerous enemy in all the seven seas, and as long as she had not surrendered he had kept firing until even he realized that the enemy had no way of firing back.

Such then, was the legend created by that one ship of the German East Asia Cruiser Squadron in just three months of warfare.

18

The Hunt

The squadron could not stay holed up in Mas a Fuera forever, and no one knew that better than Admiral von Spee. But he needed a little time to prepare for the race around Cape Horn and the dash up the Atlantic, across to the North Sea, and down to the Skagerrak and safety. The *Leipzig* and the *Dresden* should have their turns at Valparaiso, both for the physical effect of resupply and the emotional effect of even brief leave among friends. So the two small cruisers were sent to carry despatches from the Admiral for Berlin and to pick up despatches from the Admiralty. On 9 November, the day that the *Emden* was destroyed in the Indian Ocean, her sister ships sailed for the Chilean coast, unknowing.

Just before they sailed, Admiral von Spee had a message from one of the clandestine shore stations operated by Germans on the Chilean coast: Argentina and Brazil had just embargoed supply ships for the Germans, based on arguments of the British. If they intended to get away, they must be sure of their coal supplies once they got into the South Atlantic. So the *Dresden* and the *Leipzig* were given the additional task of arranging through the German embassy for more colliers to come out. The same broadcast brought news of even more gloomy portent. Tsingtao had fallen to the Japanese on 7 November. The one bright spot in that report was the story of the gallantry of the old torpedo boat *S-90*, which had defended the harbour to the last, and torpedoed a Japanese cruiser. Then, two days after the *Dresden* and *Leipzig* left, another broadcast told the story of the last fight of the *Emden*, but in such little detail that instead of wondering at Captain von Müller's marvellous exploits, the Admiral was cast into even deeper gloom. Little by little his world was being destroyed.

Admiral von Spee was desperately anxious to learn the disposition of his British enemy's naval resources in the South American area. Although he had a constant stream of information from German coast watchers in Chile and Argentina, now that Admiral Cradock's force

18 British battle-cruisers had two tiers of guns

19 and 20 British battle-cruisers *Invincible* and *Inflexible* during the chase of Admiral von Spee's squadron at the Falklands at approximately 11 a.m., 8 December. Taken from the British cruiser *Kent*

had been sunk or scattered, von Spee did not know who or where his enemies were. There was an excellent reason for this gap: the British had just been in the process of creating a dual force in these waters, and it had still not been completed. Now, too late, the Cradock warnings of several months were heeded. Von Spee was on the scene, and Britain must put up some opposing force. Had Cradock been given the *Defence* when he wanted it, and perhaps a light cruiser or two, the Admiralty would have been saved much agony and Britain would have saved many lives. For with *Defence* Cradock would undoubtedly have had the edge at Coronel, and even the von Spee squadron's excellent gunnery might not have saved them. Certainly with two or three extra ships, Cradock would have won the battle and the threat that still paralysed shipping in the South Atlantic would have been ended.

It is the irony of history that all these factors were recognized just twenty-four hours before the Battle of Coronel took place, and as Cradock went to his death, the Admiralty was belatedly trying to give him what he needed. *Defence* did arrive at Montevideo on 3 November, two days *after* Coronel. At home, the British public knew nothing of the worst naval defeat since the Battle of Lake Erie in 1813. Those who knew what was happening recognized that the Admiralty had assigned two totally inadequate squadrons to the defence of an area where one strong squadron would have been effective. That deficiency was to be remedied and soon was. Admiral Stoddart was on his way to Montevideo, and he was ordered to assemble there the battleship *Defence*, the heavy cruisers *Carnarvon* and *Cornwall*, the light cruiser *Kent* which was coming from the Canary Islands, and the *Otranto* and the *Canopus*. There was no foolishness about the *Canopus* this time; she was regarded as a support ship, and very little else. Stoddart, then, could not be caught the way Cradock had been.

But the Admiralty, reacting with great vigour if not much common sense, did far more to put an end to the depradations of the German East Asia Cruiser Squadron. The extent of the activity was an indication of the seriousness with which the whole nation regarded the threat of von Spee: And what had occasioned this remarkable change in the British attitude?

A report, cabled on 4 November from the British consul general at Valparaiso, giving remarkably accurate details of the battle of Coronel:

Have just learned from Chilean admiral that German admiral states that on Sunday (1st November) at sunset, in thick and wicked weather, his ships met *Good Hope, Glasgow, Monmouth,* and *Otranto.* Action was joined and *Monmouth* turned over and sank after about an hour's fighting. *Good Hope, Glasgow,* and *Otranto* drew off into the darkness. *Good Hope* was on fire, an explosion was heard, and she is believed to have sunk. *Gneisenau, Scharnhorst* and *Nürnberg* were among the German ships engaged.

On receipt of this stunning message, Winston Churchill had reacted with his usual decisiveness. He had called First Sea Lord Fisher to the conference table, and six hours later had worked out details for a major effort to destroy von Spee. It was done with the utmost secrecy.

Vice-Admiral Sir F. Doveton Sturdee, Chief of Staff in London, was detached and given command of a new squadron whose sole purpose was to hunt down and destroy the von Spee threat. Sturdee was given the impressive title of Commander in Chief, South Atlantic and Pacific, and his command extended from Antarctica to a line drawn along the fifth parallel 5° North Latitude, which meant Brazil, Liberia, and halfway up the Pacific coast of South America, as far west as the mind could envisage. The thinking in London at the moment was that von Spee, with all those colliers and supply ships, intended to conduct a campaign to disrupt British shipping to South Africa and South America, and if he could do this he might bring about the disruption of the British economy. London did not realize that von Spee intended to make a break and dash for the North Sea, or that the German Admiral had considered just the plan London attributed to him, but had realized that it could be effective for only a few weeks at best, and so had rejected it. So Sturdee was given *Invincible* as his flagship and sent hurriedly to the Falkland Islands, where he would take command, and direct all operations, including those of Admiral Stoddart.

Not content with this plan alone, the Admiralty created another force, whose command was given to Admiral Patey. He was ordered to prepare to move from Australia to San Clemente Island off the coast of California. He would bring the *Australia,* and would be joined by the heavy cruiser *Newcastle.* The Japanese would supply the *Idzumo,* and the cruisers *Asama* and *Hizen,* which were just then watching Honolulu harbour in case the wheezing old *Geier* should decide to come out. The assignment of a pair of cruisers to watch over an obsolete gunboat was another indication of the state of mind of the naval allies in the autumn of 1914. Also, the Japanese were going to send their 1st South Sea Squadron to patrol between Fiji and the Marquesas, lest von Spee double back and strike in the Pacific island areas once more. This squadron was reinforced to three heavy cruisers and several light cruisers, about fifty per cent stronger than the von Spee force. Another squadron was created at the Cape of Good Hope, in case von Spee came that way. The British cruisers *Goliath* and *Dartmouth* were assigned to join the battle cruiser *Albion* and the armoured cruiser *Minotaur*, Jerram's old flagship. A French squadron would patrol the area off West Africa. Rear-Admiral R.S. Phipps-Hornby was ordered to keep a sharp eye on the Panama Canal with his cruiser force, and make sure Admiral von Spee did not escape through the canal.

Churchill could move! Six hours for the plan, and that very day the battle-cruisers *Invincible* and *Inflexible* were ordered to coal at once and proceed to Plymouth to prepare for immediate foreign service. The dockyards were not in shape for such celerity, and they said the ships could not possibly be ready for sea sooner than the night of 13 November. All right, Churchill snapped back, the ships would sail on 11 November, and if necessary the civilian dockyard workmen would go along to finish the job in battle. They would be sent home from somewhere, the First Lord said airily. When the dockyard authorities received that message, they realized that the two ships would sail on November 11, and they did, with the work completed.

On their trip south, the big ships were to keep out of the shipping lanes, and to maintain wireless silence, Churchill ordered. He did not want his hand tipped to von Spee. But instead of obeying these lucid orders, the two battle-cruiser captains did just about everything else. They stopped suspicious steamers and searched them on the way south. They called in at St Vincent and forgot to warn the port authorities about the secrecy, so the St Vincent operators began gossiping with their friends at sea about the two mighty battle-cruisers that had passed through. In peacetime even the visit of such behemoths would have been an event, and now it was more, it was downright exciting. The operators did all this gossiping over the air waves *in the clear*. When the *Glasgow* arrived at Rio de Janeiro on 11 November, all battered and filthy from her battle and the long voyage, Captain Luce picked up his Most Secret messages from London, to learn that *Invincible* and *Inflexible* were coming in darkest secrecy. The captain was so impressed that he informed only his intelligence officer, Commander Lloyd Hirst and the British Minister, and then when Commander Hirst stopped in at the Club Central, which was absolutely filthy with Germans, the first thing Hirst heard was two British businessmen at the bar casually discussing the imminent arrival in South American waters of *Invincible* and *Inflexible*!

In fact, however, the dreadful gaffe worked out rather well. So well was it known that the battle-cruisers were coming that the common gossip meant little to the German intelligence network, and nobody bothered to inform Admiral von Spee, obviously assuming he knew.

Since Brazil was neutral at this stage of the war, *Glasgow* was supposed to leave port within twenty-four hours, but such was feeling in this country that when Captain Luce and the consul general asked for more time they got it. The Brazilians dusted off one clause of the neutrality regulations which said that if a warship was so badly damaged that it could not safely go to sea, then the neutral government could allow repairs to be made sufficient to enable the ship to steam to the nearest national port. *Glasgow* was quite capable of steaming on, as everyone knew, but this was a loop-hole to be used. She remained in Rio, was taken into the drydock and given a general overhaul so that when she steamed out of the harbour on 16 November, she was in better shape than she had been since the outbreak of war. Captain Luce's orders told him to go to the Falklands, so he set a course for Port Stanley.

When the *Glasgow* arrived there what a difference they found. On their previous visit, Port Stanley had been a sleepy little place, where it hardly seemed anyone knew there was a war on. But when the news was given to the public about the defeat at Coronel, suddenly the war came home, and that feeling was enhanced by a warning that the people of the Falklands might well expect a landing by the Germans in the near future. Governor Allerdyce gave the warning and then demanded immediate organization for defence. He did not take his clothes off or sleep in a bed for four nights running, so great was his excitement. He organized a home guard, equipped largely with ancient fowling-pieces, and they marched raggedly around the town square every day. Tinned foods were stockpiled at the city hall as for a siege. The word was sent out to the furthest fishing and shepherd stations. Men and women in every community slept beside their telephones, awaiting the call to arms to defend the colony. Old people and children were prepared for evacuation to the neutral mainland. Books, papers and all money and stamps were hidden along with official documents and seals. At the governor's office the codebooks and seals were buried every night and dug up every morning so that business might continue. Even the governor's tablecloths, marked G.R. (Georgius Rex) were buried lest they be stolen by the barbaric Germans. (Unfortunately they were buried in the same hole with the

Governor's silver, which was wrapped in green baize. The hole grew damp, the baize faded, and the magnificent official tablecloths were spoiled.)

The state of tension continued for about a week and then the people of Port Stanley grew tired of it. There was no sign of Germans, no sign of war. Since everyone was playing soldier, or nurse, or leader, no one was available to do business, so all the establishments of Port Stanley were locked up, and this had grown particularly tiresome. So the governor and the mayor were about to suspend the emergency and declare business as usual, when one morning the bored look-out in the watchtowers above the town started – there in front of him was a warship. She was heading directly for the wireless station and when she neared that point, turning broadside, just as would an enemy that was making ready to blast down the town's only military asset.

The look-out gave the alarm. Bugles blew, calling the home guard to arms. Men ran to the church to ring the bells and to the dockyard to alert the workers. Others saddled up their horses and prepared to do battle with the Germans. The women and children, who had not yet been sent to Chile or Argentina, were told to evacuate the town and leave the fighting to the men, and they began leaving. The warriors gathered together and stood at attention and then at parade rest and the cavalry sat atop their horses, fidgeting. What to do now? The answer was soon given by the ship: she ran up the Union Jack and sent a message, she was the HMS *Canopus* and she had come to defend them all. She had come forever in fact, for Captain Grant had new orders. He had duly reported on his voyage around South America to try to join the Cradock squadron before the Battle of Coronel. To be sure, he had indeed made 12 knots in that desperate venture – and in so doing had so strained the boilers of the *Canopus* that he had recommended she be taken home to England for a major dockyard job. The Lords of the Admiralty, with that evidence in hand, had finally decided that all Cradock had ever said about *Canopus* was true, and they had no desire to jam up their dockyards with obsolete warships, so they told Captain Grant that he was to proceed to Port Stanley and run her aground in a way that would make her most valuable as a fortress-ship.

Captain Grant came ashore and conferred with Governor Allerdyce, who was delighted with this new addition to the colony's defence. He showed the captain just where she ought to be scuttled, around behind the sand hill that stood between the town and the outside water. And very shortly and smartly it was done. The ship's topmasts were housed and she was put in position and the sea-cocks opened. She sank gently into the mud. Her side was camouflaged then to match the land and shrubbery, and from a certain distance no one would suspect that this bump on the landscape had ever been a fighting ship. But she had those 12-inch guns still, and they commanded the approaches to the wireless station and the inner harbour.

The defence of the Falklands really took on a new life then. The gunnery officer of the *Canopus*, having nothing else to do, got together with the engineering officer and the torpedo officer, who had even less to do, and they invented a new type of mine which could be made from old paint drums. These were manufactured at the boat yard in enough quantity to guard the entrance with a 'mine field'. The lighter guns of the *Canopus* were also landed ashore and moved around to strategic points as coastal defence weapons. A new signal station was built about 400 feet above the harbour, on Sapper Hill, and other stations were scattered about so that the fire from *Canopus* could be guided from many spots.

All this was accomplished before the end of November. Then everyone sat down to wait again. The women and children actually were evacuated, on the advice of authority, and that made life more difficult, but even so the tension was hard to maintain and so in early December the women and children were brought back again in a revolt against authority. Wireless messages indicated that the Germans were still in the area, and Governor Allerdyce warned everyone against any slackness, but most people wanted to get back to their storekeeping and their farms. The war seemed a long way from the Falkland Islands.

Then on 7 December 1914, Admiral Sturdee arrived with his new cruiser squadron, comprising seven powerful warships, which made the harbour of Port Stanley bristle like a real naval base. The officers and men came ashore to stretch their legs. They informed the governor that they would not trade on his hospitality for long; they had come to coal, and take on a few fresh stores, and then set off to find Admiral von Spee.

The squadron lay in the outer harbour of Port William, but the light cruisers *Bristol* and *Glasgow* took on pilots who proudly guided them through the mine field to the inner harbour of Port Stanley. Their colliers came behind them, and the two light cruisers coaled that day. Next day, the big ships would come in to the protected water and coal, starting at dawn.

That evening of 7 December, the officers of the light cruisers strolled up and down the two streets of the village, smoking and talking. They were well primed for the search, eager to be about His Majesty's business of bringing down Britain's most worrisome naval enemy. It was midsummer in the Falklands, and the gardens of the houses were filled with sweet flowers, and the householders sat on their stoops and waved to the sailors as they passed. As evening came, the temperature dropped into the 40°F. range, and the smell of peat fires rose through the village. The captains of *Carnarvon, Cornwall* and the *Bristol* asked for permission to douse their fires and thus save coal. Since there was no earthly reason to deny the request, Admiral Sturdee granted it. That would give the engineers of the ships a chance to check their boilers and propulsion systems.

So night fell on Port Stanley, and it was hard to realize that somewhere out there a war was raging.

19

The Battle of the Falkland Islands

For nearly three weeks, Admiral von Spee lay holed up at Mas a Fuera. At first he was awaiting confirmation from Berlin of his decision to round Cape Horn and make the breakthrough in to the North Sea to return to Germany. When the *Leipzig* and *Dresden* returned from Valparaiso in mid-November, they brought a message from Captain Boy-Ed, the German naval attaché in Washington, confirming the Admiral's plan. But there were also some caveats: Berlin wanted the Admiral to conduct raiding activities along the coast before he came, and he had to provide himself with all coal in the future. The pressure exerted by the British now made it impossible to charter neutral vessels. Boy-Ed had hoped to supply von Spee from New York, but he could tell it was not going to be possible.

The Admiral must see to his own coal supply until he reached the Cape Verde Islands. At that point, the German High Seas Fleet would steam out and engage the British Grand Fleet in a feinting action to draw them off, so that von Spee could come home safely to Germany.

The Admiral set about arranging the coal supply. He instructed the German minister at Valparaiso that colliers available should be sent to meet the squadron at St Quentin Bay in the Gulf of Penas, a thousand miles south of the Chilean capital. Berlin had ordered him to strip himself of all marginal vessels and specifically said that *Kronprinz Wilhelm*, the liner-turned-auxiliary cruiser, should be destroyed because she burned too much coal. But von Spee disagreed. He did, with some pangs, part with *Titania*, the squadron's despatch ship. She had served faithfully, but she had run out of coal, and become a liability. There was no way that she could be loaded up again in these waters, given the pressures of the British on the Chileans and Argentinians to abide by the letter of the neutrality laws. So on 15 November at Mas a Fuera, the sea-cocks of the *Titania* were opened and she was destroyed along with one of the captured colliers that had been emptied.

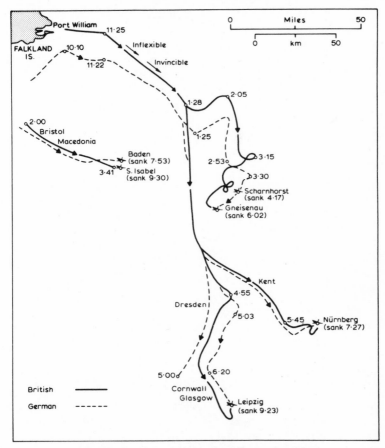

The Battle of the Falklands, 8 December 1914

Admiral von Spee was relaxed and more hopeful now that he had indications of real concern from Berlin, and a plan to get him through the British blockade. He really did not expect any trouble in South American waters since he had destroyed Cradock's squadron. He knew that on the other side of the Strait of Magellan the British were concentrating, but he felt that the British would again divide their forces and that he could deal with them.

The Admiral sent off several messages that day to New York and Buenos Aires, requesting the efforts of the consulates to secure coal. Buenos Aires should supply 10,000 tons of coal and three months supply for 1,000 men. He did not say how, but the method was

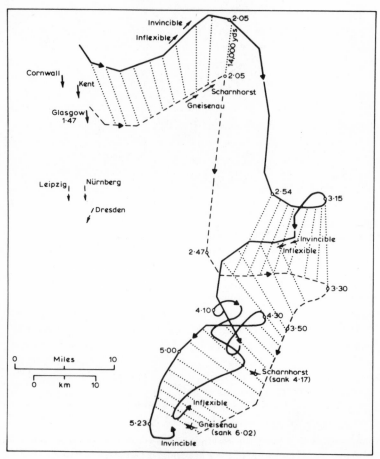

The Battle of the Falklands: the sinking of the *Scharnhorst* and
the *Gneisenau*

obvious: the consul was to use a decoy, a neutral, and charter colliers
in that name for some neutral destination. That part was not so
difficult but the supplies were something else, for who would be
sending supplies for a thousand men anywhere except a belligerent?
These had to be much more carefully camouflaged, as say, a shipment
of Argentine beef and mutton apparently destined for Sweden. But it
could be done, the Admiral was sure of that. He also planned for
20,000 tons of coal to be shipped under the same cover from New
York, to be ready in January. He did not yet give the place.

On 18 November *Dresden* and *Leipzig* returned from their visit to Valparaiso, the *Dresden* bringing along a British Admiralty steamer, the *North Wales* which she had encountered and captured on the way back. They met in mid-ocean, and the *North Wales* was sunk not far from the place where *Good Hope* had gone down. Then the squadron moved on south. At dawn on 21 November they reached the Gulf of Penas, bound by glaciers and bare rocks. But it was a secluded place and they could stop here for a time and coal again. The colliers the Admiral had ordered from Valparaiso began to show up, and the coaling was accomplished in St Quentin Bay. The men went ashore and cut Christmas trees for future use, not knowing where they might be in a month. There were honours and ceremonies. News came that the Kaiser had honoured von Spee with the Iron Cross, first and second class, and that three hundred third-class awards had been granted the crews of the squadron. Von Spee had the task of sorting these out so as to honour the proper men, and not forget anyone who had distinguished himself. The difficulty was that they had really had such an easy time so far that it was difficult to say who should get the medals. So the senior officers, and the junior officers, and petty officers received the lion's share of the awards. The Admiral distributed the medals with proper ceremony on 26 November. He had waited until the last day of their stay at this place because he wanted to bring morale to a peak as they sailed for their dangerous voyage around Cape Horn. Then, the award procedure ended, he ordered the ships to raise anchor and head into the wind. They were taking the first long step on their voyage home to Germany.

The signs looked good: all those arrangements had provided the squadron with a 17,000-ton supply of coal carried in the squadron colliers. That should get them home. The Admiral had also laid on those 10,000 tons to be delivered to Punta San Elena on the Argentine coast during the first week of December. But one problem had not been solved: he was short of ammunition after the actions at Papeete and Coronel. He had informed Berlin that he needed an ammunition ship in January, but the *Admiralstab* had not yet replied, so that problem nagged him. So did one other: the British had been putting unremitting pressure on the Chilean and Argentine authorities to stop the illegal broadcast of messages for the German squadron, and many of the stations had been closed down by the authorities. The Chileans were annoyed because those colliers that had met von Spee in the Gulf of Penas had sailed openly from Valparaiso, and the British had immediately protested so noisily that the Chilean government was embarrassed. So the Chilean naval wireless, which had been extremely helpful to the Germans in matters of weather information and messages, was no longer helpful.

German agents were located in Valparaiso and La Plata, but von Spee was out of touch with both wireless installations. This was unfortunate because on 26 November the unit at La Plata knew the whereabouts of *Glasgow* and *Canopus* and suspected that the British squadron was in the Falklands, but the message had to be given to a supply ship captain in the hope that he would encounter Admiral von Spee before the information became useless. On that day, as von Spee steamed out of his refuge, the colliers *Amasis, Memphis*, and *Luxor* headed for Chilean ports were they were not known. They carried neutral papers and would load up with coal on a pretext, and would then bring that coal to von Spee in the Argentine. The trip around the Horn was as ghastly as von Spee had thought it might be. The wind rose to hurricane strength and the waves grew so lofty that the squadron slowed to 5 knots lest they suffer some structural damage. Later that day the wind abated slightly so the speed was picked up to 8 knots, but that was the best they could do, and next day again the weather grew worse so that the colliers could not keep up the pace, and the whole fleet slowed again. By the afternoon of 28 November the waves were so high that from the bridge of the flagship *Gneisenau* could not even be seen most of the time, although she was only a few hundred yards behind the *Scharnhorst*. The Admiral estimated that the waves were 30 metres high! (90 feet) Life was utterly miserable; the stewards could not lay the tables, the wardroom crockery cabinet flew open and half the dishes crashed on the deck. Seams sprang on the smaller cruisers and they developed leaks. A man dare not go on deck unless secured by lines. On 30 November the weather abated again slightly, and on 1 December when they reached Cape Horn in a hailstorm it seemed almost good weather to them, for the waves were down to about 12 feet. Now they were in iceberg country, and sharp watch had to be kept. They sighted two icebergs that day, one of them rising 200 feet out of the water. In this difficult water they sighted a sailing ship, and *Leipzig* stopped her. When she turned out to be the three-masted British barque *Drummuir* she was taken as a prize, and *Leipzig* took her under tow. To be sure the Admiral wanted the coal cargo she was carrying, but more than that, he did not want her sailing on and giving information to his enemies of his whereabouts. He hoped to get around the Horn without being observed, and did not know that the squadron had been sighted by a Chilean vessel off the Strait of Magellan.

The squadron moved into the island chain south of Patagonia and to Beagle Channel, named for the ship on which Charles Darwin had made his famous voyage. They anchored near Picton Island to coal, relieve the *Drummuir* of her cargo, and dispose of her. They spent several days there, recovering from the effects of the storm and putting the ships to rights. *Dresden* had lost her deck load of coal in the blow, and she took on much of the coal from *Drummuir*. The Admiral and his sons continued their study of natural history, wandering around the small islands in the *Scharnhorst*'s steam pinnace, turning over rocks, picking up turtle eggs and watching the seals that seemed to be everywhere. At night the Admiral played bridge, a game he enjoyed; one evening with Captain Schultz and two senior officers of the *Scharnhorst*, and next evening with Captain Maerker and officers of the *Gneisenau*. It was a welcome distraction for the Admiral and gave him a chance to ascertain quietly the views of his subordinates.

During these games he first suggested a plan to bring discomfort to Germany's enemies. Why did they not make one last gesture of defiance by sacking the Falklands and burning British stores? When he suggested it, some of his more conservative bridge partners were appalled. To do this would be to invite an attack by the enemy naval forces, they said. Nonsense, said the Admiral. He had information from the German intelligence net in the area that the Falklands were defended by a few old men and children with fowling-pieces, who were so worried about his coming that they had evacuated the women and children to the mainland. Well they should give the islanders what they were asking for.

So inviting did this prospect become as the Admiral talked about it that on 6 December he called his senior officers to a meeting aboard the flagship and outlined his plan. The same objections were raised: it was dangerous, it was a political, not a naval gesture, and it would waste ammunition, time, and perhaps lives. The Admiral overruled these objections and added to the plan: he would also take the British governor prisoner, as reprisal for the British seizure of the German governor of Samoa, which he had learned of since they entered Chilean waters.

Von Spee's Chief of Staff, Captain Fielitz, and Captain von Schönberg of the *Nürnberg* greeted the Admiral's plan with enthusiasm, and this was all the backing he needed. He ordered messages sent to Punta Arenas, so the German settlers could mobilize their forces in Chile, Argentina and Brazil, and garrison the islands as soon as the squadron captured them. It seemed unlikely that Britain, having failed to defend the islands in the beginning, would launch anything like a major force against this forgotten spot of the southern hemisphere. He also sent word that the steamers *Mera* and *Elinore Woermann*, which were in Chilean harbours, were to be loaded up with entrenching tools, guns, cement for building blockhouses and ammunition. Then they were to be sent to the Falklands to help the new owners prepare their defences.

There was no way, of course, that Admiral von Spee could know that this entirely remarkable, audacious plan was going to find the British not only defended, but the base for a squadron of ships larger and stronger than his own. But he was the creature of his intelligence sources, and they had told him facts that had been absolutely true a few weeks earlier and were now almost absolutely false.

The audacious plan made, the Admiral lost no time in putting it into motion. At noon on 6 December, even as Admiral Sturdee's squadron was nearing the Falklands, Admiral von Spee's squadron sailed for the Falkland Islands, and on Monday, as the British ships moved into Port Stanley harbour to begin coaling, von Spee was sailing along the southern coast of the Tierra del Fuego. The weather was so fine that they could see the Argentine flag flying above government buildings as they passed one village. They moved along the rough coast of Staten Island and into the open sea; the course was set north-west, towards the eastern tip of the Falkland Island chain, and Port Stanley.

The Admiral issued his orders of the day: the *Gneisenau* and *Nürnberg* would make the landings at Port Stanley, destroy the wireless station, burn the port installations but save the town for the Germans who were coming, and carry Governor Allerdyce off into German captivity, perhaps to be exchanged for the Governor of Samoa, in time.

They moved along on schedule all day Monday, and continued in good weather on Monday evening. At two o'clock on the morning of Tuesday 8 December, the deck watch made out the land mass of the Falklands ahead, and at five o'clock the *Gneisenau* and *Nürnberg* turned sharply to the north, to reach their objective and carry out the mission. *Scharnhorst, Leipzig,* and *Dresden* followed at a more leisurely pace, for their task was to stay outside and make sure the landing operation was not disturbed by any British warships. The landing parties got ready to go ashore, the men in white uniforms, wearing gaiters and ammunition belts and carrying gas masks according to regulations. Thus attired they went to breakfast on the mess deck and then gathered on the forecastle and the upper deck to watch the coastline slide by until called to man the boats.

It was a particularly lovely day for December in these latitudes; usually it rained three days out of four but this day the sky was blue and sea was calm, and the clear air stirred only a little in the north-west breeze. The men could see the shore quite well, and occasional white houses against the brown and green of the landscape.

So, too, could a lady named Mrs Felton, the wife of a sheep farmer who lived near Point Pleasant on the coast, about twenty miles from Port Stanley, see the German ships, as she arose that morning and looked out her window at the sea. Excitedly she sent her maid and houseboy to the top of the ridge behind the house to get a better view and then report. In fifteen minutes the boy came down breathlessly to report that he had seen five warships, two of them steaming toward the entrance to the port, and three moving more slowly and further out at sea. Mrs Felton got on the telephone, and rang up the governor's house in Port Stanley to pour out the news.

Meanwhile, the *Gneisenau* and *Nürnberg* approached Cape Pembroke, the outermost point of the harbour, and from the bridge of the *Gneisenau* Captain Maerker could see a slim plume of smoke rising in the sky near the lighthouse. He picked up his glasses. At first he could not see anything else, because the broad bay that held Port William and Port Stanley was concealed from a southern approach by a long line of hills and dunes. But as the warships approached, Maerker saw fires and more smoke. Admiral von Spee had told his captains that the Falkland Islanders expected a German invasion – that was what had given him the idea – and they could be expected to destroy stores and equipment, so Maerker was not alarmed. It never occurred to him that there might be somebody inside the harbour to whom signals would be made. But that is what he saw, the island watchers of the Falkland Island Volunteers, led by Major Turner, a retired officer. They were signalling the British squadron inside the harbour that the Germans were here.

Then, almost immediately, Captain Maerker saw mastheads above the hills, two of them in the outer harbour between the lighthouse and the town, and he congratulated himself. Perhaps he had those two ships that had escaped at Coronel ... But then, as *Gneisenau* and *Nürnberg* speeded up, hoping to catch one of the ships as it moved into the channel, he saw two, three, four other sets of masts, and his experience told him that two were the masts of warships. He scribbled a message ...

It was 7.45 when Mrs Felton's first message had been received at the Government House, and a few minutes later when Major Turner began signalling. The guardship *Canopus* had the message first, and she put up flags to announce: 'a four-funnel and two-funnel man-of-war in sight from Sapper hill, steering north.' *Glasgow* was alert and had the message instantly. Captain Luce ordered a signal for the Admiral: 'Enemy in sight.' But the flagship of the squadron, *Invincible*, was not looking for trouble that morning and her watch was not alert. No one saw the *Glasgow*'s flags, and no one stirred on the decks of *Invincible*.

Captain Luce waited a few moments on his bridge, looking at his watch impatiently, and then ordered a gun fired. Perhaps that would wake them up. Admiral Sturdee was in his cabin, shaving, and he wondered aloud irritably what the commotion was about. His flag lieutenant, still in his pyjamas, rushed out of his own cabin, looked up at *Glasgow* and sped to the Admiral's quarters to snap to attention.

The Admiral lifted his razor, and turned around.

'*Glasgow* signals enemy in sight, sir.'

'Well, you had better go and get dressed.'

'Yes sir.'

As the flag lieutenant scrambled off, aboard the *Glasgow*, Commander Hirst reached the bridge of his ship, and was dispatched to the masthead with the silhouette book, to identify the enemy. He climbed up and opened the pages. '*Gneisenau* and *Nürnberg*', he shouted down. It was eight o'clock.

Lieutenant Commander Barry Bingham, assistant to the first officer of the *Invincible*, had just finished a long night, supervising the transfer of 400 tons of coal from a collier to the bunkers of the *Invincible*, beginning before dawn. He was sitting in the wardroom, having just eaten his kippers, and drinking his third cup of coffee when the commotion began.

The Admiral finished his shave in a hurry, and sat down to consider. The squadron was hardly ready for a fight. *Invincible*, *Inflexible* and *Carnarvon* had either just finished coaling or were still in the process. *Bristol* and *Glasgow* were in the inner harbour, their engines down for repairs. Only the old armoured cruiser *Kent*, 9,960 tons, built in 1901, was on guard at the mouth of the outer harbour.

The Admiral scribbled orders: every ship must be ready for action within two hours, and that meant also *Bristol*, whose captain doubted if he could manage it, and *Cornwall*, which had not yet coaled. She would have to forget it.

Admiral Sturdee despatched his messages to the signal bridge and put on his shirt. At 8.10 *Kent* was told to weigh anchor and reconnoitre the entrance to the harbour, and at 8.30 she began to move.

Aboard the *Gneisenau*, Captain Maerker saw the masts of this guardship begin to travel and he increased his speed. *Gneisenau* and *Nürnberg* were eight miles away from the port, and the other German cruisers were twenty miles away. As Maerker watched, another set of masts began to move behind the dunes. The channel twisted this way and that inside, so it was impossible to know precisely what was happening. Maerker, in fact, was watching *Kent* move out, and the auxiliary cruiser *Macedonia* move inside the inner harbour, where she had been ordered for safety. Aboard the British cruisers work was proceeding at a devil's pace to get the ships ready for battle. Stokers in holds were working at top speed, as they fed the red maws of the furnaces, and the engineers watched the steam gauges as the line crept up, little by little. The Germans were still coming on.

In her berth in the mud, *Canopus* had no worries about raising steam. Her observers had been posted on all the peaks of the south shore of the island, and her gunnery officer had gone out to the observation tower above the town. A message soon arrived aboard the flagship for the Admiral.

'*Canopus* asks permission to open fire, sir.'

'Permission granted,' said the Admiral. There, that would give the Germans something to think about, while he got ready.

It was 8.52.

Captain Maerker was puzzled at that moment. The two sets of masts moved, but no others. And then came an enormous amount of smoke drifting over the dunes. The British must be burning something valuable. (He did not realize that the smoke was the excessive burn-off of the cold boilers as the engineers struggled to bring the steam up in the anchored warships.)

Captain Maerker was now approaching the lighthouse, and he identified *Kent*, and could see into the inner harbour. There he also identified *Glasgow*, but not the old battleship *Canopus* (whose camouflage was as great as her officers believed). *Gneisenau* and *Nürnberg* would certainly be more than a match for these ships. As for the other masts in the harbour, they must be auxiliaries. Maerker asked Admiral von Spee for permission to attack. As he waited for the word, he moved ahead slowly.

At 9.15, *Canopus* fired her first shells, a salvo that landed 800 yards short of the *Gneisenau*. But the shock of being fired upon from this 'undefended' shore was enormous. It was immediately followed by another shock. Captain Maerker had brought the *Gneisenau* in close enough now that the masts of the other ships were clearly visible, and at least two of these were tripod masts, which identified battle-cruisers of the dreadnought type! Undefended was scarcely a word that could be applied to this harbour this day.

The splashes from those 12-inch shells of *Canopus*'s guns also gave Captain Maerker pause, and when the next salvo came, it was much closer to the *Gneisenau*. Maerker sent von Spee a message, telling what he had found. The Admiral was quick with an answer this time: break away and rejoin the squadron. For suddenly what had started out as a brave adventure seemed to be back-firing. Admiral von Spee did not want to meet a British squadron just now. He was short of ammunition and might have to run through the North Sea with what he had in his magazines. He would have no time to stop to repair damages to any of his ships, a ship that could not keep up would have to be sacrificed. And when Captain Maerker mentioned tripod masts, von Spee knew that his force was inferior to whatever squadron the British had assembled in such a hurry in the Falklands.

But as von Spee hurried to get away and bring up *Gneisenau* and *Nürnberg* to move around to Argentine waters, the British squadron was getting ready. At 9.45 all ships except *Bristol* reported they had steam up, and were ready for orders. *Bristol* was the one exception, she was having a bit of trouble for one boiler had been torn up when the Germans were first sighted, and she would not be under way until eleven o'clock. They would just have to do without her at the beginning then, said the Admiral, and gave the orders to raise anchor. *Glasgow* moved out into the roadstead at 10.10 with *Kent* behind her, and the remainder of the squadron started through the mine field, *Inflexible* first, then *Invincible*, then *Cornwall*, which carried Admiral Stoddart and his flag. *Glasgow* and *Kent* were detailed to chase and keep in touch with the German cruisers and inform the rest as they went.

From the crow's nest of the *Scharnhorst*, the German squadron intelligence officer could see the ships as they filed out of the harbour, and he had his own silhouette book to identify them: *Glasgow*: 4,800 tons, 26 knots, two 6-inch guns and ten 4-inch guns; *Kent*: 9,800 tons, 24 knots, fourteen 6-inch guns; *Inflexible*: 17,250 tons, 26 knots, eight 12-inch guns, sixteen 4-inch guns; *Invincible*: 17,250 tons, the same as her sister ship in all regards; *Cornwall*: 9,800 tons, 24 knots, fourteen 6-inch guns and *Carnarvon*: 19,850 tons, 22 knots, four 7.5-inch guns and six 6-inch guns.

As this word came down to the Admiral's bridge, von Spee saw that his position was no better than had been that of Cradock at Coronel. He was outshipped and outgunned. *Invincible* was faster, bigger and her guns were *twice as large* as those of *Scharnhorst*. The *Inflexible-Gneisenau* comparison was precisely the same. All the other British ships were more than a match, ship for ship for the light German cruisers. *Dresden*, the heaviest of them, weighed only 3,500 tons, a third less than *Glasgow*, the smallest British ship. What Admiral von Spee needed just then was a storm of the sort he had passed through coming around Cape Horn, but as he looked at the sky and saw the sun rising relentlessly in a cloudless day, he knew he was not going to get it. All he could do was run and hope.

The last of the British line cleared the harbour at 10.30. Off on the horizon the hulls of the German squadron were just disappearing as von Spee steamed south-west in an attempt to escape the mighty dreadnoughts that trailed the German squadron. At first it was hard for the Germans to believe that the British could really have such powerful ships in the area. *Glasgow* had sped out ahead, unleashed to trail the enemy, but *Invincible* made a signal: general chase, and that meant every vessel was free to speed as quickly as possible toward the Germans. It was then that the German watchers saw the big ships clearly for the first time, for suddenly two of the pursuers seemed to leap ahead. As they came closer the officers could see the size and the power. Admiral von Spee was under no illusions about what he faced, and some of his senior officers knew too. Soon all did. Von Spee ordered the crews mustered and told what to expect. The men were brought to muster at the end of the morning and warned the fighting would be heated, and that many would die. How many of the two thousand five hundred men of the squadron would survive this day no one knew, but they all knew they were in danger. They continued their preparations absently, watching the steam gauges, cleaning the gun barrels, checking compasses, and making sure that all was shipshape as the manuals ordered. But as the chase continued and the enemy gained ground every minute, a despair engulfed the ships. Admiral Sturdee's three leading ships were racing at 25 knots, 3 knots more than the Germans could make. At a few minutes before eleven in the morning Sturdee observed that his three ships were outdistancing the others, and he slowed to 24 knots. Then he saw that the *Cornwall* and *Carnarvon* were still losing ground, so he slowed to 20 knots. He wanted the whole squadron with him when he struck. As this slowing meant the chase would be prolonged, the captains ordered a meal for the men and sent all those who had not had time to change from their coaling gear below for a bath and a change. The Germans also ordered up meals for the men, because no one knew when the ships would be able to afford that luxury again.

At 11.45 *Invincible* and *Inflexible* were 18,500 yards from the Germans. Von Spee turned south-east and the battle-cruisers turned with him. It seemed apparent that the battle was about to begin, so von Spee ordered the battle flags broken out, and on five German cruisers the drums began to roll, and the bugles to blare, and men ran to their battle stations, stopping here and there for a brief handclasp with an old friend.

For the past hour Admiral Sturdee had been waiting for his slower ships to catch up to the leaders. *Carnarvon* was the special problem; her captain kept calling for more revolutions, but the ship straggled – she seemed only to be able to make about 20 knots this day. So Admiral Sturdee waited, until he saw the flutter of the battle flags as they were raised aboard *Scharnhorst*. Then he waited no longer, but ordered full speed ahead. The two battle-cruisers seemed to leap ahead of the other British ships and soon they were making 25 knots and closing fast. Admiral von Spee took note and moved his ships swiftly into battle formation, *Gneisenau* and *Nürnberg* on the left of the line, *Scharnhorst* and *Dresden* on the right, and *Leipzig* trailing astern, of the starboard column.

Aboard *Invincible* the buglers blew the call to action, and yet another pennant was run up the yard-arm: open fire. The range was 16,000 yards. *Inflexible* fired the first salvo, at *Leipzig*, and when the 840-pound shells struck, 100 yards behind the target, they sent geysers 150 feet in the air. The battle had begun.

Admiral Sturdee led the two battle-cruisers in at 26 knots, and at this speed and this range the shooting was not very accurate. For the next quarter of an hour the battle-cruisers fired, but made no hits. The closest to a hit was a salvo from the *Invincible* which landed so close by *Leipzig* that the men at the after guns were drenched by the column of sea water that arose. Seeing this, Admiral von Spee sent a signal to the *Leipzig*, authorizing her to proceed independently, and thus have a chance of escaping the salvoes that were coming ever closer. The Admiral had no particular battle plan. What sort of plan could he have, given the enormous superiority of the enemy in speed, guns, and numbers? He issued his orders: The armoured cruisers will engage the enemy as long as possible. The light cruisers are to use every endeavour to escape.

As the order came, *Leipzig* was already following the previous instructions and had turned away south, moving out of the line of fire of the British battle-cruisers, which shifted their attention to *Nürnberg*. But with the new order, *Nürnberg* and *Dresden* both turned south, hoping to escape as von Spee led the British squadron away. But Admiral Sturdee had discussed just such a possibility with his staff and his captains knew what to do. *Kent, Cornwall*, and *Glasgow* had already been assigned the task of pursuing the small cruisers if this occurred, so now they turned after *Leipzig, Dresden* and *Nürnberg*. If that move seemed to even the odds, even for the light cruisers, the appearance was illusory. All the British ships were faster than the Germans. The smallest, *Glasgow*, mounted two 6-inch guns and ten 4-inch guns, to the German light cruisers' ten 4.1-inch guns. *Cornwall* and *Kent* both carried fourteen 6-inch guns. So the odds were very much in favour of the British.

As for the bigger cruisers, the odds were so poor that Admiral von Spee did not even consider them. It was his duty to engage, as it had been Admiral Cradock's duty to engage him, and so he signalled to *Gneisenau*, 'follow me' and turned hard to port, bringing him on a course directly for the battle-cruisers. Up went the signal from *Scharnhorst*: open fire. It was a little premature, at 15,000 yards the range was too great for the German guns. Admiral von Spee's one chance of survival was to close quickly and find a weak spot. To close quickly with two battle-cruisers was not the easiest task in the world.

As von Spee turned, had Admiral Sturdee maintained his course, he would have moved into the range of the German cruisers in a few minutes. But just after this move at 1.30 in the afternoon, Sturdee countered by turning again, which put the British battle cruisers on a course parallel to the German. The range was 14,500 yards, maximum for the Germans, but a moderate one for the British 12-inch guns. *Scharnhorst*'s guns were pointed at the sky, as her range finders made ready. The ship was making 21 knots as the gunners opened fire. They planned their salvoes, 200 yards apart, and as the flagship of the British squadron turned away to open the range, as von Spee knew would happen, the two German cruisers concentrated on

Inflexible. One salvo came in, and then another, then a straddle, and at 1.45 *Scharnhorst*'s gunners scored their first hits. Unfortunately (for the Germans) the armour plating prevented serious damage.

The German gunners were excellent but gunnery was not going to decide that battle, as the first two direct hits on *Scharnhorst* indicated. They were a long time in coming, but when they did come, the larger shells of the British wreaked dreadful damage. One shell grazed the third funnel and exploded on the upper deck aft, near the starboard battery. Shrapnel flew all over the area, tearing off both forearms of one deck officer. A dozen seamen were wounded, but the real damage of this shell was to the ship. It bent plating and so damaged the platform of one 8-inch gun that it could no longer be aimed. The second shell crashed through the port bulwark amid ships, and landed in a magazine. The red hot shell started a fire, but before it could spread First Officer Pochhammer was there with his damage control party. They flooded the magazine, and saved the ship.

At two o'clock, the battle half an hour old, Admiral Sturdee had managed to bring the British ships back to a range of 16,500 yards, which was the outside range of the German guns. Accuracy was impossible at such distance, so von Spee turned away in what might have appeared to be an attempt to escape. Sturdee speeded up and von Spee turned back, gaining 1,500 yards in the interchange, and the German shells again began to find their targets. The German shooting was far better than the British all the way, but those lighter shells did not have the penetrating power to breach the British armour. At 2.53 the Germans turned to port again and once more Admiral Sturdee led his ships on a course that paralleled that of the enemy. Suddenly the *Scharnhorst* turned again, as if to cross the British line, a manoeuvre that startled the British. The range dropped to 13,000 yards, to 12,000, to 11,500, and the German secondary guns began to fire. Admiral Sturdee did not like this development and moved swiftly to get out of range again. There was plenty of time before nightfall and he could afford to stay off at long range and potshot at the German cruisers. But the fact was that the *Scharnhorst*'s move was not dictated by strategy but by damage. Her port screw had stopped, and she slewed around. It took some time to repair the damage, and in that time the two squadrons moved closer, closer every minute. The damage the Germans inflicted on the British cruisers was minimal compared to that done to the Germans by this coming to close quarters, for the men on the guns of the British ships were firing very accurately at these short ranges. In ten minutes *Scharnhorst* lost her first funnel, and her third funnel was so badly holed that it would no longer draw air properly. Shells broke through her decks and started fires that grew worse every minute.

In the turning the British smoke got in the way of the gunners, and the firing from the *Invincible* and *Inflexible* stopped for a few minutes. The squadrons were now about 12,000 yards apart, steaming south-west on parallel courses. The *Scharnhorst* was obviously in bad shape, lying very low in the water, with large holes in the forward section and the area around the quarter deck that were quite visibly belching flames, from the viewpoint of Admiral Sturdee's bridge. Several of the *Scharnhorst*'s guns on this side were out of action, so von Spee brought her completely around to offer the other guns opportunity to fire. The German gunners fired steadily although the British shells were hitting all around them and one by one the guns were knocked out. At four o'clock in the afternoon, the battle was two and a half hours old, but it was apparent it would not last much longer. The *Scharnhorst* was ablaze from one end to the other. From the *Invincible* the officers and men could see that whole areas of the deck had been turned into masses of twisted steel. The smoke rose black, the flames were yellow, and white steam from the broken steam pipes hissed out in half a dozen places. The Germans, all this while, were still firing in salvoes, but the salvoes came slower. Von Spee sensed that his flagship had only minutes to live. He sent a message to Captain Maerker of the *Gneisenau*: 'If your engines are still intact, try to get away.' The promise was implicit, that the *Scharnhorst* would try to draw the British fire and help. And this she did. Having sent the message, the Admiral turned the *Scharnhorst* directly toward the enemy, and came on. He headed at *Invincible*, and Admiral Sturdee sensed that he would try a torpedo attack. But even as the *Scharnhorst* limped toward the *Invincible*, the British gunners put several more salvoes of 12-inch shells into her hull, and there was a shudder, and the German cruiser's engines stopped dead. She slowed immediately.

Seeing the enemy dead in the water, Admiral Sturdee signalled von Spee to surrender, but there was no reply. A few German guns continued to fire, and the British gunners poured armour-piercing and high explosive shells into the German cruiser. Her list grew more pronounced each few seconds. Water covered the foredeck, but the battle flags still flew from the mainmast and the gaff, and the Admiral's flag was still high on the foremast. But as the men aboard the other ships watched, the German flagship heeled ever more to port, so greatly that her fore turret was only six feet above water – and still firing. Then, the bow went down further, the screws came completely out of the water and the ship began to quiver.

'What is *Scharnhorst* doing?' came a question just at that moment from First Officer Pochhammer of the *Gneisenau*, who was on the third deck down of his ship, supervising fire fighting there.

'She is sinking,' said Captain Maerker, and he watched, as a few lonely souls jumped from the side of the vessel, and she rolled, plunged, and was suddenly gone into the deep. The two British battle-cruisers then turned their full attention to the *Gneisenau*; they took no time to send boats to search for survivors, so there were no survivors.

By this time the *Carnarvon* had come up to join the big ships, so *Gneisenau* felt the fire of three sets of guns. Captain Maerker had no chance to observe Admiral von Spee's last instructions, nor would he surrender in what was obviously a lost cause. He fought on, as long as the guns of *Gneisenau* would fire. Maerker, like Captain Schultz, wanted to fight at close range, where his 6-inch guns could also be used to advantage, but the British wanted to stay out of that range. At 4.15 both battle-cruisers were firing on the German cruiser, and the *Carnarvon* was behind, throwing shells from her 7.4-inch guns. The *Gneisenau* took an enormous amount of punishment, but there was no breach of discipline: early in the battle, First Officer Pochhammer had come upon one man at the drinking fountain when he was supposed to be at his battle station. Pochhammer had pulled out his pistol and shot the man dead on the spot. With that sort of discipline, the German sailors continued the fight; there was no panic and there were no further incidents. After an hour, the ship's midsection was a shambles: the boats were smashed in their davits. The officers' mess had been opened to the outside like a sardine tin, and the remains of the last meal were still visible on the white tablecloths. Shells had broken open the livestock pens and little pigs from Easter Island scurried among the corpses and slid on the bloody steel plating. A goose waddled into the officers' pantry and sat down among the scattered potatoes on the deck. When anyone approached, the goose hissed him away.

One incident gave the picture at this hour: a shell fell into the storeroom located between the 12-inch ammunition casemate and the crew's galley, with a muffled report followed by the screeching of tortured steel. In the surge of smoke and steam that came forth it became apparent that the shell had penetrated the gun position itself and had smashed steampipes below. The battery chief was flung completely out of position, along with his two assistants. As they arose they found themselves in one huge compartment where there had been three — the bulkheads of the storeroom and the galley had disappeared. A score of men lay in the wreckage of the galley, among shattered saucepans and twisted stoves. Most of them were half-naked, their clothes torn from their bodies by the impact. The battery chief and his assistants picked themselves up and realized they were the only men alive in the whole area. They went to their guns. The guns were unhurt, and in a minute they were firing again.

At 4.25 *Gneisenau*'s guns were straddling the *Invincible*. Admiral Sturdee turned away again, outside the range of the Germans. Yet, though harried by three enemies, in the next quarter hour the *Gneisenau* scored three hits on the flagship with armour-piercing shells.

Still, there was only one possible ending to this battle. A shell destroyed the *Gneisenau*'s wireless station. Another put out the star-board guns amidships. One after another, vital positions were destroyed; a shell entered the middle stokehold and killed all the stokers, another fell into the after dressing station, killing 50 wounded men, Chaplain Rost and Surgeon Nohl. The after turret was hit by one 12-inch shell, and every man inside died. Another shell exploded on the upper deck above the 8-inch gun, swept away every man in the area, and shrapnel surged into the 6-inch gun position below and killed all but two men.

At 4.47 there came a lull in the firing. From the decks of the British ships it appeared that *Gneisenau* had struck her colours, and that seemed only sensible, for she was listing badly, much of her upper works had been shot away, and half her guns were silent. But there was no thought of surrender; the ship had lost her flags, for the third time, and she had no flags left to hoist. As the Germans kept firing, the British resumed, and moved in closer. Captain Maerker tried to manoeuvre to bring the port side to bear because the ship had a bad list to starboard and those guns had been hard hit. Soon the *Gneisenau*'s gunners became aware of another problem: the ship was running low on ammunition. There was plenty of ammunition aft, where the guns had been silenced, but to get it and bring it forward meant that the men had to run the risk of death. By 5.30 the *Gneisenau* was a shambles. All four funnels were shot away or holed. Men climbed over rubble to get to any position. The foremast had been shot away. From the deck of the *Invincible*, Admiral Sturdee estimated that the ship must have taken at least fifty hits from the 12-inch guns, plus scores of others from the *Carnarvon*, which stood close behind and pounded away.

On board the *Gneisenau*, Captain Maerker looked around, saw the condition of his guns, and fought on. Sturdee called on him to surrender, and in reply another shot from the forward turret of the *Gneisenau* struck the *Invincible* amidships. But at 5.45 Maerker could see that the end was not far away. The ship was listing badly and gurgling sounds inside indicated ominous changes below the water-line. He called for the men to come to the port side of the ship and prepare to abandon. As they assembled, crawling out of holes in the blackened steel, the officers stood by and handed out hammocks and spars to help the men save themselves.

'His Majesty the Emperor!' shouted Captain Maerker, speaking from the bridge.

'Hurray', shouted the crew of *Gneisenau*.

'Our good and brave *Gneisenau*', shouted the captain.

'Hurray', shouted the crew.

'Deutschland, Deutschland, uber alles ...' sang the captain.

'Über alles in der Welt ...' sang the crew.

And then the ship began to shudder, and the men began slipping over the side and swimming away to escape the suction that would come. Someone had found a red, white, and black ensign in the wreckage and it was hoisted aloft on the wireless rod which had slid down the truck of the mainmast, and it flapped heroically in the breeze, as the ship heeled.

'All men overboard', shouted Captain Maerker, from his bridge. All men went overboard, save the captain. Four hundred of the crew, not quite half the assigned number, slid into the water and waited for salvation from their enemies.

The British ships slowed, and as the *Gneisenau* plunged into the sea, they began to send out boats.

20

The Chase

After Admiral von Spee released his light cruisers to let them try to escape the superior force of the British squadron, the Germans formed into a triangle, with *Dresden* at the apex, *Leipzig* on her starboard and *Nürnberg* on her port side, and headed toward the straits, hoping to escape into the maze of islands. They were making 23 knots. At 2.45 in the afternoon, as the battle raged behind them, the German cruisers were eleven miles ahead of the *Cornwall* and *Kent*, but *Glasgow*, which had been speeding along at 27 knots, was overhauling them. At 12,000 yards *Glasgow* opened fire, hoping to put enough shells around the *Leipzig* to force a course change, which would speed up the process of getting into reasonable range. But Captain Haun was not to be intimidated, and he pressed on. It was not long however, before *Glasgow* came to within 10,000 yards, and Captain Haun and Captain von Schönberg saw that if all three cruisers turned briefly, and opened fire on this single enemy with broadsides, they might damage her and then be off to escape. But Captain von Lüdecke, who was not of the squadron or its tradition, fled on, determined to save his ship if possible, and without consideration for his fellows. *Glasgow* saw her danger and bore off, and the *Leipzig* and *Nürnberg*, resumed their course. *Dresden* had gained at least a mile in this proceeding, and was running into patchy weather, with squalls and clouds ahead.

Captain Luce saw by the manoeuvres of the German ships that he had to make a basic decision. He could go on and catch *Dresden*, if she did not escape in the heavy weather, but if he did so, all three German cruisers might conceivably get away, because *Leipzig* and *Nürnberg* were both faster than *Kent* and *Cornwall*. 'Are you gaining on the enemy?' he asked *Cornwall* and *Kent*.

'Yes', they both replied but Luce could see that the gain was hardly perceptible, and as senior officer present he was responsible to the Admiral. So reluctantly, he decided to let *Dresden* get away, while he supervised the destruction of the other two enemy cruisers. That decision made, he set to the work of war. Just before 3 p.m. *Glasgow* fired a salvo and one shell struck forward of the third funnel, killing Seaman Nicholas, the talker on the third 4-inch gun. The body was moved out of the line of action, and since Nicholas was first to fall, his body was covered with a flag. Soon there would not be enough flags or enough time for such niceties.

Captain Haun moved his ship to port, and prepared to do battle in earnest. Soon *Leipzig*'s shells were falling around *Glasgow*, and her shooting was accurate. In a few minutes she should begin scoring. But each time Captain Haun wanted to fire at the enemy with effect, he had to turn to bring his broadsides to bear, and this cost him distance, so the other British cruisers did indeed begin to catch up. At 3.35 Captain Ellerton of the *Cornwall* was nearly in position to begin firing, and he signalled the *Kent* that he would take the *Leipzig* and that *Kent* should fire on the *Nürnberg*. This meant that *Leipzig* had two enemies to meet, and had to make his choice. He chose to fire on *Cornwall* as the larger target, and so rapid was the *Leipzig*'s rate of fire that the linoleum baffles between pairs of guns grew hot and burst into flames. But, said the gunners, there were so many splashes around the ship by this time that the British shelling put the fires out for them. That was a pleasant joke; the reality was more grim. One shell struck the No. 1 starboard gun and killed its gunners. And almost unnoticed, a 6-inch shell fell into the clothes press between decks, and started a fire. Fifteen minutes later the blaze was burning so furiously that the damage control party called for help; they could not get near the source of the fire.

At this point there was one last look at the *Dresden* as she turned sharply to port and sped south-west into a heavy bank of cloud. Some men spat over the side, airing their feelings about Captain von Lüdecke. Captain Haun looked wryly after the other cruiser and observed that she was losing no speed in getting away. He said no more.

Zigzagging, *Leipzig* managed to put some distance between herself and *Glasgow*, but *Cornwall* came after her, and soon the British cruiser's shells began to straddle *Leipzig*. Just then *Glasgow* came up on the same side, to produce a maximum firing effect. Fifteen minutes later the two British ships had holed *Leipzig* several times below the water-line, and Captain Haun heard from the engine room that the capacity of the engines had been reduced to 20 knots. This was the disaster for which Haun had been waiting, knowing it would come and there was nothing to be done. As the cruiser's speed dropped, the

British closed, and their fire grew more deadly. A shell fell in the small arms magazine and bullets began whizzing about the deck like firecrackers. Gunners were killed by their own ammunition as they aimed shells at the enemy. Still, they kept firing, and they were doing damage to the British cruisers, too. *Glasgow* was hit three times: one shell passed through the foretop without exploding but took off the hand of a signalman. One shell hit the mast and knocked out the ship's electrical system. *Cornwall* was taking fire from the *Leipzig*, too, and suffering damage. The battle joined, Captain Haun kept trying to bore in, and his men's shooting was excellent, but the British moved away, to take advantage of their greater range. *Cornwall* was a little slow: the men of *Leipzig* put ten shells into her in a few minutes, before she got out of range.

As darkness began to come down at 5.45, the British ships' captains became concerned. The sky was much darker than it should be at this hour in this season, and the weather was worsening rapidly. But for the Germans came worse news: they were running out of ammunition. Captain Haun had begun the battle with 1,800 shells for his 4.1-inch guns, but after two and a half hours of fighting there were only 200 shells left, and most of these were amidships. The after guns were almost completely out of ammunition. The problem was to get the ammunition aft from the positions forward, and there were no spare men to do so. Four deck lieutenants volunteered for the dangerous job. Just then the British changed over from ordinary shells to the more powerful lyddite. Soon the *Leipzig* was raging with fires, and Captain Luce came to the erroneous conclusion that the ship was about done for. She had nearly stopped firing, and that seemed to settle the matter. But what Luce did not realize was that the ammunition had finally been exhausted altogether, and the last shell fired at 7 p.m., and that Captain Haun was even then planning a torpedo attack on his enemies. *Cornwall* had grown a little careless as the rate of fire from *Leipzig*'s guns slacked off, and came in close.

Lieutenant Schiwig, the *Leipzig* torpedo officer, had a considerable problem in launching this attack. The electrical system of the *Leipzig* was gone, and the emergency system had just failed, so he had no working direction finders, no distance estimators, and no communications with the bridge save by runner. But Captain Haun turned, and they headed for the *Cornwall*.

Darkness had fallen and Captain Luce queried the Germans by searchlight about surrendering. A signalman was sent aloft to watch *Leipzig*'s flat, with instructions to sing out if it dropped, and then

Luce would cease firing. But Haun had no intention of giving in yet, and as *Cornwall* came in to within 4,700 yards, *Leipzig* loosed two torpedoes at her, which she managed to evade, and thereafter *Cornwall* was more cautious. Haun circled, and Captain Luce's searchlight made a fine target. Another torpedo went off against the *Glasgow*, but it too missed.

At 7.20 came the word, 'the ship is sinking' and Captain Haun ordered all men on deck, and they prepared to abandon ship. Before they could do so a tremendous explosion in the boilers shook the *Leipzig*, just as a British shell took down the mainmast and killed the gunnery officer and the communications officer. *Cornwall* and *Glasgow* were circling, firing occasionally, but seeing the condition of the German cruiser, restraining themselves, and asking continually for surrender. The fact was that in the dark, Captain Haun did not ever see one of their signals.

On the main deck a group of men tried to lower the port cutter, but as they got it moving, a British shell struck in their midst and the cutter became a mass of scrap lumber covered with parts of bodies. Others rushed to the starboard cutter, but it was half filled with water still, and the ship's list was too great to launch her. Captain Haun looked at his circling enemies, not understanding their question to him, and wondered what sort of men these were who would continue to massacre the men of a defeated enemy ship. Dr Schaafhausen, the surgeon, shook his fist at the damned Englishmen. Down in the engine room several men had volunteered to keep the ship moving until the last, and they did so. Using manual steering Captain Haun tried to keep the ship stern on to the enemy, to cut down the death toll, but the British shells swept the deck until perhaps only a hundred men were left alive, and then even these leaped overboard, until at the last there were only a half dozen officers, a dozen seamen, and Captain Haun aboard. *Leipzig* was sinking slowly, filling with water from below.

Glasgow came up to within 500 yards, and circled, Captain Haun ordered all his men off the deck, for he felt the ship going. They called to him to come, but he said he would wait until she sank and then swim away from her. Just before 9.30 she heeled over, and thick clouds of steam came from the boilers. Then a mighty explosion shook her, and her stern went up and her bow went down. Two minutes later she disappeared.

21

The End of the Enemy

After *Nürnberg* and *Leipzig* turned back to fight the British squadron, Captain Luce assigned *Nürnberg*'s destruction to the eleven-year-old cruiser *Kent*. That ship made 23.7 knots, according to specifications, and since *Nürnberg* was logged at 23.5 knots, on the basis of the record her lead should give her a chance to get away. But the men of *Kent* were determined, and they ran the ship's engines up so she was making 25 knots. Captain von Schönberg could not manage more than 22 knots from the little cruiser after all these months at sea. So the *Kent* overhauled the *Nürnberg* steadily, and at five o'clock in the afternoon *Kent* was close enough to begin shooting with her 6-inch guns.

The tale of the *Nürnberg-Kent* duel was almost a duplicate of the story of the *Leipzig*, except that in this case a single British ship was involved. At first the Germans shot better and scored more hits, an indication of their training and discipline, but the more powerful 6-inch shells soon began to take their effect on the German cruiser. One shell hit the after steering flat and killed every man there, and another shell, crashing through the deck amidships, damaged the steam system, so that at 5.35, with no warning, two of *Nürnberg*'s boilers burst, and her speed fell to 19 knots almost immediately. From that point on Captain von Schönberg knew there was no escape, and it was a question of going to their end still fighting. British superiority in guns was matched by that in explosives, the new lyddite shells did far more damage in comparison to their size than the old style German powder shells. By six o'clock the *Nürnberg* was afire in half a dozen places. The mainmasts toppled, and her funnels were torn half away. Only two of her port guns were still in action. Fifteen minutes after the mast fell, the ship was a complete wreck. Just before seven o'clock Captain von Schönberg ordered the battle flag hauled down, to stop the carnage, for his guns had quit, and the men were taking a terrible beating. He gathered the men for the three cheers for the Kaiser, they were given, and then he advised them to abandon ship or remain, as they pleased, to await the British. One boat was launched, to carry the wounded, lest the ship sank before the British arrived. But the boat sank on launching and many of the wounded were lost. Twenty minutes after the flag came down, *Kent* launched her boats, just at the moment that *Nürnberg* turned over on her starboard beam and sank. *Kent* had turned a searchlight on her to direct the boat crews, and in that light they saw a group of German sailors standing on the fan-tail, waving a flag, just as she turned. Then she was gone under, and the boats hurried to the spot to search for survivors.

Thus the battle of the Falkland Islands ended, in a defeat as resounding for the Germans as had been their victory a few weeks earlier at Coronel. Once the shooting stopped the British cruisers picked up survivors, but they were woefully few. By the time *Gneisenau* sank if there had been any men left alive from *Scharnhorst*, immersion in the 40-°F. water for several hours had finished them. Not one seaman or officer survived to tell the story of the flagship in battle. When *Gneisenau* was sunk, the nearest British cruiser was six miles off, and it took some time to reach the collection of flotsam that represented the cruiser. Most of the wounded had died by then. Two hundred men were picked out of the water, but fifty of them died that night of exposure and their wounds.

The survivors of the *Nürnberg* were most unlucky. Hundreds went into the water but when the captain of *Kent* went to launch his boats he found that all of them had been shot up in the battle, and only two could be patched up in a short time. They were patched, and launched, but the process took several hours, and when they reached the area where the *Nürnberg* had gone down, they found only 12 half frozen men. Five of them died of exposure or wounds that night.

Aboard the *Leipzig*, Captain Haun sat in the wrecked ship and shared out the contents of his cigarette case. The British kept firing, for the *Leipzig*'s flags were still flying, and to the British that meant she was fighting, although no fight was coming from her. The men of the *Leipzig* sat there, helpless, and watched their comrades die as new shells came piling into their wrecked ship. Some men leaped over the side with impromptu rafts and flotation devices, hoping to drift down on the British and be saved. But the current carried them away from the British, and there was nothing Captain Haun could do about it, save sit and watch. He could not bring down the flags because both masts were ringed with flames and no man could get through. Finally the hulk sank, flags still flying, and only then did the British stop shooting, and send their boats. Six officers and nine men were saved.

That night Admiral Sturdee and his staff sorted out the events of the battle. They soon had all the essential parts, except the story of *Kent* and *Nürnberg*, for *Kent*'s wireless had been shot out in the early stages of the battle and she could not communicate. But Admiral Sturdee, while not quite certain, suspected that the *Dresden* had escaped the net, and he queried all his captains. Captain Luce of *Glasgow* had the most reliable information, having seen the *Dresden* heading off south-south-west as *Leipzig* had turned to fight. It was not until the following day, however, when the squadron assembled in Port Stanley, that the *Kent* story indicated the certainty of *Dresden*'s escape. She was the only ship of the German squadron to get clean away. Admiral von Spee's colliers, which he had left behind at Point Pleasant, off the Falklands' coast, were intercepted late on the day of battle by the *Bristol*, which finally got her engines going, and the *Macedonia*, the armed merchant cruiser. The *Seydlitz*'s captain had smelled trouble and cleared out, but he was a victim of the changed attitudes in these waters following the resounding British victory. He went into the Gulf of San Mathias, and his ship was immediately seized by the Chilean authorities for violation of neutrality. The *Baden* and *Santa Isabel* were slow getting away and the *Bristol* caught them and sank them both. So only the *Dresden* was left, somewhere in the hundreds of isles and inlets along the southern tip of South America.

On the night of 8 December, Admiral Sturdee was also assessing the damage to his own ships, before sending his battle report to London. *Invincible*, the flagship, had been hit twenty-three times by shells from the *Scharnhorst*. The Admiral's tactics had certainly paid off, for although the German fire was extremely accurate and much of *Invincible*'s upper works had been damaged, because of the long range, the German shells had very little angle of penetration, and so the hull was almost intact. The battle over, the men of *Invincible* could laugh about some of their narrow escapes. One shell had come into the wardroom and smashed the grand piano, then ploughed on through the bulkhead. The paymaster's money chest had been hit and broken open, scattering a thousand gold sovereigns about the ship. Many of these were never found, at least not by authority. One dud shell was found in the captain's mess storeroom, on a shelf next to a Gorgonzola cheese. But one hit at the water-line indicated what might have happened had the German guns more range, or had von Spee been able to close more successfully: one shot that hit at the water-line had made a hole seven feet long, and three feet wide, and two coal bunkers had been flooded. A few more such hits and *Invincible* would have been in difficulty.

The *Inflexible* suffered far less damage, since the British flagship had been the major target of *Scharnhorst* and *Gneisenau*. The gunners of the *Leipzig* had hit *Cornwall* eighteen times, but their 4.1-inch shells did not penetrate the armour of the British ship's decks except on one occasion where a shell flooded one coal bunker and gave *Cornwall* a decided list to port. *Glasgow* had fought *Leipzig* too, at long distance, and had only six shell holes. *Kent* had been hit thirty-seven times by *Nürnberg*, but most shells had glanced off her armour and done little damage. The wireless station was gone, and a direct hit through the gunport of one six-inch casement had destroyed that installation. But that was all.

The immense difference in casualties represented the reality of the battle better than anything else. The British squadron lost only 6 men killed, and a few wounded, all of these aboard *Kent* and *Glasgow*. There were no casualties at all on *Invincible, Inflexible, Carnarvon* and *Cornwall*. As for the Germans, the squadron had numbered 2,500 men aboard the four ships that were sunk, and 182 officers and men were saved, most of them from the *Gneisenau*. Even these figures were not accurate, because at Valparaiso the squadron had enlisted dozens of volunteers from the merchant ships in the area, and the records had gone down with the ships.

All the information available was collected and the story was sent to London, where it did wonders to raise the morale of the government and of His Majesty's Navy. It was, said the naval experts, a victory in the tradition of Nelson. For Lord Fisher it was also vindication: he had been severely criticized for involving the government in the building of the mammoth battle-cruisers in the first place, and then for sending these huge ships to the end of the earth on what his critics considered to be a wild-goose chase. Now, the battle-cruisers had put an end to the greatest threat to British shipping that existed in the early part of the war, and the immediate revival of the South Atlantic trade was the proof of it.

One task remained, important enough to warrant consideration, although not the full attention of the Sturdee squadron: the hunting out of the *Dresden*. Even so, Admiral Sturdee took with him *Invincible, Inflexible*, and *Bristol*, enough firepower to deal with any three heavy cruisers in the Kaiser's Navy. At 10.30 on the morning of 9 December, Admiral Sturdee was within fifty miles of Staten Island in thick fog. He decided the weather was hopeless – being new to the area perhaps he did not know that this sort of weather was normal for the barren wastes around the tip of South America. He turned north-west, and *Bristol* was sent off to the Western Falklands. They searched for twenty-four hours, and then gave up to return to the Falklands and Port Stanley. So *Dresden* had got away.

One might have expected that when the news of the Battle of the Falklands was given to the Admiralty, that Admiral Sturdee would have become an overnight hero. But when Winston Churchill learned that Sturdee had let *Dresden* escape him, no one could say anything good about the man. Admiral Fisher was even stronger in his condemnation; he regarded Sturdee's finding of the Germans as the purest luck (which it was – von Spee's Teutonic pride had sent him straight into the hands of his enemies when by simply steaming on past the Falklands he would have got away scot free and could easily have made the Canaries and the dash homeward that Berlin wanted). Further, Fisher saw on studying the account of the battle that Sturdee had done nothing to assure the destruction of all ships. With *Glasgow, Kent* and *Cornwall*, he had on the scene a ship-to-ship ratio. Captain Luce's decision to concentrate on *Leipzig* at the expense of allowing *Dresden* to get away was not highly regarded. For public relations reasons it would have been so much better had the British been able to make a clean sweep, and here they had created a new folk hero of the sort that had bedevilled them since the *Goeben* ran through the Mediterranean Fleet to reach Constantinople. Churchill and Fisher regarded Sturdee as a bumbler who had let the fox escape a whole pack of hounds. The memory of *Dresden*'s sister ship *Emden* and her exploits was much too fresh in London. Churchill, as a politician, was desperately worried lest *Dresden* prove as much an embarrassment as *Emden* had done.

The First Lord of the Admiralty need not have worried. In Captain von Lüdecke he had no von Müller to worry about. It would never have occurred to von Lüdecke to take this opportunity to carry on a campaign like Müller's. And, as he ran south away from the battle on that fateful day, he became thoroughly frightened when all his calls for German vessels went unanswered. He was heading for Picton Island, where Admiral von Spee had stopped, and when no supply ships replied, he decided he must go to Punta Arenas inside the Straits of Magellan. He did not stop to think that by so doing he would most certainly alert the British, who had their own intelligence system operating in the area. It did not occur to him that the resounding defeat of his own squadron would change the tide of public opinion. Captain von Lüdecke was not a combat officer, and the wisdom of the German Admiralty in sending him out even to exchange one ship for another, could have been brought under question as things turned out.

Von Lüdecke's caution did bring him to realize that the British might expect him to head back through the Straits, and might have a warship posted there. He agonized with that consideration and forced himself into a bold action, to take the tricky, narrow Cockburn Channel into Punta Arenas by the back route, so to speak. So, on 10 December, as Admiral Sturdee searched fruitlessly for the *Dresden*, she was on her way to Punta Arenas. But true to his own cautious nature, having decided to risk Punta Arenas, von Lüdecke then fell short. He stopped some sixty miles south at a place called Sholl Bay, and sent his men ashore to cut *green timber* for his furnaces. There were still 160 tons of coal aboard the ship, but Captain von Lüdecke was assailed with second and third thoughts. What if there was no coal in Punta Arenas? What if the British got there first? What difference it would have made, von Lüdecke did not get around to reasoning out; but he kept his men cutting green timber and loading it. As luck would have it, the Chilean gunboat *Almirante Condell* came upon him in these not very protected waters that same day and, when the captain had ascertained what this strange character was doing, issued the general warning that the ship must be out of Chilean neutral waters in twenty-four hours. Even von Lüdecke must have recognized the change in Chilean naval attitudes; a week earlier a Chilean vessel would have ignored him politely. So now he had the worst of all worlds, a load of green timber instead of coal, and the assurance that he must not return to Chilean waters for another three months. But having alerted the Chileans, and the enemy, to his presence without getting any help from it, von Lüdecke now decided to go into Punta Arenas and see if there was not some coal there. It was fortunate that he was dealing with an admiral who was perhaps as unimaginative as himself; had Sturdee continued the search, he almost certainly would have taken *Dresden* on 12 December, when she pulled into Punta Arenas, for Sturdee had expected her to head there.

Von Lüdecke was delighted on arrival to learn that the American collier *Minnesotan* was in port, carrying a cargo of coal ordered by Captain Boy-Ed in Washington, to be delivered to the squadron. But the news of the Falklands battle had penetrated here, and the American captain pleaded the position of a neutral in neutral waters — and refused to give von Lüdecke a bag of coal.

Von Müller, under the circumstances, would have suggested that unless he had this *German-owned* coal within the hour, that the cruiser's guns might just accidentally be trained on the collier, but von Lüdecke was not made of that stuff at all. Luckily for him, as he turned away empty-handed, the German consul advised him that the German Roland liner *Turpin* was in port. She had been anchored there since the war began, sheltered in Chilean neutrality. From *Turpin* Captain von Lüdecke secured 750 tons of coal. It would take some time to load it, and so the twenty-four hour rules were ignored. Since *Dresden* was the only warship in the harbour, there was no one to challenge. But the Chilean government now informed the British, and at Whitehall the Foreign Office informed the Admiralty. Winston Churchill grunted and had a message sent to Sturdee, privately even more furious that he was having to do the man's intelligence work for him. The *Dresden* was preparing to coal at Punta Arenas he told Sturdee, and she must be destroyed before the Chilean government got the idea in its head to intern her.

When this message arrived at Port Stanley, in the small hours of 13 December, the Admiral was in bed. But the urgent tone of the message prodded the officer of the communications watch to have him roused, and when Sturdee saw the note he prepared to act. But action was impossible. The men of *Inflexible, Glasgow*, and *Bristol* were scattered, half of them ashore on overnight permission. None of the ships had more fires going then those necessary to operate the electrical and heating systems. Once again, Admiral Sturdee was caught in his cabin. It was past nine o'clock in the morning before the three ships managed to move out.

As the Admiral's ships sailed, *Dresden* was coaling furiously in Punta Arenas. That night just before midnight the job was completed and the ship sailed south.

The *Bristol* arrived in Punta Arenas the next day, and learned that the quarry had escaped. She turned and headed south. A few hours later the *Glasgow* came into port, and Captain Luce, smarting in his understanding of what London thought about his actions at the Falklands, took out his wrath on the Chilean port authorities for allowing the German ship to violate their neutrality. That did hardly any good at all, and in an hour, *Glasgow* also sailed out to search for the *Dresden*.

The squadron did not find the *Dresden*. On leaving Punta Arenas, Captain von Lüdecke sailed back through Magdalena Sound and Cockburn Channel to Hewett Bay at the south-west end of Barbara

Channel. All the way, von Lüdecke was calling up German colliers in the naval code, and demanding that they meet him. He was in luck, the collier *Amasis* responded and was waiting when he arrived at the meeting point. These messages, and one in the clear to German stations in the Argentine were intercepted by the British, but again, they did not have the German naval code on hand, and must send the intercepts back to London for deciphering. So the *Dresden* escaped.

The British heard more of her. Von Lüdecke sent the *Amasis* into Punta Arenas to take off the coal from *Minnesotan*, and the Chileans, thoroughly cowed by Captain Luce, not only refused permission, but interned the *Amasis* for trying to break the neutrality laws. The whole British squadron came out and steamed about, searching, calling at every port and searching some channels into the fjord country. The Japanese cruisers *Idzumo* and *Hisen* came to help. The *Australia* came over to give her assistance. None of them went to Barbara Channel, so they did not find the *Dresden*.

By Christmas the hunt had lost its urgency. Winston Churchill had begun to recall from foreign waters all those ships that had been tied down by von Spee and the *Emden* over the past five months, for there was no longer any major threat to British rule of the seas. Admiral Sturdee, in command of the sleek battle-cruisers, was ordered home. Admiral Fisher was so furious with Sturdee that he would have liked to assign him to the *Bristol* or the *Glasgow* and keep him in exile for the rest of the war, but Churchill, the politician, sensed that denigrating the Admiral in charge would arouse speculations about the Navy that did not need airing. Nobody ever indicated that the Falklands battle compared with Trafalgar – at least nobody outside Sturdee's circle of friends – but the job had been done and von Spee was no more. That in essence was the important matter. *Dresden*'s continued life was an embarrassment, but since she lay holed up in the Tierra del Fuego region, and did not bother any shipping, she was no more than that.

Fisher had let Sturdee know how matters stood. A series of telegrams in January from the Admiralty had been no better than rude to the gallant commander, indicating that he had missed his big chance. In February, Sturdee came back through London with his battle-cruisers, to take command of the 4th Battle Squadron, which had been ordained earlier, and which Churchill did not wish to change, since denial of the command would raise the whole question of Coronel over again. But when Sturdee came to the Admiralty, Lord

Fisher gave him a brisk five minutes and no compliments. He did not even *mention* the Falklands battle.

Fisher's private view, aired almost everywhere, was that Sturdee was 'criminally inept'. How inept he did not know, perhaps fortunately. For on Boxing Day 1914, Captain von Lüdecke was pursuing his strange delusion once more, cutting green timber for fuel, although he was not using any fuel. Ashore, his men encountered a group of sailors from the French motor sailer *Galileo*, who had come in for water. In the conversation that followed, the Germans pretended they were Norwegians, but the French caught glimpses of the German naval tattoos on some arms, and when the motor sailer reached Punta Arenas a bit later, the captain rushed to the British consulate and told Consul Aylward that they had seen the *Dresden*'s men, though not the ship, in Barbara Channel. The consul immediately wired the story to Admiral Sturdee, who scoffed: for their charts showed positively that there was not a decent channel in that whole area. The Frenchmen were drunk. No cruiser could get in there. What the Admiral forgot was that those charts had been drawn by the navigator of the *Beagle* a long, long time ago, and never really improved. So Sturdee really did seem to bear out Admiral Fisher's estimate of him.

Von Lüdecke did not know what to do. It never occurred to him to do what he was expected to do, go raiding. He got in touch with Berlin, and someone in the Admiralty, who must have known him, suggested that his only course was to come home. They would arrange colliers from Berlin to meet him *en route*. Von Lüdecke pondered. Steam all that way without any protection, and only the off-chance of meeting colliers? He guessed not. He refused. He would go into the Pacific Ocean and go raiding, maybe out by Australia. The Admiralty vetoed that plan; it could not be bothered to try to arrange colliers so far away. Von Lüdecke was ordered to follow the sailing ship routes, stay off the steamer lanes, and try to make it into the North Sea.

The prospect was so unappealing that Captain von Lüdecke decided to think about it for a while. A German otter hunter happened by and directed von Lüdecke to a new hiding place, in a deep, virtually unknown channel south of Santa Ines Island. There, thinking things over, he decided his best course was to go into the Pacific, where there seemed to be fewer British warships, and hide in that wide ocean, raiding commerce when it was safe. So he headed out. He would work the sailing ship routes; sailing ships were unlikely to do much damage to a cruiser. He had one collier, the *Sierra Cordoba*, and others awaited him at various places.

Meanwhile, Consul Milward at Punta Arenas was more than a little annoyed with the Navy. Admiral Sturdee's scoffing at his report on the *Dresden* did not sit well. He continued to have reports and transmitted them, and got the same treatment. So one day he chartered a motor sailer and went into those waters where the Admiralty said there were no channels. He drew a chart for the Royal Navy. So finally credence was given to Milward's reports, but the squadron did little to augment them. One day, quite by accident, the *Kent* came upon *Dresden*, steaming her way to the Pacific, but the surprise was so great that Captain von Lüdecke was able to react quickly, and the captain of *Kent* did not. Although the *Dresden* was stopped and coaling at the moment, and was only nine miles from *Kent*, the German ship got moving with remarkable speed, and *Kent* never came within 12,000 yards of her that day, which was the outside range of *Kent*'s guns.

All that night von Lüdecke drove the ship. Early on the morning of March 9 1915, von Lüdecke took the ship into Cumberland Bay and stopped there. Captain von Lüdecke took stock. He had only 80 tons of coal left in his boilers, and his nearest collier was many miles away. He had already complained bitterly to Berlin about the need for a refit, for more colliers, for more ammunition. In reply Berlin had finally told him that he might as well intern in Chile, as continue, so he prepared for this. But that day the local lighthouse keeper came aboard the *Dresden* and informed him, in his capacity as governor of the region, that the *Dresden* must move out. The lighthouse keeper then went away and informed the British that *Dresden* was there. So the *Glasgow* and the *Kent* came back on the morning of 14 March. They appeared in the distance and Captain von Lüdecke got up steam. But when the British came in firing, he saw that this battle could have but one end so he ran down the German ensign and ran up the white flag of surrender. The crew took to the boats, leaving a demolition party that set charges in the main magazine. Then the demolition men left and at 12.15 the charges exploded and the *Dresden* sank.

The Germans went ashore, and declared themselves interned. The British came ashore and declared that the Germans were prisoners of war. But the Chileans decided the Germans were internees. The British were mollified somewhat when the Chileans claimed that they had damaged a Chilean schooner and thus caused the death of a thousand lobsters. The British took over the lobsters and ate them, leaving the damages to the consular powers to digest. As they ate, they could consider the whole adventure a success, although their part in it was not one to make Winston Churchill fill the air with the squadron's praises. Indeed, from beginning to end, this squadron's successes were more a matter of bungling than anything else. But the fact was that the sea was cleared of German cruisers, at this point, eight months after the beginning of the war. The whole East Asian Cruiser Squadron of the Germans was gone. The cruiser *Karlsruhe*, which no one had been able to find, had actually blown up and sunk off South America after an internal explosion. The cruiser *Königsberg*, which, with the *Emden*, had so frightened everyone in the Indian Ocean, was bottled up in the Rufiji River of German East Africa, never to emerge. And so the fleet that had so frightened England and English commerce throughout the world was no more, and there was no question at all but that Britannia ruled the waves.

Bibliography

The material for this book was gathered over a number of years during which I wrote several studies of German naval operations in the period of the great European war of 1914-18. These include *The Last Cruise of the Emden, The Raider Wolf, The Elusive Seagull* (Moewe), *Ghost of the Atlantic, The Karlsruhe Affair, The Germans Who Never Lost, The Fall of Tsingtao,* and *Disaster at the Dardanelles.*

The major source for the life of Maximilian Johannes Maria Hubertus, the Graf von Spee, is Fritz Otto Busch's *Admiral Graf Spee's Sieg und Untergang.* Another useful book about the Admiral was Eberhard Koebssll's *Die grauen Wölfe des Grafen Spee; die Heldenfahrt des deutschen Südseegeschwaders.* Other works, more in the order of their importance than in alphabetical configuration are: Hans Pochhammer's *Before Jutland*; Admiral von Spee's Last Voyage. Pochhammer was executive officer of the *Gneisenau,* and knew his Admiral as well as nearly anyone who survived the war, which he barely did after the ship was sunk at the Falklands. I used the translation by H.J. Stenning.

Richard Alexander Hough's *The Pursuit of Admiral von Spee* was interesting as a modern treatment but not extremely detailed. Older works that might be considered primary are W.L. Godshall's *Tsingtau under Three Flags,* Jefferson Jones' *The Fall of Tsingtau*; H.M.S.O., *Kiaochow and Weihaiwei*; Walther Hubatsch's *Der Admiralstab*; C.B. Burdick's *The Siege of Tsingtau* (a new book, 1976, quite detailed); D. Hutter's *Das Uberseeische Deutschland*; Mary E. Townsend's *The Rise and Fall of Germany's Colonial Empire,* Jakob Marquart's *Die Fraue in Schantung,* A.J. Marder's *From the Dreadnought to Scapa Flow,* E.L. Woodward's *Great Britain and the German Navy,* Grand Admiral Alfred Peter Friedrich von Tirpitz's *My Memoirs,* Peter Padfield's *The Great Naval Race,* and J. and K.P. Moses' *Germany in the Pacific and Far East, 1870-1914.*

I am indebted to archivists at the Imperial War Museum for assistance in research and for photographs. I also owe a debt to the librarians at Yale University for much assistance over the years.

Index